D1795462

Political Communication in Britain

Titles in this series

- R. Worcester and M. Harrop (eds.) *Political Communications: The General Election Campaign of 1979* (George Allen & Unwin)
- I. Crewe and M. Harrop (eds.) *Political Communications: The General Election Campaign of 1983* (Cambridge University Press)
- I. Crewe and M. Harrop (eds.) *Political Communications: The General Election Campaign of 1987* (Cambridge University Press)
- I. Crewe and B. Gosschalk (eds.) *Political Communications: The General Election Campaign of 1992* (Cambridge University Press)
- I. Crewe, B. Gosschalk and J. Bartle (eds.) *Political Communications: Why Labour Won the General Election of 1997* (Frank Cass)
- J. Bartle, R. Mortimore and S. Atkinson (eds.) *Political Communications: The General Election Campaign of 2001* (Frank Cass)
- D. Wring, J. Green, R. Mortimore and S. Atkinson (eds.) *Political Communications: The General Election Campaign of 2005* (Palgrave Macmillan)
- D. Wring, R. Mortimore and S. Atkinson (eds.) *Political Communication in Britain: The Leader Debates, the Campaign and the Media in the 2010 General Election 2010* (Palgrave Macmillan)
- D. Wring, R. Mortimore and S. Atkinson (eds.) *Political Communication in Britain: Polling, Campaigning and Media in the 2015 General Election Campaign* (Palgrave Macmillan)

Dominic Wring · Roger Mortimore
Simon Atkinson
Editors

Political
Communication
in Britain

Campaigning, Media and Polling
in the 2017 General Election

Editors
Dominic Wring
School of Social Sciences
Loughborough University
Loughborough, UK

Simon Atkinson
Ipsos MORI
London, UK

Roger Mortimore
King's College London
London, UK

ISBN 978-3-030-00821-5   ISBN 978-3-030-00822-2   (eBook)
https://doi.org/10.1007/978-3-030-00822-2

Library of Congress Control Number: 2018954966

© The Editor(s) (if applicable) and The Author(s), under exclusive license to Springer Nature Switzerland AG, part of Springer Nature 2019
This work is subject to copyright. All rights are solely and exclusively licensed by the Publisher, whether the whole or part of the material is concerned, specifically the rights of translation, reprinting, reuse of illustrations, recitation, broadcasting, reproduction on microfilms or in any other physical way, and transmission or information storage and retrieval, electronic adaptation, computer software, or by similar or dissimilar methodology now known or hereafter developed.
The use of general descriptive names, registered names, trademarks, service marks, etc. in this publication does not imply, even in the absence of a specific statement, that such names are exempt from the relevant protective laws and regulations and therefore free for general use.
The publisher, the authors and the editors are safe to assume that the advice and information in this book are believed to be true and accurate at the date of publication. Neither the publisher nor the authors or the editors give a warranty, express or implied, with respect to the material contained herein or for any errors or omissions that may have been made. The publisher remains neutral with regard to jurisdictional claims in published maps and institutional affiliations.

Cover credit: Steven Scott Taylor/Alamy Stock Photo Tommy London/Alamy Stock Photo Flag Icon © Kelsey Chisamore/Noun Project
Cover design by Tjaša Krivec

This Palgrave Macmillan imprint is published by the registered company Springer Nature Switzerland AG
The registered company address is: Gewerbestrasse 11, 6330 Cham, Switzerland

PREFACE AND ACKNOWLEDGEMENTS

This volume marks the tenth instalment of a series that has charted the evolution of political communication in Britain over the last four decades. Collectively the books cover a period that saw both Margaret Thatcher and Tony Blair each win three successive elections, the Liberal Democrat (and their antecedents') surge and eventual fall away, as well as breakthroughs for once marginal forces like the SNP, UKIP and the Greens. Allied to this there have been significant developments in the way campaigns are conducted and cumulatively this series provides invaluable insights here from the vantage point of those most responsible for pioneering strategic and tactical innovations. The transformation of electioneering is closely entwined with changes in the reporting and polling of elections, two other subjects that have featured prominently in the *Political Communications* books. Successive volumes demonstrate how news coverage of campaigns has evolved during an era in which broadcast and newspaper journalists have experienced a significant challenge to their past dominance. Central to this has been a fragmentation in audiences for mainstream print and television news that once provided voters with most of their information about rival parties, leaders and policies. This in turn has led the polling industry to experiment with new methods to cope with the growing complexities of understanding how (and if) the public engages with the contemporary electoral process.

Like its predecessor volumes this book offers comment and analysis on the momentous event that was the 2017 General Election. It is fair to say that although several previous elections may have been a tad predictable, even relatively uneventful, they remain important to study because cumulatively these campaigns provide insights into the continuities and changes in political communication. The 2017 race was both interesting and innovative for reasons explored in this book. When any election is called it piques media if not necessarily public interest even though, in this case, most opinion forming commentators concluded the outcome was in little doubt: Theresa May and the Conservatives were assumed to be on course to a comfortable victory with the only uncertainty being the size of her majority. Successive polling figures and results from the local elections held just after the campaign began reinforced this perception. There had been surprise when the characteristically cautious May had reneged on her promise not go to the country before the current parliament had run its course in 2020. But this was as nothing to the shock felt when it became clear that the Prime Minister had gambled and lost her Commons' majority. It was an unenviable position to be in for a once seemingly unassailable leader now trying to govern an already complex Brexit process.

The editors are very grateful to numerous people for their help. On this anniversary marking our tenth volume we would like to pay a special tribute to past contributors and, in particular, our predecessors who have served on the editorial team: John Bartle, Ivor Crewe, Brian Gosschalk, Jane Green, Martin Harrop and lastly, and by no means least, Bob Worcester who did so much to support the *Political Communications* series following its inception. We are delighted to present chapters from a varied group of practitioners and academics that collectively explain and analyse what happened. Each contribution brings a different perspective in addition to offering invaluable insights into this most fascinating of campaigns. We are extremely grateful to our authors for their efforts. We would also like to express our gratitude to the following: Andrew Chadwick, Jon Crannage, Dipesh Dhimar, Klara Isaiah, Rachel Mackenzie, Olly Swanton, Dane Vincent, Denise Wade, Xing Wang and Judy Wing of Loughborough University. Thanks to Helen Tighe of the University's Institute for Advanced Studies; Jim Kelleher and Suzanne Owens of Ipsos MORI; and Ric Bailey, Sydney Budgeon, Chris Carman, Ivor Gaber, Erik Geddes, Gaby Hinsliff, Dan Holden, Dan Jackson, Michael Jermey, Dennis Kavanagh, Adam Langleben, Kerry-Ann Mendoza, Darren Mott, Anthony Mughan, Charles Pattie, Mike

Smithson and Gideon Skinner. Special thanks go to Jo Sheriff and Tilly Wring. We would also like to sincerely thank Ambra Finotello, Oliver Foster, Imogen Gordon Clark and Sooryadeepth Jayakrishnan of our publishers Palgrave Macmillan for their invaluable help and patience.

Loughborough, UK   Dominic Wring
London, UK   Roger Mortimore
London, UK   Simon Atkinson

CONTENTS

Notes on Contributors

Simon Atkinson is Chief Knowledge Officer at Ipsos.

Jay G. Blumler is Emeritus Professor of the Social and Political Aspects of Broadcasting at the University of Leeds.

Paul Brand is a Political Correspondent for ITV News.

Paul Carroll is Associate Director in the Qualitative Social Research Unit at Ipsos MORI.

Greg Cook is Head of Political Strategy for the Labour Party.

David Deacon is Professor of Communication and Media Analysis at Loughborough University.

John Downey is Professor of Comparative Media Analysis at Loughborough University.

Craig Gent is Senior Editor at Novara Media.

Isla Glaister is a Journalist at Sky News.

James Gurling was Chair of the Liberal Democrats' 2017 General Election Campaign.

Suzanne Hall is Head of the Qualitative Social Research Unit at Ipsos MORI.

Emily Harmer is Lecturer in Media at the University of Liverpool.

Will Jennings is Professor of Political Science and Public Policy at the University of Southampton.

Damian Lyons Lowe is Chief Executive of Survation.

Declan McDowell-Naylor is a Teaching Fellow in Politics and International Relations at Queen Mary, University of London.

Roger Mortimore is Professor of Public Opinion and Political Analysis at King's College London and Ipsos MORI's Director of Political Analysis.

Keiran Pedley is Divisional Director at GfK.

Angela Phillips is Professor in Journalism at Goldsmiths, University of London.

Abi Rhodes is a Doctoral Candidate in Critical Theory and Cultural Studies at the University of Nottingham.

Anthony Ridge-Newman is Lecturer in Digital Media at Liverpool Hope University.

David Smith is a Research Assistant in Communication and Media at Loughborough University.

Rosalynd Southern is Lecturer in Political Communication at the University of Liverpool.

James Stanyer is Professor of Communication and Media Analysis at Loughborough University.

Michael Walker is host of the TyskySour video podcast at Novara Media.

Dominic Wring is Professor of Political Communication at Loughborough University.

List of Figures

LIST OF TABLES

Seven Weeks Is a Long Time in Politics

Dominic Wring, Roger Mortimore and Simon Atkinson

The 2017 General Election will live longer in the popular memory than many recent campaigns. It provided another dramatic outcome comparable to that of the Brexit referendum and the American presidential race in the preceding twelve months. If the victories of Leave and Donald Trump stunned most commentators, this election also confounded the many who had predicted its result was a foregone conclusion from the start. There was a prevailing consensus that Theresa May's calling of the election would deliver the new Prime Minister a landslide victory. Such a result would cement her hitherto commanding reputation as an assured politician who could get things done. As May said in justifying her sudden announcement, a decisive public vote of confidence from the electorate was vital for her and her government going forward into the potentially fraught negotiations over the country's withdrawal

D. Wring (✉)
Social Sciences, Loughborough University, Loughborough, UK
e-mail: d.j.wring@lboro.ac.uk

R. Mortimore
King's College London, London, UK
e-mail: roger.mortimore@ipsos-mori.com; roger.mortimore@kcl.ac.uk

S. Atkinson
Ipsos MORI, London, UK
e-mail: simon.atkinson@ipsos.com

© The Author(s) 2019   1
D. Wring et al. (eds.), *Political Communication in Britain*,
https://doi.org/10.1007/978-3-030-00822-2_1

from the EU. Seasoned observers predicted this would therefore be the 'Brexit election' albeit, they surmised, without the drama and unpredictability of the referendum campaign. But when the exit poll was broadcast on election night it contradicted most expert predictions by correctly anticipating voters would return the second hung parliament in a decade and only the third since the Second World War. Speaking after the full results were known, the broadcaster Jon Snow confessed he 'knows nothing' such was the shock of what had just happened. It was a remarkable climax to a frenetic seven weeks of campaigning and one that left the future direction of British politics and government in some considerable doubt.

Theresa May and the Conservatives received the largest UK wide vote share of 42.4%, up from 36.9% in 2015, and ordinarily this would have been enough to secure a commanding majority in the House of Commons. But with only 317 MPs returned, the party was down 13 seats and thereby forfeited the right to form a government on its own. This was because the growth of support for Jeremy Corbyn and Labour in successive polls during the campaign materialized on election day, securing them 40.0% of the vote. The Parliamentary Labour Party grew from 232 to 262 seats in the Commons and thereby denied May her widely anticipated majority. The Scottish National Party (with 35 MPs, down from 56 in 2015, on a UK wide 3.0% share of the vote this time) and Liberal Democrats (12, up from 8 seats, on a 7.4% share) came third place in terms of seats and votes won respectively in a disappointing outcome for both. The election also marked a setback for the Greens who retained their sole existing seat but fell back in terms of vote share. More spectacularly UKIP suffered a haemorrhage in support in the aftermath of a Brexit referendum that had delivered on their core demand for British withdrawal from the EU. Northern Ireland's main parties fared better with both the Democratic Unionist Party and Sinn Fein further asserting their electoral dominance within the province. The 10 DUP MPs would subsequently provide Theresa May with the vital support necessary to ensure she continued as Prime Minister after her electoral setback.[1]

---

[1] This volume focuses on what might be called process aspects of this General Election as others in our series have traditionally done. The book also complements others that have appeared on the 2017 campaign, each taking a distinct focus of its own. *The British General Election of 2017* offers a comprehensive account of a dramatic election, drawing on interviews with many of the key people involved (Cowley and Kavanagh 2018). *Britain Votes*

THE ROAD TO 2017: BREXIT AND ITS AFTERMATH

Theresa May's calling of a snap election surprised the large numbers of professional pundits who comment on politics. It proved to be a bold move for a politician hitherto noted for a cautious approach that had served her well in her ascent to the highest office. Previously May had repeatedly denied that she would go to the country and seek her own parliamentary mandate in place of the slender one she had inherited from David Cameron. The Prime Minister had originally emerged as Cameron's most likely successor following his resignation in the aftermath of Remain's defeat in the 2016 Brexit referendum. The subsequently truncated contest for the Conservative leadership involved only two rounds of voting among MPs and confirmed May's frontrunner status as various pro-Leave figures vied to present themselves as credible alternatives. Despite her previous support for Remain, the Home Secretary's reputation only grew as those of rival candidates Boris Johnson, Michael Gove and Andrea Leadsom suffered under intense media scrutiny. They and others bowed to the seemingly inevitable and were voted out or withdrew from the race, enabling May to be anointed leader and the new Prime Minister.

Theresa May's coronation and her declaration that 'Brexit means Brexit' helped the Conservatives avoid a potentially protracted leadership contest that had threatened to reignite the divisions over Europe that had long divided the party. By contrast Labour was convulsed by the fallout from the Brexit referendum despite having outwardly promoted a relatively united pro-Remain message during the campaign. Party leader Jeremy Corbyn came under sustained criticism that led to a major challenge from his parliamentary colleagues. An unprecedented number of frontbenchers resigned in protest at what they claimed had been Corbyn's ineffectual campaigning on behalf of Remain, a charge he himself denied. A no confidence ballot of Labour MPs calling on him to

contains a wide-range of chapters on all aspects of the election including the rival parties, voter behaviour, key debates and how the campaign affected the different constituent parts of the UK be they geographical or demographic (Tonge et al. 2017). The *Britain at the Polls* volume is especially useful in setting the varying fortunes of the contending parties in the dramatic context of the last two years (Allen and Bartle 2018). *Betting the House* offers a journalistic account of what happened (Ross and McTague 2017) while Steve Howell, a campaign advisor working for Jeremy Corbyn, offers his perspective on Labour's dramatic recovery and is suitably entitled *Game Changer* (Howell 2017).

resign was passed by a large margin, but the leader refused to step down, having been emboldened by extra-parliamentary support from the party grassroots and trades union affiliates. In a critical showdown Labour's National Executive Committee narrowly allowed Corbyn to participate in a new leadership contest forced by his opponents. After a protracted debate a majority on the NEC agreed that incumbency negated the need for the leader to attract the requisite number of fresh nominations from MPs he might have found difficult to obtain. The National Executive vote over whether the leader should be able to defend his position against eventual challenger Owen Smith proved closer than the subsequent ballot of members which overwhelmingly returned Corbyn by a slightly larger margin than in his initial victory of 2015.

Against all prior expectations, including those of his supporters, Jeremy Corbyn had won the 2015 leadership contest following the resignation of Ed Miliband. First elected in 1983, the veteran left-winger and anti-austerity campaigner had struggled to gather sufficient nominations from fellow MPs and only got on the ballot paper by gaining several endorsements from non-supporters who thought his inclusion would broaden the debate over Labour's future. Corbyn subsequently articulated a message that found huge resonance with the large numbers who swelled the ranks of the party and contributed to his extraordinary campaign. This gave him the momentum that proved unstoppable as he overcame former Cabinet ministers Andy Burnham and Yvette Cooper as well as Liz Kendall to triumph in the first ballot with just under 60% of the votes. And although comfortably re-elected leader in 2016, many of his internal critics remained hostile to Corbyn's vision, believing he was turning Labour into what several of them complained was 'a party of protest not power'.

Theresa May's initial experiences as party leader could not have been more different to those of Jeremy Corbyn. The new Prime Minister enjoyed consistently favourable coverage from her many supporters in the press and this proved useful in maintaining a sense of unity and purpose within government, particularly during the initial negotiations regarding Brexit. This comparatively calm period in office made what subsequently happened during the 2017 campaign all the more of a surprise, wrong-footing the many commentators who believed there would be a landslide Conservative victory. Unfortunately for May the election she herself had called marked the period where her fortunes abruptly changed—for the worse. Despite having had the element of surprise and having also reassembled the team of strategists who had guided the party to success two years before, the Conservative leader appeared underprepared for the weeks ahead that would come to define her premiership.

The travails surrounding the Conservative and Labour leaderships dominated the political landscape between the elections of 2015 and 2017 to the detriment of other parties vying for exposure. Following the extraordinary media phenomenon of 'Cleggmania' in 2010, new leader Tim Farron struggled to attract attention for the Liberal Democrats in the aftermath of their electoral rout in 2015. The party hoped 2017 would enable them to recoup much lost ground (see Chapter "The Liberal Democrat Campaign"), buoyed by a performance in the local elections that was their best since joining the Coalition government in 2010. The by-election capture of Richmond Park from Zak Goldsmith in December 2016 had also boosted their confidence and hopes that they could make gains in this campaign through virtue of being the only major party that unequivocally opposed Brexit.

Some parties approached this election with considerable anxiety and none more so than UKIP who had won an eighth of the vote in 2015 under Nigel Farage's leadership when the demand for a referendum on EU membership had been very much a live issue. But the party found it difficult to re-establish a raison d'être now that the vote for Brexit had been won. It also didn't help that Farage's immediate successor Diane James stepped down as leader days after having been elected to the post in September 2016. Under James' replacement Paul Nuttall, UKIP suffered sweeping losses in the local elections and it became clear that in many constituencies they would not nominate a candidate for the general election. Since Theresa May was appealing for a mandate to implement Brexit it seemed reasonable to expect much of party's votes might swing to the Conservatives. Labour candidates in seats that had delivered a "Leave" majority in the referendum, particularly in the North of England, were reportedly nervous that the Tories could be poised to capitalize from UKIP's demise.

If the Tories' positioning weakened UKIP, a more radically inclined Labour party presented an obvious threat to the Greens now jointly led by their only MP Caroline Lucas. The similarly left-leaning Scottish National Party also faced a potentially stronger challenge from a reinvigorated Corbyn led opposition having previously won 50% of the votes in Scotland and all but three of the seats in 2015. It would be a difficult feat to repeat, particularly as the party and leader Nicola Sturgeon, now in power at Holyrood, were receiving lower ratings for their performance than they had two years before. The First Minister had recently called for a second referendum on Scottish independence in the aftermath of the UK wide vote for Brexit. While the country had supported Remain, voters were more divided over separatism and the issue contributed to the resurgence of the Scottish Conservatives under their youthful, pro-unionist leader Ruth Davidson. Together with a modest recovery by Labour in one of its former traditional heartlands it made it more difficult to predict the electoral outcome north of the border.

FOREGONE CONCLUSION? THE VOTERS DECIDE

When Theresa May called the election, most observers believed her government would be returned with a substantially increased majority. The opinion polls at the time were almost unanimous in giving the Conservatives a lead of twenty or more percentage points and there was widespread speculation that Labour might be facing a more devastating defeat than in the nadir that was the election of 1983. The assumption that May was on course for victory, possibly by a landslide, was shared by many in the Conservative dominated press as well as several despondent Labour candidates, some of whom argued May's calling of an election should and could have been more forcefully resisted. The local elections on 4 May appeared to confirm such fears when Labour received the national equivalent vote share of just 28%, the worst performance by the opposition in the years these figures have been calculated including those during the leadership of Michael Foot in the early 1980s. Writing two weeks later Trevor Kavanagh, Associate Editor of *The Sun* (22 May), was still confidently predicting that: 'Mrs May will have to settle for a paltry 94 (majority)... don't worry she'll do much better than that'. What came next, however, completely confounded most commentators' initial expectations as to what would happen, producing one of the most dramatic election campaigns and certainly one that generated some of the largest recorded movements in the polls.

During the seven week long campaign Labour increased its support from an average 26% share of the vote in the polls immediately after the election was called to 41% in the eventual result,[2] the biggest sustained

---

[2] These figures measure share of the vote in Great Britain, as is the practice of almost all opinion polls; the share of the vote for the whole United Kingdom, including Northern Ireland where Labour runs no candidates, is slightly lower.

movement in party support during a British election campaign in at least three-quarters of a century. Much of this movement was evident at the time from the opinion polls, although most of the polls significantly under-estimated Labour's final vote and there was still a general expectation of a clear Conservative victory on election night; with the benefit of hindsight, and the help of further data, it is possible to observe a clearer picture of what happened. Although the Conservatives lost support during the campaign, their losses were much more moderate than Labour's gains and in fact they achieved a substantial increase in their total vote compared to the previous election. They lost some votes to Labour, especially among those who had voted "Remain" in the referendum, but picked up other votes from Labour among "Leavers", and direct switching from Conservative to Labour probably made a relatively small net contribution to the overall swing.

The polling in this campaign followed on from the 2015 debacle when none of the final polls by the major research companies had anticipated the Conservatives winning an outright majority. This time around, the overwhelming consensus among the published polls was that the Tories were on course to win handsomely if not by a landslide (see Chapter "The Polls in 2017" on the performance of the polls). There were two notable outliers whose findings pointed to the eventual result. Survation's final poll indicated Labour would secure at least 40% of the vote and that this was likely to lead to another hung parliament (see Chapter "'Yer Jaiket Is Hanging by a Shooglie Peg!': Fear, Groupthink and Outliers"). You Gov research also suggested a potential upset was on its way. Despite headline voting intention figures in line with those of rival companies, the firm also used new statistical techniques to make detailed constituency-level projections that surprised commentators and even attracted ridicule. Significantly these studies forecast possible Labour victories in the previously safe Conservative seats of Canterbury and Kensington, and, overall, also pointed to a hung parliament.

The turnout in 2017 was the highest for some years, and this was an important element in the swing: most of these new voters voted Labour. Early post-election estimates of the vote suggested a dramatic increase in the turnout of 18–24 year olds: this "youthquake" was interpreted in some quarters as the primary and even sole explanation for Labour's near success, and there was much discussion of how much it owed to developments in the party's campaigning practices so as to reach and win over young voters more effectively. But data from the British Election Study has since cast doubt on whether there was really a significant rise

in turnout among the youngest group, suggesting this factor is not so crucial to explaining the increase in Labour's vote. More importantly there is,
however, agreement that Labour achieved a greatly increased share among
those younger citizens who did vote, not only as regards the 18–24 year
olds but within all age groups under 45. The so-called 'youthquake'
might be better termed a 'youthful quake' and this more than offset the
swing of older voters to the Conservatives by giving Labour a higher share
of the vote among the younger age groups than for many years; age is,
for the moment, the clearest dividing line in British voting behaviour (for
further analysis of this see Chapter "Seismographs for Youthquakes—How
Do We Know How the Public Voted in British General Elections?").

One of the most prominent aspects of political communications in
modern elections is the publication of opinion polls. At the simplest level,
they can make up a significant part of the subject matter that is reported
by the media, especially the voting intention polls whose measurements
allow coverage of the "horserace", which is sometimes the biggest part
of the media's narrative (see Chapter "Why Polling Matters: The Role of
Data in Our Democracy"). They also allow the voters a channel of communication with the parties, giving feedback on what is being done and
said, which can sometimes prompt changes in the conduct of a campaign.
Further, they can be agenda setters, influencing understanding of the context in which the election is being fought, which comes to be reflected
in the way journalists frame their stories and in how editors distinguish
the important from the unimportant whether reporting events, issues or
personalities. An important part of that context, of course, is the standing
of the parties, which may have implications for the very meaning of the
votes that will be cast. Somewhat paradoxically, the criticism of the polls
arising from their collective failure to anticipate what came as a surprising
result in 2015 meant there was less noticeable reporting of their findings
in 2017 and yet the headline trend, suggesting the Conservatives were on
course to win, still clearly informed a great deal of the media coverage.

Because of the shift in party support over the seven weeks of the
campaign, there has arguably never been a modern British election in
which the political context changed so dramatically between the opening manoeuvres and polling day. In April, it seemed almost certain that
the government would win easily, and that a vote for Labour was a vote
to restrict the increase in Theresa May's majority; seven weeks later
the Conservative lead had evaporated and a vote for Labour was, in
a very meaningful sense, an endorsement of Jeremy Corbyn as Prime
Minister. Without the opinion polls, the voters would have had only the

judgments of the journalists and the claims of the politicians on which to base their understanding of the contest in which they were participating. But although they reflected the direction of movement during the campaign correctly, many polls under-estimated the final Labour vote and left most observers expecting a Conservative majority rather than the hung parliament that followed. One of the main talking points of the 2017 election was, once again, the discrepancy between the final projections of the polls and the results as they emerged on election night (for further commentary on this see Chapter "Election Night: The View from Sky News").

TRADING PLACES: A TALE OF TWO LEADERS

Announcing the election against the backdrop of Downing Street, the Prime Minister pointedly used the term 'strong and stable' three times in her brief speech. But an obvious problem in communicating the party's message became self-evident once Theresa May began campaigning. Her seeming over reliance on (and yet apparent awkwardness in repeating) the party's core slogan 'Strong and Stable in the National Interest' detracted from the impression strategists wanted her to convey. If the phrase made for potentially decent print advertising copy it sounded unconvincing when uttered by the leader herself. May's robotic use of the words in speeches and a Party Election Broadcast might not have mattered had the ensuing campaign turned out differently. But it would subsequently prove near impossible to avoid the slogan given it adorned all aspects of the party's election branding together with the leader's personal battlebus. The Prime Minister's central rationale for asking the public to give her an endorsement to strengthen her hand in forthcoming negotiations over Brexit was also not without problems in that it placed considerable emphasis on telling the electorate what they could do for her government, rather than primarily what her government could do for the country.

When the Prime Minister opted not to participate in the face to face leader debates this sent out a contradictory message from a politician who had explicitly stood on a platform of being 'strong'. May's strategists had likely calculated appearing in a televised encounter was an unnecessary risk because of the Conservative lead in the polls and given the format could boost the prominence of rival politicians in the way it had Nick Clegg and Nicola Sturgeon in 2010 and 2015 respectively. The Prime Minister explained her refusal to appear in the televised debates (that attracted millions of viewers) was because she preferred to meet the public and listen to what they had to say. But this claim was undermined by news footage of her on the campaign trail knocking on doors and receiving no response. When May did meet a member of the public in her one of her rare campaign encounters with a voter in Oxfordshire it was to receive criticism of the government's welfare policies.

Theresa May's approach to campaigning revolved around making short speeches to supporters in controlled locations in the hope of generating favourable photo-opportunities and media exposure. The format suited May's style but produced predictable copy and staid images (see Chapter "'Strong and Stable' to 'Weak and Wobbly': The Conservative Election Campaign"). This might not have mattered so much but for the drama that unfolded in the aftermath of the Conservative manifesto launch. Initially the document had been praised as an effective programme for government which marked a break with the past and a new direction for the party and country. This narrative soon changed when ordinarily supportive commentators in newspapers like the *Mail* and *Telegraph* criticized the party's proposals relating to social care provision for the elderly. The policy was attacked for its potentially negative impact on people seen as natural Conservative supporters who had saved prudently to become home owners.

Although it took a weekend for the implications of this manifesto pledge to get fully picked up, May's response failed to assuage doubts about the proposal. The Prime Minister subsequently claimed her clarification of the policy did not amount to the change many media commentators and others were calling it. But the veteran observer of British elections, Sir David Butler saw it differently, tweeting "In the 20 general election campaigns I've followed, I can't remember a U-turn on this scale – or much that could be called a U-turn at all." The overall impact of this incident was to raise significant doubts as to whether the apparently panicked May was as 'strong and stable' as her slogan suggested (for discussion of voter reactions see Chapter "An Ever-Changing Mood: Qualitative Research and the 2017 Election Campaign").

May's initial spell in Downing Street prior to the election had gone well if judged by successive polls on her leadership, the party's standing and the government's handling of Brexit. The campaign brought this to a humiliating end and in the most highly public of ways. The confusion over what became known as the 'dementia tax' caused significant problems for an incumbent who had called an election because of her desire, as she explained, to guarantee 'strong and stable leadership with me in the national interest where what you see is what you get' before warning the alternative would be a 'coalition of chaos under Jeremy Corbyn'. This gamble ultimately failed in that it denied her the large majority she craved although the Conservatives' standing in the polls never collapsed. Rather what successive opinion surveys picked up was the narrowing of the Tory lead over Labour, the only other party with a realistic chance of forming a government. For their part Jeremy Corbyn and his colleagues appeared to benefit from a surge in enthusiasm from among their core voters and younger people including students. Corbyn's own support network Momentum played a role in cultivating this support (Chapter "Movement-Led Electoral Campaigning: Momentum in the 2017 General Election"). Growing confidence and an outbreak of unity in Labour was reinforced by a distinctive and broadly well received manifesto which included pledges on housing, education and the NHS that collectively marked a break with the prevailing pro-austerity consensus (see Chapter "The Labour Campaign"). The document's title 'For the Many, Not the Few' also provided the party's main campaigning slogan.

The 2017 election was a turning point for a Jeremy Corbyn now liberated from having to defend his leadership on a regular basis including, by coincidence, on ITV Good Morning Britain a couple of hours before May announced the election would be taking place. When asked by presenter Piers Morgan to name one mistake he had made, Corbyn disarmed his interviewer by saying he couldn't because there were 'too many'. This lightness of touch would prove an asset in the coming weeks. Corbyn clearly benefitted from his considerable experience as a campaigner although he was not as central to his party's branding as May was to hers, perhaps an acknowledgement that his personal ratings trailed those of the Prime Minister. But perceptions of both were about to change, and it would be the Labour leader who emerged stronger and more stable from this election. During the early stages of the campaign Corbyn was compared with Michael Foot, a fellow left-winger who had been leader when the former was first elected an MP. The spectre of 1983 was invoked by several commentators who saw parallels with that landslide defeat and one they believed was again about to befall Labour. But rather than 2017 heralding another meltdown, the leader was met with seemingly genuine enthusiasm wherever he appeared.

Like Michael Foot, Jeremy Corbyn wanted to take his message out directly to the electorate by addressing large crowds in public gatherings as part of an attempt to bypass impartial broadcasters and the largely hostile press. Such events appeared even more compelling because of their apparent spontaneity and an authenticity that set them apart from the rival gatherings involving May, not to mention most Labour leaders since Foot. The sheer scale of the crowds also acted as a buffer against interventions by detractors that might have otherwise diverted the focus away from the goodwill being generated. Corbyn's reception provided favourable images that repeatedly went viral on social media and cumulatively helped underline his growing credibility as an alternative prime minister rather than, as mainstream news media had often framed him, a beleaguered leader of the opposition.

GAME CHANGERS? THE RIVAL MEDIA

Jeremy Corbyn had been the significant beneficiary of social media in his successful campaign for the party leadership. When neither of the two Labour sympathizing national newspapers endorsed him in the 2015 contest, potential Corbyn backers could look beyond the *Guardian* and *Mirror* to a burgeoning range of web-based sources for more supportive commentary and analysis about him. The new online platforms that either emerged or grew during that campaign helped the veteran left-winger win and then defend his position in the 2016 leadership race. This experience helped forge an independent network of supportive sites including The Canary, Another Angry Voice, Skwawkbox, Evolve Politics, London Economic and Novara Media. These and a myriad of other like-minded web-based operations proved valuable to Labour going into the 2017 election because they facilitated the swift mobilization of activists who were able to rapidly share messages and memes on Facebook, Twitter and elsewhere throughout the seven-week-long campaign (Chapter "Alternative Media: A New Factor in Electoral Politics?"). In one notable post, the leader was seen in conversation with musical artist JME in a widely circulated video that urged people to register to vote. This and other encounters between Corbyn and celebrities popular among the young appeared more natural when compared to the contrived meeting between his predecessor Ed Miliband and eventual endorser Russell Brand in 2015 (see Chapter "#GE2017: Digital Media and the Campaigns").

In the two years since the 2015 election there has been a rapid development in online news be it of a mainstream or alternative character, and whether it was attached to a traditional provider. Prominent among the latter, established brands were the *Guardian* and *Mail* who had successfully pioneered UK originated digital platforms, albeit with much American oriented content (Chapter "Alternative Agendas or More of the Same? Online News Coverage of the 2017 UK Election" includes a study of these and other sites). Familiar media organizations like the *Mirror* and *Sun* have also invested resources in their web content as their print sales have declined. The increasingly varied market for news has been further complicated by growth in online only sites including those likely to appeal more to younger adult audiences and that have taken a specific interest in reporting on British politics such as Huffington Post, Vice and BuzzFeed.

The 2015 election and 2016 referendum underlined the apparent potency of the traditionally partisan national newspaper despite the marked reduction in hard copy sales. Like the previous campaign, 2017 saw another concerted attempt by pro-Conservative titles like the *Sun*, *Mail* and *Express* to question and undermine the credibility of the Labour leadership (Chapter "A Tale of Two Parties: Press and Television Coverage of the Campaign"). Corbyn was accused of being an apologist for, or even a supporter of, various groups involved in political violence. This potentially mattered because these and other print newspapers remain popular with older people, the age demographic traditionally most likely to exercise their right to vote. The press also has a still enduring significance beyond its immediate readership in that it can and does influence the wider news agenda (Chapter "The Agenda-Setting Role of Newspapers in the UK 2017 Elections"). The most obvious example of this are the dedicated slots that are routinely given over by the major radio and television outlets to reviewing stories that originate from paper copies of the said publications.

Partisan press content can and does shape media narratives that inform˙ how leading politicians are treated by broadcasters (for a wider discussion of how television covered the election, see Chapters "Broadcasting the Snap Election: Surprising Politics but Familiar Production" and "BBC Campaign Coverage Policy"). At the outset of the campaign the veteran BBC journalist David Dimbleby joined more radical commentators in expressing concern over what he suggested had been the excessively critical mainstream news coverage of Jeremy Corbyn. Nonetheless Corbyn subsequently found himself repeatedly questioned over his past links with various causes including in his main set-piece interrogations by the BBC's Andrew Neil and Sophy Ridge of Sky News. Perhaps somewhat paradoxically an increasingly confident Labour leader was able to defend his record when dealing with such robust questioning whereas Theresa May attracted varying degrees of ridicule for her awkward responses to seemingly innocuous queries from ITV's Julie Etchingham and other journalists about her formative experiences and personal life during supposedly 'soft', human interest orientated interviews on network television. This performance, together with her decision not to debate opponents live on air, detracted from May's attempt to portray herself as a strong leader and despite appearances in more conventional programming where she appeared to cope better when being interrogated by Neil, Ridge and the other leading interviewers.

STRUCTURE OF THE BOOK

This volume is divided into three main sections, each devoted to the media, campaigning and polling aspects of the election. The first section of the book, focusing on how the race was covered, is introduced by a piece from the Loughborough University team who monitored the mainstream print and television news organizations' outputs during the campaign. David Deacon and his colleagues provide a comprehensive assessment of the issues and personalities that defined this election. In marked contrast to 2015, reporting of the 2017 race was dominated by the two major parties and particularly their leaders Theresa May and Jeremy Corbyn to a far greater degree. Coverage of the so-called 'electoral process' was once again to the fore but not as much as last time, reflecting the way Labour's leaked manifesto together with the Conservative's 'dementia tax' problems helped boost reporting of policy related matters. Significantly the fallout from the debate over May's social care plans led to some Tory supporting press titles to briefly switch from attacking Corbyn to criticizing the government. And despite the recency of the EU referendum, and the related controversy over immigration, this topic was not as dominant as some predicted at the beginning of the campaign. This reflected the way other issues, such as security in the aftermath of the Manchester Arena and London Bridge attacks, asserted themselves on the news agenda.

The media section of the book features three contributions that complement one another by focusing on different aspects of the news services provided by the main television channels. In his chapter ITV Political Correspondent Paul Brand reflects on his experiences covering a surprise election and an ensuing campaign that would have ordinarily been the subject of considerable planning. The piece notes the extent to which 2017 was dominated by the two major parties to the exclusion of rivals that had enjoyed far more coverage in 2015. The contrasting approaches of the Conservatives and Labour to journalists are discussed: whereas Theresa May tended to be remote and guarded in her carefully controlled appearances, Jeremy Corbyn appeared to be more accessible and expansive in the various open public meetings he attended. Paul Brand also acknowledges the impact of other factors on the campaign, not least the terrorist atrocities, as well as the decision by Ofcom to relax some of the rules previously governing the reporting of elections, a move that has enabled journalists some greater degree of editorial freedom in deciding which parties to cover in a given locality.

Jay Blumler takes the reader behind the BBC's cameras to consider how editorial policy is formulated and implemented by considering the decision-making process in this and the previous elections. In doing so he draws on his extensive knowledge of the topic to highlight the major trends in contemporary political journalism and the challenges as well as the threats facing broadcast news providers. He notes the Corporation must simultaneously balance the need to remain relevant to audiences with the demands from rival politicians anxious to promote a favourable impression of themselves and their manifestos. Jay Blumler also conveys how BBC editors, despite the prevailing 'groupthink' that the result of this election was a foregone conclusion, were determined to offer quality journalism that scrutinized the rival policies on offer. The piece ends with some reflections and observations on the future role of the BBC as a public service broadcaster reporting on elections.

Isla Glaister provides another invaluable insight into the editorial process from her vantage point of having worked on the Sky News Election Night programme. Her account captures the drama of the unfolding events as well as the considerable challenges facing a live broadcaster forced to have to rapidly change schedules because of a sudden revelation or, as in this case, the publication of an exit poll that contradicts the dominant narrative of the preceding weeks of campaigning. Moreover Isla Glaister offers a detailed account of how breaking news works over the course of a historic night where claims and counter-claims had to be sourced, quickly evaluated and then aired (or not).

If television news continues to provide many voters with their key source of information Angela Phillips explores another medium, the press, which has also been the subject of intense debate in relation to the role and nature of its impact on elections. She notes that the leading newspaper brands are now successfully publishing online as well as in their traditional print format and how they still make an important journalistic contribution during campaigns through their extensive reach and influence on the wider news agenda. Angela Phillips contends that whether in print and digital copy terms the press is (still) a force to be reckoned with, particularly when the *Mail* and other ordinarily sympathetic titles briefly turned on the Conservatives. This came at a critical point in the campaign during the calamity over a so-called 'dementia tax' that was widely perceived as being particularly detrimental to the interests of older people, the demographic most likely to vote and also still buy a hard copy of their favoured newspaper.

Many voters, especially younger people, access their news from online only sources. Emily Harmer and Rosalynd Southern explore the important and still growing digital role in politics with a content analysis of five major websites that reported on the campaign. The study considers the most popular news providers of this kind be they of the established (the BBC, Mail Online and Guardian) or newer, online only varieties (Huffington Post, and BuzzFeed). Aside from focusing on the familiar journalistic preoccupation with the electoral 'horserace' as was as substantive issues including Brexit, the analysis also reveals a keen interest (particularly on the part of the latter two websites) in allegations of bias in traditional media coverage. Harmer and Southern assess the gendered nature of online news and how and whether this departed from the male dominated television and print reporting given the prominence of women politicians on both of the two main parties' frontbenches. Despite this being a markedly presidential campaign featuring a female Prime Minister, online news coverage of the election emulated that of its offline rivals in that it was also dominated by men.

In media terms several relatively new digital platforms made a significant contribution to the election, helping generate numerous stories that went viral. The more influential of these were pro-Labour and offered an important source of support for Jeremy Corbyn's leadership. Craig Gent and Michael Walker from Novara Media, one of the most prominent of these left websites, reflect on their experiences of the campaign. They provide considerable insights into how the new online radical presence including their own organization originated and developed in a changing media ecology. Various innovative features and stories by Novara Media helped promote Corbyn and Labour policies once the election was called and also defended him against his prominent critics within the mainstream media. Gent and Walker demonstrate how the online left including The Canary, Evolve Politics and their own operation mounted a sustained and formidable attack on the Conservatives that successfully reached a wide audience while promoting certain issues that might otherwise not have attracted so much public attention.

The Conservative campaign 'won' the election in terms of gaining the largest vote share and one that was significantly better than that achieved in 2015 yet 'lost' the party the critical number of seats that deprived it of an overall majority. Opening the section on campaigning Anthony Ridge-Newman explores why this happened, focusing on the ultimately flawed strategy that centred on promoting Theresa May. Drawing on various post-mortems into the campaign that have taken place, notably on the influential website ConservativeHome, the chapter compares the 2017 setback with the success of 2015 and the ambivalent outcome in 2010. The snap election came as a considerable shock but what also proved a surprise to many was May's unpreparedness to exploit this advantage because of her soon to be revealed limitations as a campaigner. Anthony Ridge-Newman also discusses the party's failure to capitalize on previous innovative work done in the realm of digital based forms of voter engagement.

Party insider and strategist Greg Cook provides an insightful account into how Labour approached a snap election that headquarters had already been contemplating might happen despite pronouncements by the Prime Minister to the contrary. He notes the local elections and other forecasts suggested the party looked like it was in serious trouble but how a greatly enlarged activist base together with lessons learned from the previous campaign helped with preparations this time. Although Theresa May's mishandling of her manifesto commitment on social care proved a turning point, Greg Cook suggests this was one among a range of other factors that changed the dynamic of this election. He discusses the kinds of voters, including younger people, who were sympathetic to Labour and contributed to the significant closing of the gap between the major parties' vote shares.

The Liberal Democrats were still recovering from their comprehensive defeat in the 2015 general election. Leading party strategist James Girling explains how the party benefitted from approaching the 2017 campaign with many candidates already selected, the manifesto largely prepared and the basis of a strategy in place. However limited resources and the added complexity of having organized for local government elections meant the Liberal Democrats were restricted in terms of their planning. Tim Farron also faced problems in this his first (and ultimately only) election as leader largely arising from the media. Aside from this the Liberal Democrats' ability to promote their case was diminished by the relaxing of broadcast regulations that had previously helped the party gain a larger share of news attention than they traditionally receive outside of formal campaigns.

Momentum activist Abi Rhodes discusses how the group emerged from the campaign that supported Jeremy Corbyn's successful bid for the Labour leadership. Her chapter explains how the organization subsequently came to play a role in efforts to mobilize the party's vote in the election. Significantly the grassroots movement based, labour intense style of campaigning favoured by Momentum provided a contrast with the top down consultancy driven approach that has dominated contemporary British politics. There is a detailed explanation of the work of the organization that took place both offline and online and was designed to ensure Labour's message reached the maximum number of potential voters as possible. Abi Rhodes also discusses how the group benefitted from advice and training provided by members of the team behind Bernie Sanders' US presidential bid in 2016.

Declan McDowell-Naylor examines the impact of digital media on campaign communication by considering the growth of news websites and other platforms as significant conduits for political information, particularly among younger voters. The chapter focuses on the different approaches taken by the Conservative and Labour in this election. The well-financed, targeted advertising-based Tory strategy is contrasted with the more organic efforts involving a diffuse group of left-wing websites that helped galvanize an online community of committed activists. The intervention by the apparently influential network of pro-Labour websites is considered alongside the alleged shortcomings of a Conservative digital operation developed by the same people responsible for helping win in 2015.

As in previous volumes, our chapters on polling cover a wide range of perspectives, from practitioners presenting new findings that help understand the course of the election to analysis of the performance of the polls in 2017 and discussion of the role of reports of polls in modern British politics. Will Jennings examines the performance of the polls in 2017 and puts this into useful historical perspective. Among other findings he shows that it is not true, in any meaningful sense, that the polls are getting "worse"—so if they could contribute to the political communication of elections in the past, they ought still to be able to do so in coming campaigns. The chapter also analyses the polls in 2017 and compares their outputs with those from the notorious election of 2015 as well as others stretching back to 1945, the campaign where the method first cemented its reputation as a useful analytical tool. Consideration is also given over to the impact of YouGov's successful innovations in constituency polling which first pointed to some of the shock results to come.

Damian Lyons Lowe is chief executive of Survation, the only major polling company whose polls predicted the election correctly, and he explains some of the methodological decisions that made his polls different from the others. His piece also helpfully reflects on the pressures facing a researcher whose findings are out of line with the rest of the industry, and what implications this may have for pollsters' ability to contribute reliably to the reporting of the political tides beyond the unique case of 2017. As his account of a testing pre-election TV appearance shows, these pressures are sometimes a direct product of the way in which the media report opinion polls. His experience highlights two of the inherent dangers of current practice. One is that the mainstream media can have a tendency to settle upon a predominant narrative and understanding of the election, becoming much more questioning of any evidence that contradicts those assumptions than of any that supports them. The other is that television, particularly in the form of a confrontational live interview for which limited time is available, can be a poor forum for weighing the strength of technical evidence such as doubt on the standing of the parties in an election which arises from a methodological disagreement between pollsters.

Paul Carroll and Suzanne Hall trace the course of the election campaign and the changing mood of the electorate through qualitative research, a revealing approach which arguably is too little used both by journalists and academics; here the voters have the chance to speak in their own words, and this adds an extra dimension to the accounts published elsewhere based on quantitative polling. The research picks up growing frustration with leading politicians and Theresa May, particularly in the aftermath of her now infamous difficulties over the 'dementia tax'.

Roger Mortimore explores the strength of the evidence that is available on perhaps the most controversial question that has arisen in interpreting the 2017 election: whether or not Labour benefitted significantly from a "youthquake". The issue here is one of conflicting indications given by different polls and surveys, ranging in type from an instant online poll for a music website to the months-long weighty academic survey of the British Election Study; but resolving the question is not as simple as concluding that one survey is more accurate or reliable than another. He concludes that the case is not proven either way—none of the evidence is of sufficient strength to preclude the possibility that the alternative reading is correct. However, he also notes that the way in which the findings from all of these varied sources have been published has been in some ways less helpful than it might have been to the lay observer hoping to weigh up the competing claims against each other, an issue of relevance beyond the immediate puzzle of the real or phantom youthquake.

Keiran Pedley, an experienced public opinion researcher who was not involved in conducting polls in 2017, expands on some of the themes touched on by Damian Lyons Lowe and Roger Mortimore, suggesting that some of the most problematic aspects of the impact of polls in recent years may arise more from their reporting than from the way in which they have been conducted. Like Will Jennings, he puts the experience of 2017 in a wider context, considering the polls at other recent British elections and referendums, and also the reporting of polls of public opinion away from elections. He argues that excessive concentration on voting intention polls to report the "horserace" is damaging, raising expectations of a degree of accuracy which it is clear that the polls cannot always guarantee to provide, and at the same time diverting attention from the more useful evidence which the polls can give on the public's views of the issues and personalities. One of Keiran Pedley's conclusions is that, misused and misunderstood or not, opinion polls are an essential part of a modern British election. The recent House of Lords committee report on polling came to the same conclusion, rejecting the idea of banning or restricting the publication of polls during elections, although arguing that the self-regulation of the polling industry should be strengthened and criticising some aspects of the media's reporting of polls. Certainly, without polls the voters' experience of the 2017 election would have been very different.

References

Allen, N., & Bartle, J. (Eds.). (2018). *None past the polls: Britain at the polls 2017.* Manchester: Manchester University Press.

Cowley, P., & Kavanagh, D. (2018). *The British general election of 2017.* London: Palgrave Macmillan.

Howell, S. (2017). *Game changer: Eight weeks that transformed British politics.* London: Accent Press.

Ross, T., & McTague, R. (2017). *Betting the house: The inside story of the 2017 election.* London: Biteback.

Tonge, J., Leston-Bandeira, C., & Wilks-Heeg, S. (Eds.). (2017). *Britain votes 2017.* Oxford: Oxford University Press.

PART I

Media

A Tale of Two Parties: Press and Television Coverage of the Campaign

David Deacon, John Downey, David Smith, James Stanyer and Dominic Wring

Election campaigns are still shaped by mainstream news narratives despite the rise and continuing growth of alternative forms of online reporting and commentary. Moreover a significant section of the population continues to receive much of their political information from print and television sources. This in turn helps explain why the rival parties

D. Deacon (✉) · J. Downey · D. Smith · J. Stanyer · D. Wring
Social Sciences, Loughborough University, Loughborough, UK
e-mail: d.n.deacon@lboro.ac.uk

J. Downey
e-mail: j.w.downey@lboro.ac.uk

D. Smith
e-mail: D.Smith5@lboro.ac.uk

J. Stanyer
e-mail: j.stanyer@lboro.ac.uk

D. Wring
e-mail: d.j.wring@lboro.ac.uk

© The Author(s) 2019   23
D. Wring et al. (eds.), *Political Communication in Britain*,
https://doi.org/10.1007/978-3-030-00822-2_2

have remained committed to trying to manage the news in the hope of promoting a favourable impression to the widest possible audience or, at the very least, rebutting claims made by opponents. 2017 proved to be a more exciting, eventful campaign than most. Theresa May declared the snap election having looked unassailable since becoming Prime Minister in the aftermath of the Brexit referendum. Hardly any of the many media commentators predicted this campaign would deliver the surprise result it did. May lost her commanding position in parliament but also in terms of a carefully cultivated persona that was undone in the critical weeks running up to polling day.

This chapter is based on a detailed content analysis of news coverage produced on each weekday (Monday–Friday inclusive) between 5 May and 7 June, i.e. the final five weeks before polling day. The sample covers the major broadcast and print outlets. The television content comprises: Channel 4 News (7 p.m.), Channel 5 News (6.30 p.m.), BBC1 News at 10, ITV1 News at 10, Sky News at 8–8.30 p.m. The team analysed all election news found in the aforementioned TV programmes. The press material includes: *The Guardian, The I, The Daily Telegraph, The Times, The Financial Times, The Daily Mail, The Daily Express, The Mirror, The Sun, The Star*. For these newspaper titles the material sampled includes election news on the front page, the first two pages of the domestic news section, the first two pages of any specialist election section and the page containing and facing the papers' leader editorials.[1]

[1] More information on methodology is available at http://blog.lboro.ac.uk/crcc/methodology-2/. Thanks go to the coding team: Shani Burke, Gennaro Errichiello, Simon Huxtable, Jack Joyce, Herminder Kaur, Jade Markham, Nathan Ritchie, Lukas Stepanek, Ian Taylor, Rosie Tinker and Lou Tompkins. Intercoder reliability tests were conducted on all key variables:
A reliability test using a random sample of 11 newspaper stories was conducted early on in the coding process with 10 coders. It is customary to provide an inter-coder reliability measure for each variable on a coding sheet. We have focused here on the more subjective variables that require coder judgement and the scores below are for these variables on the coding sheet.
Two measures are used, average pairwise percent agreement (APPA) and Krippendorff's Alpha. Given the number of coders and the amount of training time ahead of this snap election our confidence level was set at 70% for APPA and 60% for Krippendorff's Alpha.
The identity of actors in the news: APPA 78.324%; Krippendorff's Alpha, 0.733776976662.
Disposition of actors in the news: APPA, 72.9761904762%; Krippendorff's Alpha, 0.633986079743.

This study explains what the campaign was about. It does so through measuring the visibility or presence of the different parties as well as other organizations and individuals in the news. The latter included the various rival politicians and comparisons are made with recent elections, especially the previous one in 2015. The chapter also identifies the issues that attracted most news attention and, by extension, those that were less prominent than might have been expected when the campaign began. Finally there is some consideration of the role of the (partisan) press, focusing on the negativity versus positivity of the coverage that appeared in print.

Parties

The Conservatives were the most prominent party in terms of the frequency of their representatives' appearances on TV and in print. Incumbent governing parties have tended to benefit from this advantage in the past (Miller et al. 1990), although the resulting news attention—especially in this campaign—was not always necessarily favourable. Some of this coverage was, for instance, devoted to the furore that followed in the wake of the debate over the so-called 'dementia tax', and the perceived failure of Theresa May to reassure journalists that she had not committed a 'U-turn' on her social care manifesto pledge. Together with their principal Labour rival, the Conservatives dominated the news coverage of this campaign, particularly in terms of the way the major newspapers reported the election (Fig. 1).

Between them both major parties accounted for 84% of all politicians reported by the press. In TV terms the two accounted for 67% (Fig. 2), reflecting the sensitivity of the broadcasters to reporting the various third parties. This greater diversity of voices is in part a reflection of the regulatory codes governing the provision of television news. This also helps explain why, when appearances by their representatives were compared, the margin of difference between the Conservatives and Labour was greater for the press (9.6%) than the broadcasters (2.1%). But overall

The themes of news items: APPA, 76.2962962963%; Krippendorff's Alpha, 0.684490950537.
Overall story evaluation: APPA, 86.7824074074%; Krippendorff's Alpha, 0.644939179375.

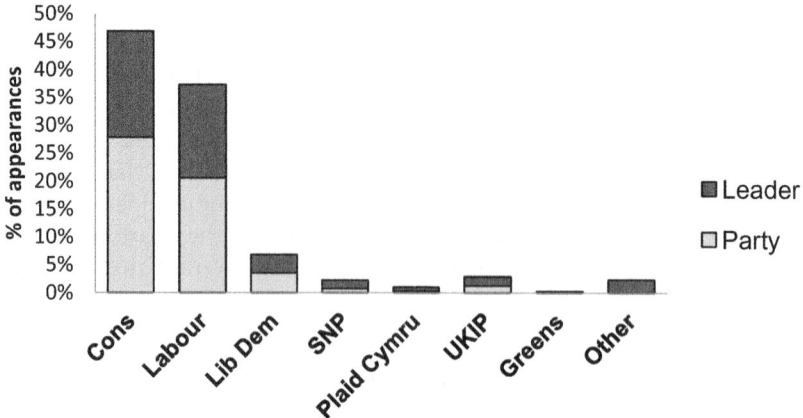

Fig. 1   Prominence of parties and their leaders in the press (5 May–7 June)

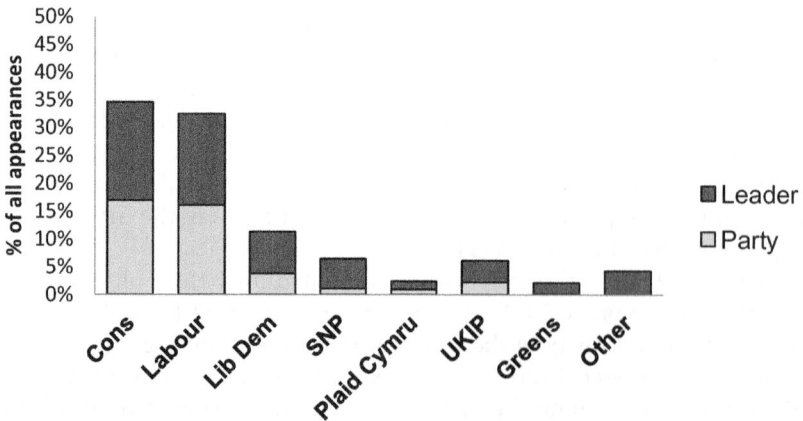

Fig. 2   Prominence of parties and their leaders on TV (5 May–7 June)

this was very much a two horse race where politicians from other parties played less of a role in terms of media coverage during the campaign. This was in striking contrast to the previous election of 2015 where there had been more diversity in respect of the representatives featured, with the Liberal Democrats, SNP and UKIP enjoying greater prominence (Deacon et al. 2017).

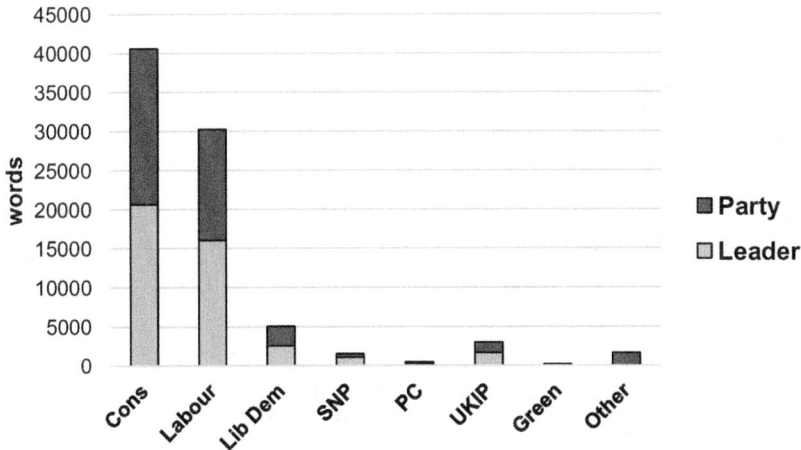

Fig. 3 Direct quotation of parties and their leaders (press)

The Conservatives' advantage in terms of their being able to attract greater news coverage during the 2017 election was reinforced by them also having representatives who were most likely to be directly quoted in the press reports (Fig. 3) and heard on TV news bulletins (Fig. 4). Once again, reflecting the Tory sympathizing leanings of the newspaper industry, Conservatives were more likely to be quoted than their Labour rivals. There was, however, greater balance in the equivalent measure of television coverage.

Broadcasters were as likely to give direct airtime to comments made by Theresa May as they were Jeremy Corbyn. By contrast the smaller parties were largely overshadowed in this respect: individually and collectively they received a relatively small amount of quotation time. This was perhaps to be expected from the largely pro-Conservative newspapers keen to promote the government and attack Labour. But television news similarly marginalized what were, in media terms at least, the 'minor' parties. This was in sharp contrast with the 2015 election where the widespread anticipation of a hung parliament had heightened interest in the various junior partners in potential coalition scenarios. Two years on, and with most polls predicting the return of a majority Conservative government, there appeared to be comparatively little reporting of the SNP, UKIP, Greens and even the Liberal Democrats.

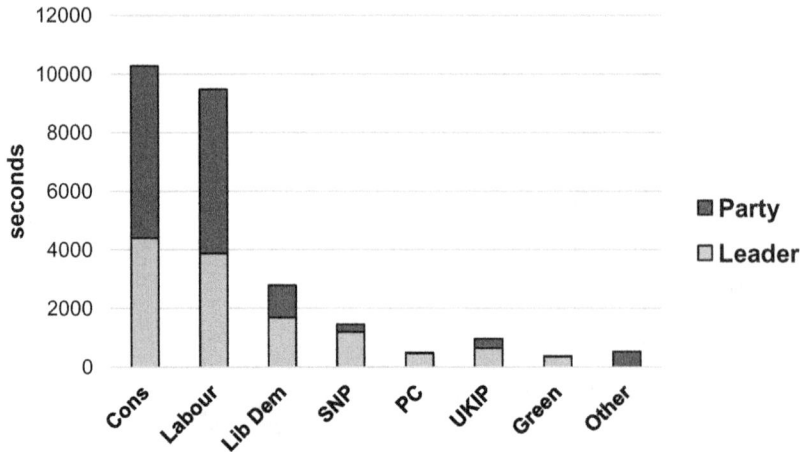

Fig. 4   Direct quotation of parties and their leaders (TV)

Representatives including the leaders of the various third parties were somewhat marginalized in this election, although they were more likely to be directly quoted on television than in the press. And as with the two major parties this larger news access was necessarily a positive. Tim Farron, for instance, spent the early part of the campaign embroiled in a controversy surrounding the discrepancy between his party's and his own stance on same sex marriage. Paul Nuttall also had a difficult start to his race with limited media attention he received largely taken up by him defending the continuing relevance of UKIP in the aftermath of a referendum vote that had delivered Brexit, the party's raison d'etre.

Aside from the changed political landscape since 2015, another significant factor that influenced coverage of this campaign was the revision of the broadcast guidelines by the regulator Ofcom. These afforded news organizations greater freedom to exercise their editorial judgement as to the degree they reported on rival leaders, parties and candidates in this election. Cumulatively the impact of the revised Ofcom guidance may have further diminished the third parties' already limited access to the airwaves. It would appear the live debates failed to help boost the profile of non-Labour/Conservative leaders in terms of the wider media

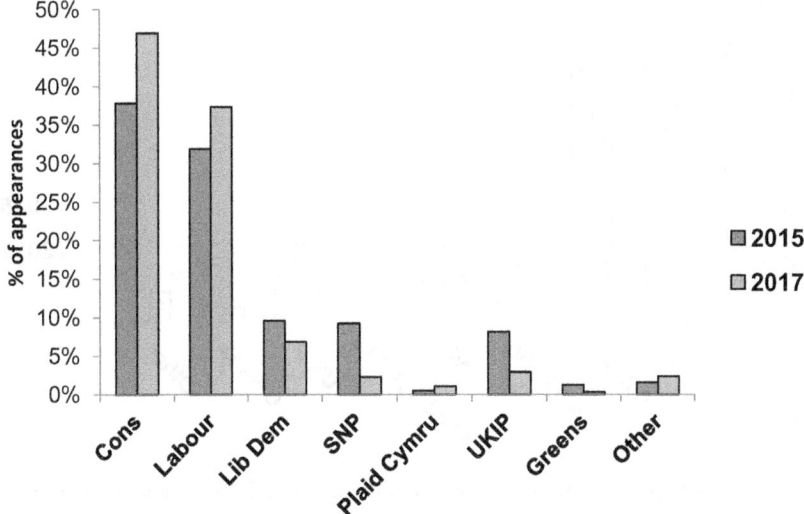

Fig. 5 Party prominence in press coverage in the 2015 and 2017 general elections

coverage certain leaders had received following such encounters in the 2010 (i.e. Nick Clegg) and 2015 (Nicola Sturgeon) campaigns. The marked decline in the news devoted to the third/minor parties since the last general election was a notable trend of this campaign.

The 2017 campaign saw the resumption of Labour and Conservative dominance in terms of their joint share of the electoral coverage, not to mention the actual vote itself. This two-party squeeze was most evident in press reporting. In the 2015 campaign 69.7% of politicians covered in the newspapers were Conservative or Labour whereas by 2017 this had increased quite significantly to 84.3% (Fig. 5). This trend was also noticeable in terms of TV news coverage too (Fig. 6).

In 2015, 55.7% of all appearances by politicians on television were made by representatives from the two main parties. By 2017 the equivalent figure had gone up, though not as drastically as the figure for print reporting. Nonetheless the total for Conservative and Labour representatives combined was just over two thirds at 67.1% of all broadcast appearances.

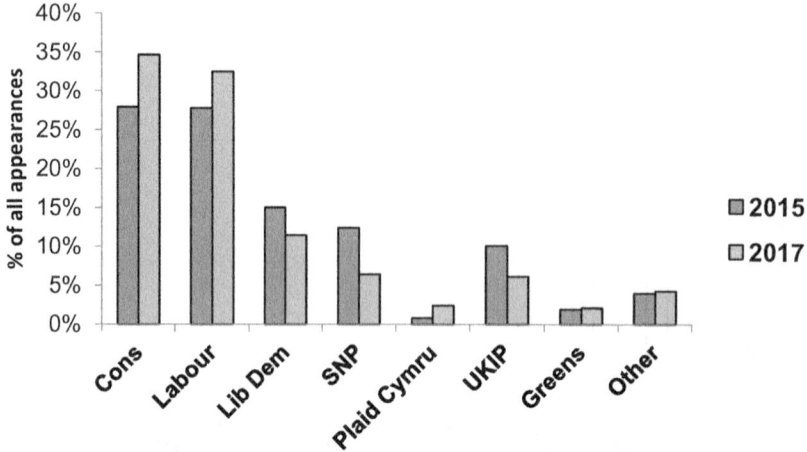

Fig. 6   Party prominence on TV news in the 2015 and 2017 general elections

CAMPAIGNERS

Media coverage in elections tends to focus on certain personalities, most notably those with any realistic chance of becoming Prime Minister. Table 1 highlights the extent to which Theresa May and Jeremy Corbyn dominated the reporting of individual protagonists involved in this campaign. Both leaders on their own received approximately four times the coverage afforded Tim Farron, the third placed most prominent figure. This is a significant issue for politicians representing parties other than the 'big two' because campaigns have traditionally been an opportunity for them to gain greater exposure than might normally expect in routine political coverage (Blumler and McQuail 1968).

Aside from their prominence, May and Corbyn also received roughly twice as much news attention as their respective predecessors achieved in the 2015 election (Deacon et al. 2017). Conversely others including Farron, Nicola Sturgeon and Paul Nuttall saw their equivalent leaders' profiles plummet in line with the decline of their respective party's prominence in the news. Apart from these five leaders, the six other most high profile politicians were the holders of the 'Great Offices of State' (Chancellor, Foreign and Home Secretaries) and their Shadows on the Opposition frontbench. The coverage of these portfolio holders

Table 1 Most
prominent politicians in
campaign coverage (total
news appearances)

1	Theresa May (Cons)	30.1%
2	Jeremy Corbyn (Lab)	26.7%
3	Tim Farron (Lib Dem)	6.8%
4	Nicola Sturgeon (SNP)	3.7%
5	Boris Johnson (Cons)	3.6%
6	John McDonnell (Lab)	3.4%
7	Paul Nuttall (UKIP)	3.4%
8=	Amber Rudd (Cons)	2.8%
8=	Diane Abbott (Lab)	2.8%
10	Emily Thornberry (Lab)	1.8%
11	Philip Hammond (Cons)	1.7%
12	Michael Fallon (Cons)	1.5%
13=	Ruth Davidson (Cons)	1.4%
13=	Caroline Lucas (Green)	1.4%
15	Jeremy Hunt (Cons)	1.2%
16	David Davis (Cons)	1.1%
17=	Leanne Wood (PC)	1.1%
17=	Jonathan Ashworth (Lab)	1.1%
19=	David Cameron (Cons)	1.0%
19=	Angela Rayner (Lab)	1.0%
19=	Vince Cable (Lib Dem)	1.0%

reflected the significance of Brexit and security concerns in this campaign as well as the perennial issue of the economy (see below). And despite their presence on the platform in the largest set-piece debate between the party leaders, the Greens' Caroline Lucas and Leanne Wood of Plaid Cymru received comparatively modest amounts of attention in terms of how the wider campaign was covered by the news.

The two major party leaders were, as has already been noted, the dominant figures in what was a highly presidential campaign. This of course reflected the initial strategic choice of the Conservatives to brand their campaign with the name of the Prime Minister. Although the accompanying descriptive slogan 'strong and stable' later became notorious, this personalized approach contributed to Theresa May becoming the most prominent politician over the course of the election. Aside from Jeremy Corbyn, who was a clear second, other politicians commanded a fraction of the attention over the duration of the campaign. Home Secretary Amber Rudd, who deputized for the Prime Minister in the live televised leader debate, was the eighth most prominent figure overall but still received less than a tenth of the coverage that May garnered.

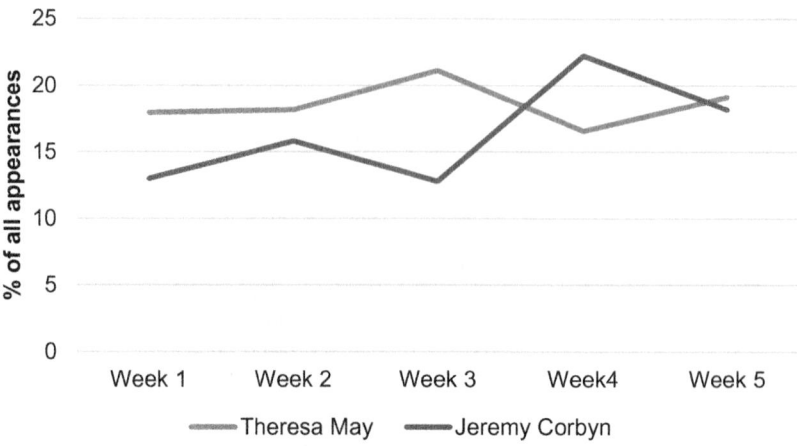

Fig. 7 Proportional presence of the two main party leaders by week

Theresa May was the single most high-profile politician of the campaign but her lead, in media coverage terms, was not continuous throughout the race. During the penultimate week before polling day Jeremy Corbyn managed to overtake the Prime Minister as the most prominent figure before May regained a slender lead in the final days before the election (Fig. 7).[2] The surge in the coverage of Corbyn marked a significant transformative period in the campaign. This change followed on from what turned out to be the defining weekend in the race when the Labour leader was warmly greeted by a crowd of young people attending a concert in Merseyside. By contrast the same period saw the self-proclaimed 'strong and stable' May struggling to re-assert her authority after the launch of her manifesto became mired in (counter-) claim and confusion over the details of her plans relating to social care for elderly people. Senior citizens are normally regarded as being more reliably pro-Conservative, so the party suffered from the ensuing uncertainty caused by a policy change quickly interpreted as being detrimental to a significant group of core Tory supporters.

[2]Sample days for the respective weeks were the weekdays between: 5–11 May (week 1), 12–18 May (week 2), 19–25 May (week 3), 26 May–1 June (week 4), and 2–7 June (week 5).

Initially the Conservative manifesto launch in Halifax had appeared to go to plan. By contrast Labour published their programme for government following the leaking of a draft version of the document. But far from damaging the party, the additional publicity generated may have succeeded in helping promote the manifesto. Whether by design or not the impact of this preview meant the party's policies were widely discussed before and after their formal announcement by Corbyn and his colleagues. This also contributed to the election debate being more decidedly policy rich than was the case in 2015 when a good deal more of the media focus had been on the so-called 'process' including the 'horse race' aspects of the campaign.

It has already been noted how anticipation of a hung parliament emerging after the 2015 election appeared to significantly boost media interest in those parties that might play a role in one of the various possible coalition government scenarios. In the event the Conservatives won an outright majority, rendering this kind of journalistic speculation (a marked feature in the latter stages of that campaign) redundant. Ironically this election did result in a hung parliament despite most polls indicating another Conservative victory was the likeliest outcome. The polling industry had, of course, suffered much criticism and an inquiry following their performance in 2015. But despite this it is noteworthy how the media nonetheless still internalized the dominant trend in the polls in terms of the way the campaign was covered. An important manifestation of this was the already noted decline in news attention devoted to the various third parties whose support a Conservative or Labour led minority administration would need to govern.

Few in the extensive network of political commentators retained by the print and broadcast media entertained the possibility of a hung parliament. This reflected the tenor of much coverage. A strong indicator of this was the lack of any sustained reporting on the Democratic Unionist Party (Table 2). After the election the Conservatives became reliant on the DUP's 10 MPs to stay in office. The party inevitably attracted a considerable amount of media interest but their virtual absence prior to polling day reinforced the degree to which little serious attention had been given to the possibility of another hung parliament being returned. Paradoxically the dominant, misplaced narrative of the 2015 campaign about a future coalition government would have been far more appropriate for this race.

Table 2   'Coverage' of the DUP (total news appearances)

Politician	N	% items
Arlene Foster MLA (Leader and Northern Ireland First Minister in the suspended administration)	5	0.2
Nigel Dodds (Deputy and Westminster Leader)	2	0.1
Other	3	0.1
Total appearances	10	0.4

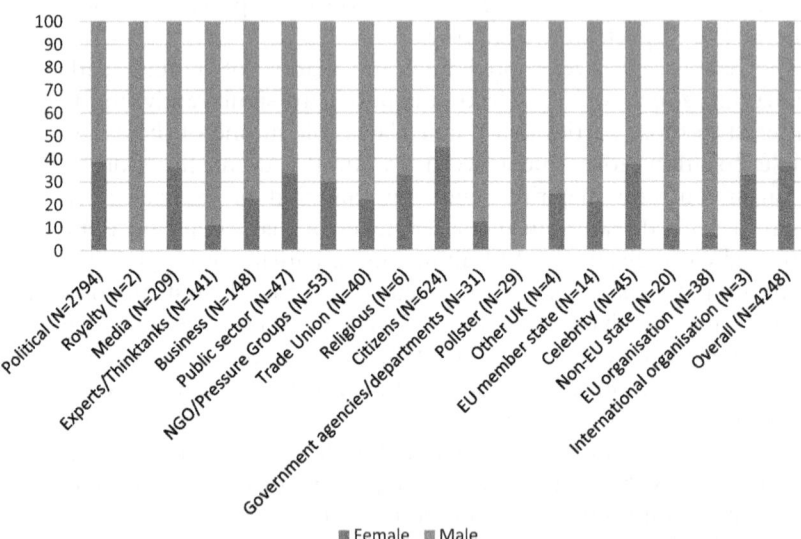

■ Female ■ Male

Fig. 8   Gender balance across sources

Arlene Foster was one of several women to lead parties into this election. Others included the comparative veteran Scottish First Minister Nicola Sturgeon of the SNP, Plaid Cymru's Leanne Wood and Caroline Lucas, having previously returned to (co-)lead the Greens for a second time. Further to this the position of women had been advanced through their now occupying senior frontbench positions including some of the major offices of state and their shadows. And for the first time since Margaret Thatcher a woman was in Downing Street while leading a major party. This election might have been expected to herald something of a potential breakthrough for women, at least in terms of their presence in the news coverage.

Figure 8 identifies the different kinds of gendered actor who appeared in the election reporting. Overall the percentages demonstrate women were still in the minority whatever their role with nearly two thirds (63%) of the coverage featuring men. Females are in the minority whatever the category but achieved their best representations in the groupings for 'politicians' and 'citizens' with shares of approximately 40% on both cases. Conversely there were comparatively few women identified as 'experts' and none featured as 'pollsters' in the coverage.

ISSUES

This most striking trend in terms of coverage during this campaign was the significant fall, compared with 2015, in the amount of reporting devoted to 'electoral process', a category including so-called 'horse race' journalism (Table 3). A corollary of this trend was that the amount of news attention given over to substantive policy concerns. There was greater coverage of the rival manifestos and their implications for

Table 3 Most prominent issues in news coverage

		2017 general election (%)	*% difference from 2015 general election*
1	Electoral process	32.9	−12.5
2	Brexit/European Union	10.9	+7.8
3	Defence/military/security	7.2	+4.7
4	Health and health care provision	6.7	=
5	Taxation	5.7	−1.1
6	Economy/business/trade	5.5	−5.9
7	Social security	4.6	+2.4
8	Immigration	4.2	+0.8
9	Devolution and other constitutional	3.3	−1.0
10	Standards	3.0	−0.3
11	Education	2.9	+1.6
12	Public services	2.3	+1.7
13	Employment	1.6	−0.7
14	Housing	1.3	−1.5
15	Other issues	7.9	

government that had been the case, particularly in the previous general election where there was considerably more media interest in the polls, personalities and other aspects of this campaign. 2017 was different, most obviously because of the impact of the leaked Labour manifesto together with the furore that ensued following the confusion over the Conservative plans for social care.

Prior to the campaign there had been considerable speculation as to whether 2017 would be the 'Brexit election'. The European question was indeed the single most prominent issue, reflecting the salience of the topic in view of the UK's impending negotiations to leave the EU. But aside from Brexit several other substantive policy areas received significant news attention. Coverage of defence and security issues, marginal in 2015, was much more prominent in 2017 following the controversy surrounding the renewal of Trident as well as the responses to the Manchester and London terror attacks. Education related matters, including the debates over school meals and university tuition fees, received more attention than they had in 2015. News coverage of health and health care remained as prominent in 2017 as it had in the last campaign.

Some substantive policy areas received less news media attention despite their salience in previous years. For example, the important issues of housing, transport and the environment rarely featured in coverage, reflecting a similar pattern from the 2015 campaign. More surprising was the relative marginalization of immigration, an issue that had been a major factor in the reporting of the EU referendum campaign in 2016 if not so much in the previous election. One topic that was substantially down in terms of its prominence was the news coverage devoted to business and the economy this time. In past campaigns this had been a major issue. In 2015 David Cameron had led the Conservatives to victory having repeatedly attacked Labour for its alleged failure to manage the economy.

Compared with 2015 the issue of the economy was more marginal in media terms and became ever more so as the campaign progressed (see Fig. 9). Although traditionally the most prominent category, interest in the electoral process declined midway through the campaign as the debate over health (including social care) peaked following the controversy over the Conservatives' so-called 'dementia tax'. It is noteworthy that Brexit was the substantive issue that attracted most news attention in two different weeks but not throughout the campaign. In the final days of the election race the Manchester Arena bombing and latterly the attacks near London Bridge led to increased coverage of defence and

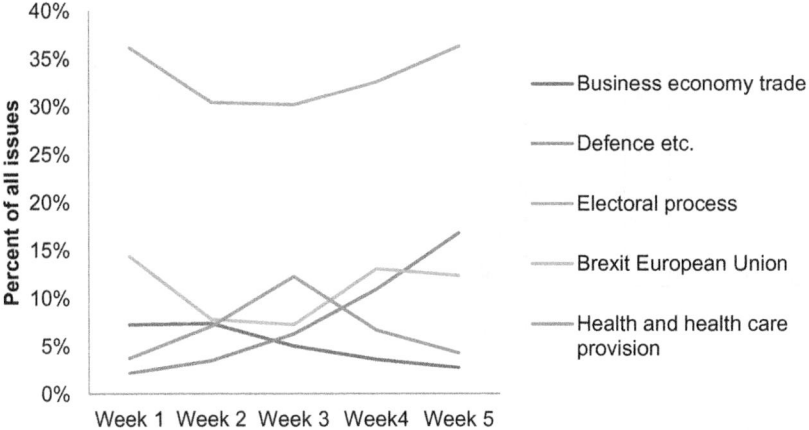

40%
35%
30%
25%
20%
15%
10%
5%
0%

Percent of all issues

Week 1 Week 2 Week 3 Week4 Week 5

——— Business economy trade

——— Defence etc.

——— Electoral process

——— Brexit European Union

——— Health and health care provision

Fig. 9 Proportional prominence of issues, week by week (all media)

security related matters, thereby making it foremost among the policy areas discussed in the media during the closing days of the race.

PARTISANSHIP

The print media report on elections, and politics more generally, free from the legal constraints imposed on their broadcasting counterparts. Newspapers are therefore able to editorialize in ways that favour a party or, as is common, denigrates another. The Conservatives have traditionally benefitted from this kind of press partisanship: the extent and nature of this support is examined as well as the degree to which the coverage was positive or negative.[3] Figure 10 shows the overall directional balance

[3]This is not solely a measure of overt support or criticism by a journalist of a party (although these instances would be included in the count). Rather it is a broader measure of the extent to which newspapers report on issues/comments/developments that have positive or negative implications for parties. We only coded these instances where these were overtly referred to in the piece. In term of scoring If an item mainly or solely focused on positive matters for a party, it was given a value of +1. If it was mainly/solely focused on negative matters for a party, it was assigned a value of −1. Items where there was no clear evaluation or they contained positive and negative issues in broadly equal measure were coded as zero. Items where no reference was made to the party were excluded from the calculation. The scores in Figs. 10–12 are calculated by subtracting the total number of negative stories from the total of positive stories.

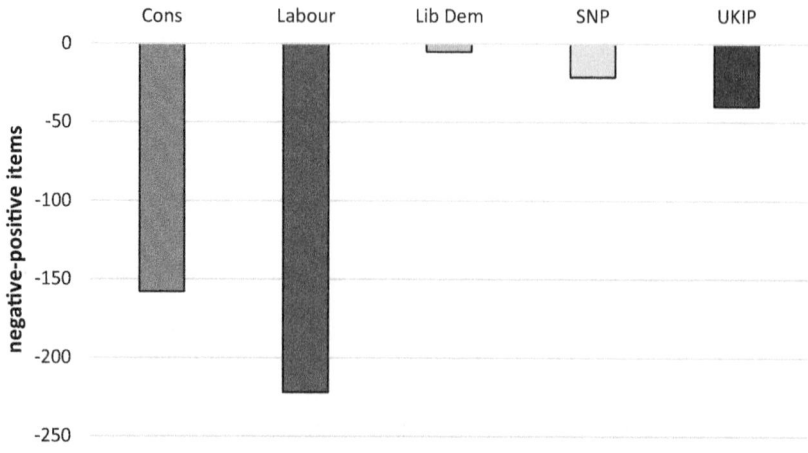

Fig. 10   Overall evaluations in newspapers (unweighted)

of stories relating to the respective five parties that received the most electoral votes.

Although the media preoccupation with the major two is pronounced with Labour attracting the most adverse commentary, what is particularly noteworthy is that all columns in Fig. 10 are negative: the tenor of the press coverage was 'a plague on all your houses'. Admittedly the Liberal Democrat score is negligible but what limited newspaper attention the SNP and UKIP managed to attract appears to have been primarily critical. Most striking is the considerable amount of negative coverage the Conservatives received. Much of this was concentrated in the period after the 'dementia tax' when there was criticism of the party's social care plans as well as the wider manifesto, the campaign strategy and then the leader herself (for further discussion, see Chapter "The Liberal Democrat Campaign").

Figure 11 presents the overall impact of press evaluations when these are weighted by the Audit Bureau of Circulation statistics for the respective newspapers. This pattern is more beneficial to the Conservatives, the only party to benefit from a positive rating overall. Whereas the other three received slightly negative scores, Labour's deficit is even more pronounced than in Fig. 10, reflecting the considerable amount of 'knocking copy' they received from the 'Tory press'.

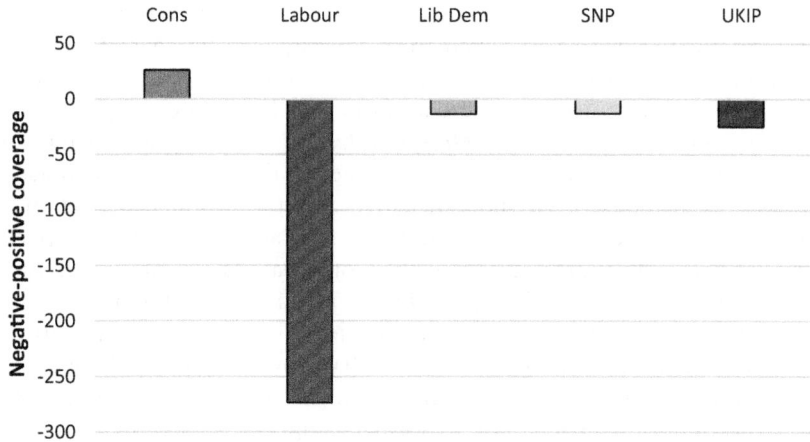

Fig. 11   Overall evaluations in newspapers (weighted by circulation)

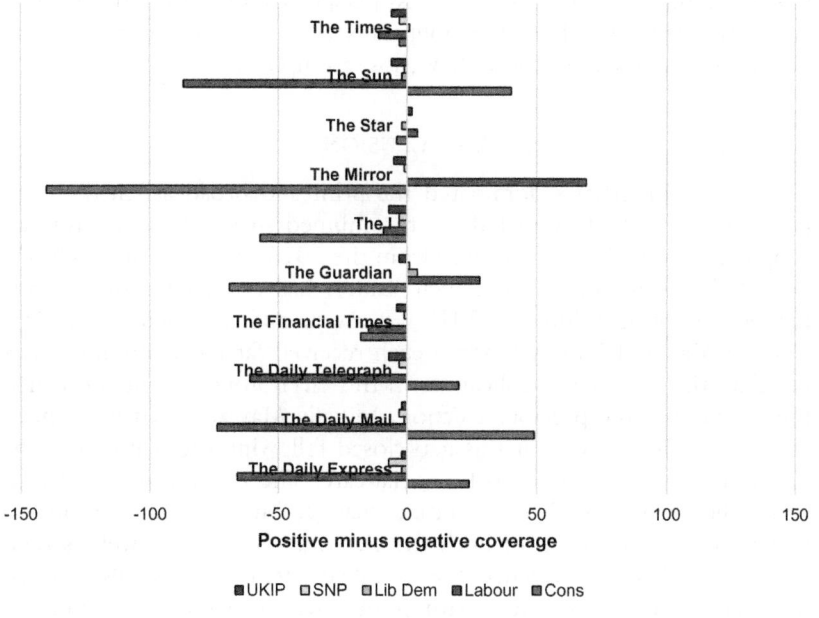

Fig. 12   Evaluations by newspaper (unweighted)

The various major newspapers differed in their partisanship but also in terms of the degree to which their coverage can be characterized as positive and negative. Figure 12 explores how the various titles evaluated the rival parties drawing on the data from Fig. 10. Six newspapers (*Sun, Mirror, Guardian, Telegraph, Mail* and *Express*) were highly partisan in their reporting, offering positive coverage of the party they endorsed as well as all being even more negative about the principal rival they opposed. This trend does not, however, take account of these papers' circulations: if these are considered the Conservatives advantage increases because of support from the best-selling *Sun* and *Mail* for them.

The remaining four titles were less strident although the *i* was noticeably more critical of the Conservatives than any other party despite the newspaper's policy of not making electoral endorsements. The *Star* was the only other paper not to formally support a party in this election. The newspaper also offered the least partisan coverage of any of the ten national dailies, reflecting its avoidance of the campaign in favour of celebrity based human interest stories. The remaining two newspapers, *The Times* and *Financial Times*, endorsed the Conservatives but were not positive about the party. From a press perspective this election was more about the press attacking the politicians they most feared rather than promoting the vision of those they chose to support.

CONCLUSION

The two major parties dominated the print and broadcast media campaign in a way that emulated their combined share of the electorate's support. This marked a departure from the 2015 campaign in which several of the minor parties and their leaders had attracted a significantly higher level of news interest. 2017 was a very different media campaign. Theresa May and Jeremy Corbyn each received far more attention during than their rivals and colleagues in this election not to mention their predecessors in the previous election. Initially May attracted more news coverage than Corbyn but this gap closed following the hiatus over the Conservative manifesto plans for social care. The Prime Minister denied this policy represented a significant change, but the incident proved to be a catalyst in terms of both the electoral dynamics as well as their reporting. There is evidence the so-called 'dementia tax' also muted newspaper support for May with print coverage largely consisting of 'knocking copy'. Admittedly most of this negative press was primarily about Labour but some of it was also aimed at a faltering Conservative campaign.

Reporting of the electoral process, encompassing aspects of the campaign such as the polls, mishaps and other events, was the main category in terms of news media coverage of this election. But the leaking of the Labour manifesto and the drama surrounding the Conservative 'dementia tax' generated ample copy to make this a more decidedly policy centred debate in terms of the print and broadcast reporting. There was also considerable interest in security and defence matters reflecting the heightened concern over public safety in the aftermath of the Manchester and London atrocities during the campaign. There was news media interest in Brexit but the key related issue of immigration was some way down the list of news priorities in terms of election coverage. With hindsight the Conservatives might have fought a different kind of campaign by placing greater emphasis on another issue central to the referendum but not as critical a part of this campaign as it might have been: the supposed strength and stability of the economy.

REFERENCES

Blumler, J. G., & McQuail, D. (1968). *Television in politics: Its uses and influences*. London: Faber and Faber.

Deacon, D., Downey, J., Stanyer, J., & Wring, D. (2017). The media campaign: The issues and personalities who defined the election. In D. Wring, R. Mortimore, & S. Atkinson (Eds.), *Political communication in Britain: Polling, campaigning and media in the 2017 general election*. Hampshire: Palgrave Macmillan.

Miller, W. L., Clarke, H., Harrop, M., LeDuc, L., & Whiteley, P. (1990). *How voters change: The 1987 British election campaign in perspective*. Oxford: Clarendon.

Broadcasting the Snap Election: Surprising Politics but Familiar Production

Paul Brand

A colleague once described general elections as the Olympics of polit-ical journalism. Well, 2017 were the Games for which none of us had trained. For the first time since the 1970s, we were presented with an election we hadn't spent four or five years anticipating. Indeed, since 2010, fixed-term parliaments had pretty much enshrined our planning period in law. But this time, we would have little more than seven weeks to build our stadiums and hone our athletes.

As journalists cancelled holidays (or a honeymoon, in my case), man-agement drew up game plans that largely replicated the best of the 2015 coverage and weaved in other innovations from the 2016 EU referen-dum. The snap election simply didn't afford time to tear up the tem-plate and rethink our approach, as is often attempted between major votes. Familiar studio sets and graphics were dusted down, target teams assigned in the traditional way and energy necessarily focused on the pol-itics over the production.

As electrified as we were by the prospect of a surprise election, broadcasters were slightly less enthralled by the apparent predictability

P. Brand (✉)
ITV, London, UK
e-mail: paul.brand@itn.co.uk

© The Author(s) 2019
D. Wring et al. (eds.), *Political Communication in Britain*,
https://doi.org/10.1007/978-3-030-00822-2_3

of the result. Early discussions were mostly about the exact margin of the Conservative win, with little jeopardy to excite pundits or captivate audiences. In 2015, the explosion of multi-party politics had led to an obsession with polling percentages and coalition conundrums—only for the electorate to return a surprise Conservative majority. Ironically, this time expectations played in reverse: journalists anticipated a Conservative majority, only for Britain to deliver a hung parliament and a coalition (of sorts).

Initial projections helped shape what was already set to be the most presidential campaign on British television. While in 2015 UKIP, the SNP and even the Greens provided for interesting side shows, this time two party-politics was back, with the election almost exclusively focused on who would make the best Prime Minister. Both the Conservatives and Labour actively fostered this narrative, with almost all campaign events fixated on their respective leaders, to the virtual exclusion of other party figures.

The Conservative campaign was particularly tightly controlled this time around. The focus was of course on Theresa May's 'strong and stable' leadership, but it was the strong-arm of the press office which initially got journalists talking. Most televised campaign events were incredibly restrictive, usually involving the Prime Minister delivering a short speech to a carefully selected audience of party members, or sometimes to the staff of a company (who'd been warned not to speak to the media).

David Cameron had followed much the same formula during the previous two general elections, but this time events felt even more closely controlled. For example, in 2010, I recall offering a box of crisps to Cameron at one rally, so that he could choose his favourite flavour (a far more sophisticated TV stunt than it sounds!). I cannot imagine ever slipping a box of crisps past Theresa May's team, despite her penchant for a packet of salt and vinegar. The unexpected and the spontaneous were actively avoided to a degree few broadcasters had experienced before.

To her credit, the Prime Minister always took questions from journalists at these events, but at first they were strictly policed. The press and broadcasters would be led to a waiting room before each visit, where a lucky few would be told that it was their turn to be called on by the Prime Minister. But on several occasions, Conservative press officers asked what the questions would be—a red line for all broadcasters. The press office denied that this had any bearing on whether a question might be permitted, but at one event in Leeds it led to a very public row between *Channel 4 News*'s Michael Crick and a Tory staffer. Indeed, after the restrictive nature of the Conservatives' campaign began to become a story in itself, journalists were quickly granted more freedom, with the Prime Minister taking a greater range of questions without prior warning of their content.

In contrast, Labour's campaign was the polar opposite. Many of Jeremy Corbyn's events involved addressing thousands of unvetted supporters at huge rallies, often out in the open with little security. Typically, these events would begin with a few hundred party members, but quickly swell to thousands of people, as members of the public were drawn in by the excitement or via social media. These rallies were often held in safe Labour seats, or seats where they feared defeat, rather than in marginals the party was hoping to capture.

Because few in Jeremy Corbyn's press team had any experience of organizing an election, nor had been anticipating one, their operation often lacked the military precision of the Conservatives'. But Labour events were a feast for the cameras—the colour of the crowd, the rallying cry of the leader and the freedom to talk to pretty much anyone we liked all made for good television. And whether the spontaneity of their events was by accident or design, it set them apart from a clinical Conservative campaign.

However, several journalists reported hostility towards the 'mainstream media' at some Labour events, with a section of the crowd harbouring a long-standing cynicism and suspicion about the way newspapers and the BBC in particular had reported on Jeremy Corbyn's leadership in the past. At one event, a television reporter was pelted with biros while she tried to address the camera. On another occasion, a satellite truck was surrounded by an angry mob. But more generally, Labour were welcoming of broadcasters and actively courted our coverage, even if Jeremy Corbyn took fewer questions from journalists at his events than Theresa May did, although he could sometimes be grabbed for a clip before or afterwards.

More generally, neither leader did a vast array of interviews with broadcasters this time around, aside from a series of discussions with the BBC's Andrew Neil and ITV's Julie Etchingham. On the final day of campaigning, Jeremy Vine complained it was the first election in 40 years that a sitting Prime Minister had refused to go on Radio 2. On the same day, his colleague John Humphrys complained it was the first time he could remember a leader of the opposition refusing to go on Radio 4's *Today* programme. *Channel 4 News*'s Jon Snow had to chase down Theresa May in the final hours of campaigning to secure a spot with her. LBC and several other outlets also said they were let down by both leaders.

As for the smaller parties, the battle was to get on, not off, the airwaves. Compared to 2015, the Liberal Democrats struggled to be heard, in part thanks to their near electoral-wipe out, but also due to a more presidential campaign. In the initial stages of the election, it looked as if the Lib Dems had found cut-through thanks to their unique positioning on Brexit—a topic that had been expected to define the campaign. Indeed, the main broadcasters did assign journalists to the Lib Dem battle bus. But after tangling himself up in a controversy about his views on gay relationships, their leader Tim Farron largely faded from the coverage. Instead, broadcasters tended to include the Lib Dems on merit, rather than in every report, contrary to previous elections.

The same was true of UKIP, but to an even more dramatic extent. Following their complete obliteration in the local elections of May 2017, their broadcast coverage dwindled. Again, they tended to be included in reports about Brexit and immigration, but their domestic agenda received little coverage, save for the more controversial elements. Broadcasters did assign journalists to keep an eye on UKIP's campaign, but by the middle of the election their press conferences in London barely contained more than a handful of hacks, with very little television coverage.

Indeed, it is unclear whether UKIP would even have been designated as a *major party* this time, if Ofcom had not done away with the term altogether shortly before the election. Traditionally, the broadcast regulator issued a list of *major parties* which should be given 'due weight' in a general election. In 2015, this included the Conservatives, Labour, Liberal Democrats and, for the first time, UKIP. In practical terms, this meant that television and radio reports often had to contain sound bites from each of the four different parties.

But after commercial broadcasters called for change, in March 2017 Ofcom did away with its list of *major parties*, theoretically granting far more freedom in the coverage of campaigns. The new rules were quickly put to the test during the subsequent snap election, with broadcasters able to make their own decisions about who to include in reports, basing their calculations on parties' past and/or current support. The new rules are particularly liberating with regards to constituency reporting, where previously candidates from all *major parties* had to be interviewed, regardless of whether they had any track record of support in a constituency or not.

For the first time, too, the Ofcom code applied to the BBC in addition to the commercial broadcasters, following a change earlier in the year. But in practice, all of the regulatory adjustments came too soon before the general election to make any real difference. The BBC did not alter its approach significantly, partly because its own editorial guidelines were already closely aligned with Ofcom's. Meanwhile, commercial broadcasters approached the election in much the same way as 2015, with little time to consider how best to capitalize on the changes. In future, it may well be that broadcasters are liberated to think more creatively about their coverage, but the snap election did not afford enough warning for such innovation.

One way in which the broadcasters' approach did differ this time was in relation to polling. In 2015, outlets such as *Sky News* and *Newsnight* had regularly run party-by-party predictions based on the latest polls, with forecasts heavily influencing the news agenda. Party leaders were regularly asked which permutations of coalition they were willing to entertain, and the Conservatives in particular played on the possible outcomes in their campaigning. But given that the polls proved so inaccurate in 2015, this time the broadcasters made far less mention of them. There was initial interest in the large lead the Conservatives exhibited over Labour at the outset of the campaign (after all, Theresa May had undoubtedly been banking on it herself), with further interest as the gap subsequently closed. But in general, broadcasters' analysis of polling was nowhere near as intense as it was in 2015.

Another noticeable difference in 2017 was the television debates. In 2010, and to a lesser extent in 2015, head-to-head debates had dominated the campaign and disrupted its traditional rhythm, much to the frustration of several party leaders. Once the Prime Minister had given her refusal to take part in 2017, the assumption was that the TV debates would have less influence on the media cycle this time around. The lack of any head-to-head with Jeremy Corbyn—especially as he too chose to sit out the ITV debate—was expected to reduce the potential to change the course of the campaign.

Arguably, reporting of the content of the debates was diminished this time. However, they did retain an important influence on the campaign, as the Prime Minister's absence, coupled with Jeremy Corbyn's last-minute attendance at the BBC debate, became a major narrative in itself. Indeed, perhaps the most important legacy of the 2017 debates is that it will be difficult for a sitting Prime Minister to refuse to take part again, thanks to the damage done to the Conservative campaign. 2017 demonstrated that the debates are now an established and expected feature of any general election, independent of the wishes of any one party leader.

Another reason why the TV debates did not set the rhythm of this election in quite the same way is because that rhythm was disrupted by extraordinary and tragic events. Two major terrorist attacks on British soil, costing dozens of lives, irreversibly changed the course of the campaign.

On exceptional occasions, ITV executives will crash into the usual schedule of programming to broadcast rolling news of a breaking story, in what's called an 'open-ender'. In the nine years I have worked for the station, I can recall just a handful of times that this has happened prior to 2017. But having already broadcast two open-enders to cover the Westminster terrorist attack in March, plus the announcement of the snap election in April, incredibly ITV broke into its schedule twice more during the campaign itself, to report on both the Manchester Arena attack and the London Bridge attack. On both occasions, the political parties abandoned their campaigning and the broadcasters abandoned their coverage of it, as reporting of the lives lost rightly dominated news bulletins for days.

Debate about the parties' response to the attacks will be had elsewhere, but terrorism fundamentally altered the course of the campaign for journalists. In the case of the London Bridge attack, there were just five days left until the election. But even by the date of the Manchester bombing, the broadcasters' election coverage was already well mapped out: the main issues had been identified and special reports had been commissioned. Broadcasters had to adapt quickly to the changing agenda, as the topic of security dominated and other issues were quickly squeezed out. This arguably left the issue of the economy, for example, relatively under-reported compared to 2015.

If the topics of debate were curtailed, viewer participation in this election was not. The emergence of social media allowed for far greater online discussion than ever before. Broadcasters embraced new technologies, streaming campaign events and special interviews via *Facebook Live* to foster a two-way conversation with viewers, who were able to comment on or 'like' videos in their millions. At times, 2017 even became the emoji election, with ITV's *Facebook Live* interview with the Prime Minister almost completely covered with angry faces at one point, as viewers clicked along in real time.

This was also the first election in which recently established alt-left and alt-right blogs competed with the analysis of journalists online. Indeed, research by BuzzFeed found that in the first two weeks of the campaign posts by these blogs went more 'viral' on social media than those by mainstream outlets. Anecdotally, many journalists felt this contributed to a more polarized campaign than in previous elections, with broadcasters working harder than ever to separate fact from 'fake news' and provide a balanced account.

The political parties employed their own social media strategies, with Labour's by far the most effective, complemented by cleverly produced videos from their sister campaign, Momentum. These clips received up to eight million views each during the campaign, far outstripping anything produced by the Conservatives. But often, it was content initially generated by broadcasters which really lit up the internet, from Diane Abbott forgetting her figures to Theresa May's wheat field confession.

When it came to results night tradition was restored. The broadcasters largely adopted the studios and production techniques they'd developed in 2015. David Dimbleby fronted the BBC's coverage, despite the fact that Huw Edwards had been expected to take over after 2015, while Tom Bradby was chosen by ITV to front a second election, employing the double act of Ed Balls and George Osborne to great effect. Many struggled to believe the exit poll when the broadcasters first announced it, but as political careers rose and fell over the course of the evening, it was eventually proven to have been spot on.

In conclusion, 2017 was a surprise campaign from start to finish—unexpected in its timing, its unfolding and its result. But some predictability could at least be found in the way broadcasters approached the campaign. Time did not allow for major innovations on air, even if coverage did change significantly online. But whether it was participation in TV debates or regulatory change, this election did set some interesting precedents for the next—whenever that may come.

BBC Campaign Coverage Policy

Jay G. Blumler

The literature of empirical research on public service broadcasting organizations is relatively ample for their relations to government, content analysis of their news outputs, and evidence of audience reception and effects—comparatively against more commercially funded provision and comparatively across different countries. It is relatively scant, however, on PSBs' *policies* for political coverage, their main features, how they were considered, internally discussed and formed, and what influences played on their decisions. This chapter steps modestly into that territory with an account of BBC policy formation for coverage of the UK's 2015 and 2017 General Election campaigns, based on semi-structured elite interviews planned and conducted jointly with Professor Christopher Anderson.

Four sections of analysis follow. Section "System Turbulence", there is the systemic context in which BBC policy makers and news personnel worked at the time—including a surrounding public arena that sometimes seemed governed by the assumptions of Niccolo Machiavelli and Thomas Hobbes more than those of John Stuart Mill or Jurgen Habermas. Sections "Election Campaign Coverage Policy at the BBC in 2015" and "Election Campaign Coverage Policy at the BBC in 2017"

J. G. Blumler (✉)
University of Leeds, Leeds, UK
e-mail: jayblumler@sky.com

© The Author(s) 2019   51
D. Wring et al. (eds.), *Political Communication in Britain*,
https://doi.org/10.1007/978-3-030-00822-2_4

present the campaign coverage policies that were formulated and implemented at the BBC in 2015 and 2017, respectively. These parts of the chapter are not judgmental though in some places judgmental perspectives in the literature are mentioned. The section "Taking Stock and Looking Ahead" discusses some of the challenges and issues that may arise for BBC coverage of the next election campaign whenever it is called. The essay concludes on a more philosophic note.

SYSTEM TURBULENCE

By the second decade of the twenty-first century British political journalism was operating in radically different conditions from those that had obtained previously. Major changes, extra-media and intra-media alike, had occurred.

On the 'external' side, some of these included:

- increased polarization around deep opinion divides (generational, financial, cultural)
- emergence of a more dissonant public sphere than the consonance that had tended to prevail in the past
- fragmentation of the public sphere, entry to it of an increasing number and variety of increasingly active non-party groups campaigning to gain media and public attention
- the declining authority of established institutions, including especially political parties, making voters' preferences less predictable and Leaders' holds on power less secure
- communications regarded by significant actors more as weapons of warfare than as aids to enlightenment
- a coarsening of political discourse, including premiums on outrageous statements and a working assumption that being fast and loose verbally won't necessarily be lastingly damaging, since it can always be lost to view in the flux of ever-changing events and controversies.

On the 'internal' side, key challenging developments included:

- a furthering of communication abundance with more, and more diverse, media outlets, channels and news providers
- proliferation and diversification of the devices through which people receive communications, including political news

- shift from a low-choice to a high-choice information environment, in which the relative supply of news in schedules is lessened, and media organizations, including their news departments, must pursue their goals in an 'attention economy'
- breakdown of the business models to which mainstream journalistic organizations had adhered
- transformed newsroom conditions, especially reduced resources and intensified time constraints
- increased incentives for editors and reporters to adapt stories for attention-worthiness, accenting news values of drama, sensation, conflict, personalization, human interest and to heighten their emotional and/or entertaining elements
- reduced patronage of mainstream news media by younger people in favour of online sources
- the increased salience of social media—for direct expressions of opinion by ordinary citizens as well as for political actors to reach them.

These have been ongoing currents of change. From the 1980s until recently, however, one more or less constant feature has structured the conduct of campaigning in many electoral democracies, including the UK: 'a thoroughgoing professionalization of political advocacy' (Blumler and Gurevitch 1995: 217). This professionalized paradigm (the 'Modern Model of Campaigning' in Swanson and Mancini's phrase 1996: 249) has been analyzed in an extensive literature, from which the following main components can be derived:

- a substantial upgrading of publicity priorities among most would-be opinion-shapers, especially political parties—in resources, staffing, and voice in policy
- news management: adaptation of political rhetoric to the presumed susceptibilities of mainstream journalists, including the projection of clear simple messages in soundbites (or 'nuggets, nutshells and golden phrases' as put by a leading politician when interviewed by Blumler et al. 1978: 29)
- news management: proactive agenda-setting ('entering the news cycle in the earliest possible time and repeatedly re-entering it with stories and initiatives so that subsequent news coverage is set on your terms', as recommended by Gould 1998: 294)

- aim to influence mass *perceptions* of key political issues and events (not necessarily their realities)
- event management for symbolism, visual appeal and signs of support
- relentless attack campaigning on opponents' points of vulnerability and instant rebuttal of their claims and charges
- centralized campaign management to ensure message discipline among all spokespersons
- introduction to the system of a new and highly influential actor role in order to direct and advise on all the above—that of the expert political consultant.

ELECTION CAMPAIGN COVERAGE POLICY AT THE BBC IN 2015

By 2015, BBC news executives and journalists had long since recognized the major parties' commitments to professionalized publicity endeavour. One informant confessed even to 'admiring' in particular the Conservatives' professionalism, describing its products in 2015 as having been 'slick', 'sharp' and 'efficient'. This could be advantageous for pressured journalists. You could usually count on being offered material that would be readily adaptable, verbally and visually, to standard story formats. The same informant commended the Conservatives' 'brilliant' provision of pictures to accompany leaders' appearances—bringing to mind Gandy, Jr.'s (1982) concept of 'information subsidies'.

But the same process could seriously challenge the performance by journalists of their independent informing role. In fact, it had been concluded at the BBC that in 2010 'we may not have dug deep enough' into politicians' assertions. To the norm of 'due impartiality', had to be added, then, 'fairness to the now highly skeptical audience', whose members, in present-day conditions of communication abundance and social media presence, demanded greater consideration than they had been given in the past. In order to maintain trust in the BBC, it was essential, not only to present campaign news accurately, clearly and accessibly and to place it in some explanatory context, but also to hold the campaigning politicians to account for what they had done in the past and intended to do in the future.

A Corporation-wide determination persistently to probe the veracity and credibility of the parties' promises and claims during the 2015 campaign followed from this—to 'press them hard', as an informant put it.

Of course the main instrument of such probing was the political inter-view. Blumler and Esser (2018) have identified five question types used by BBC interviewers during the 2015 campaign, drawing on previous research by Bull and Elliott (1998), Clayman and Heritage (2001), and Voltmer and Brants (2011). They were:

- Assertiveness—example: 'By playing the Sturgeon card, aren't you putting the Union at risk?'
- Adversarialness—example: 'Isn't your pledge not to raise VAT, income tax and national insurance irresponsible?'
- Threat to public image—example: 'When would Labour clear the deficit? Given your past economic record, how much credence can we give to your pledge on that?'
- Challenging an answer—example: 'Your NHS spending pledge seems unfunded. Where will the money come from?' [A: 'We won't raise taxes'] [Q: 'That's not an answer']
- Accountability—example: 'In your proposed welfare reforms, why won't you tell us where the 12 billion pound benefit cuts will fall?'

Election Campaign Coverage Policy at the BBC in 2017

How BBC news people assessed this effort in post mortems on their 2015 performance will be considered below. But first the implications of a fundamentally transforming change in the British political communi-cation system that was set in train after the 2015 election result must be built into the policy picture. As a consequence of Jeremy Corbyn's victory in the contest to become leader of the Labour Party, British journalists and voter/audience members became exposed to two rad-ically different strategies of campaign communication management: a political-consultancy-led model, followed by the Conservatives, versus a social-movement-led model adopted by Labour. Boiled down to their essences as eventually witnessed during the country's 2017 election campaign, the consultancy-led model relied on a repetition of sound-bit-ten slogans; had a limited view of the desire and ability of the average person to take in political information; was relatively policy-light; and was also relatively ethics-light. In contrast, the social movement-led model favoured elaborations of larger social and political visions; was policy-heavy; presumed an appetite among many citizens to learn more broadly what politicians intended to do if given power; and mobilized and systematically organized activists in new modes of grass-roots campaigning.

Throughout the first half of 2017, a widely shared conventional wisdom maintained that the latter model could not prove to be an electoral winner, especially under Jeremy Corbyn's leadership of the Labour Party. Evidence to support that assumption included opinion poll ratings, the results of recent local government elections, and signs of continuing disaffection among some 'moderate' Labour MPs. Nevertheless Theresa May frequently declared her intention to occupy 10 Downing Street for a full parliamentary term. And then suddenly in April, she reversed course, specifying the country's need for a period of assured strong and stable leadership to justify the calling of a General Election, designating June 8th Polling Day.

The snap election caught BBC policy makers on the hop. As an informant described the situation: Told at a morning meeting that the PM would be making a statement later in the day, I said, 'My god, she will call an election'. Whereas the 2015 election (like most others before it) had been a pre-scheduled event, there was now a 'truncated period to prepare'. Quick decisions had to be taken ('something for which the BBC is not known') on a host of matters with insufficient time to convene committees to deliberate over them. Who will cover the parties' campaigning activities? How can the 'massive logistics exercise' involved in such coverage be organized and mounted? What set-piece programmes, beyond regular news bulletins, should we produce? When and how will party leaders be available for interviews? What kind of service will the audience expect of us? 'What should our core brand, our core message, be – in the way that "making it clear" had been in 2015?' And all these questions had to be faced within the limits of a budget for General Election News that had been cut 'line by line' by about 75% since 2015.

Some of the available time had to be spent on negotiations with the political parties over leader debates, which involved 'a lot of politics with a small p'. Theresa May's refusal to appear in debates was unbudging. Her line was that debates were a distraction from a 'traditional campaign where we can get out and speak to all the voters and so they see them personally'. A Change.org petition calling on the broadcasters to 'empty chair' a party leader refusing to take part in a debate had attracted well over 100,000 signatures. For the BBC, however, this was normatively unthinkable:

> If we had said, we'll go ahead without you, we would
> have been making a political statement. Should a public
> service broadcaster be doing that?

The scheduling one week before Polling Day of a Question Time Special, in which Theresa May and Jeremy Corbyn were separately interrogated by members of a studio audience, was at least 'an audience-facing exercise'.

After dealing with these matters, a senior executive spoke to us about how what he called a 'groupthink' had prevailed 'across the media' as to 'how much Theresa May was going to win by'. 'All the polls, the papers, the politicians were clear: he's {Jeremy Corbyn} going to be hammered'. His account of this assumption's role in the coverage seemed complex. The 'received wisdom' about the expected election result had to be discussed at the BBC. They were 'clear that it wasn't their job to predict the winner'. Yet it was 'hard for "groupthink" not to bleed into your thinking'.

In two respects this may have happened. Early on for one thing, BBC2 commissioned David Modell to prepare a political documentary for transmission after the election, in which four Labour MPs—three of them with reservations about Jeremy Corbyn's leadership—were followed and talked to from start to finish of the campaign. According to Mr. Modell in interview, the programme was based on the premise that 'Labour would be wiped out at the ballot box'. That was the 'only trajectory' envisaged. There would then be a 'fight to create a new kind of Labour Party after the election', in which some of the MPs featured in the programme 'would have roles afterward to reform the Party'. In a thoughtful personal communication (2017) Professor John Corner expressed appreciation of how a:

> ...disaster-inflected idea of following three MPs critical of
> Corbyn as they went about their campaigning business
> produced fascinating and frank material...I thought the
> programme managed to engage, sometimes rather subtly,
> with what remains a continuing set of questions about
> Labour's prospects as a party of electoral success.

BBC journalists' uses of vox pops is another area in which conventional wisdom may have been reproduced. Professor Mark Wheeler (2017) formed the impression that 'Labour leader Jeremy Corbyn's obituary was written' by apparently 'honest voices' in many vox pops. Corner (2017) felt that 'The shifts in the BBC's coverage of the campaign lagged the changed reality on the ground rather badly'. Some empirical confirmation of these impressions was provided by Stephen Cushion's (2017) finding (based on analysis of the evening news bulletins of four TV networks) that 'between a fifth and almost half of all sources' aired were 'citizens' views in vox pops' As he goes on:

> These were often short in length and substance, with
> the public mostly asked to respond to questions about
> the horse race, leaders' personalities and, to a far lesser
> extent, the parties' policies.

A broader pattern of which all this is a part is the attention that journalists normally pay to the 'game' or 'process' aspects of election campaigning (the horse race, party strategies, politicians' mishaps, polling, etc.). Traditionally dominant—amounting to 34% of the themes covered in BBC1 nightly news during the 2015 campaign—it was reduced to 29% in the same bulletins in 2017 (Deacon 2017).

That, however, did leave more time for substantive coverage of the 2017 campaign than at previous elections. Two main consequences followed. For one thing, Labour enjoyed a more balanced crack of the coverage whip over its policies and the public appearances of its Leader than some felt had been the case in pre-campaign times. In fact, a content analysis conducted by scholars at Loughborough University (Deacon et al. 2017) showed that of the party actors appearing in BBC1 coverage of the 2017 campaign, 26% were Labour and 25% Conservative politicians (Deacon 2017). As an informant explained to us, the advent of an election triggers especially rigorous applications of the 'due impartiality' norm.

For another, BBC coverage spanned a broader range of issues than previously, such as the NHS, the cost of living, the state of the economy, social care and Brexit options. According to our informant, this stemmed from 'a very conscious decision' at the outset (rather than a mid-campaign response to release of the Labour and Conservative parties' manifestoes, as has been suggested) 'that if voters were to be adequately informed, all the main issues had to be covered'. 'We kept asking ourselves have we done all the things we should' across the palette of BBC news programmes. In part, this was a reaction against the 'superficiality' of the Brexit campaign with 'too much on the personalities and too many photo-ops'. But it also derived from a strengthened understanding of the BBC's informing mission in contemporary political conditions. As enunciated by Director of News James Harding in January 2017:

> The world is living in an age of instability. Normal rules have been disrupted by low growth and high inequality, technological innovation spurring behavioural change and job insecurity, identity politics supplanting the old parties and fuelling narratives of exclusion. We need to explain what's driving the news. We need slow news, news with more depth, data interrogation, analytic expertise - to help us explain the world we're living in.

An important offshoot of this informing mission was the provision of 'reality checks' in campaign news. According to our informant, 'A certain amount of this had been done in 2015, but, on an ad hoc basis, it wasn't central enough; we had to do more.' A major change was accordingly introduced in January 2017. A reality-checking team was formed as an established part of the News Division's structure. And a formal process was established whereby on a daily basis the team would decide what topics likely to be in the news might warrant reality checks and would then put their suggestions to the morning meeting for consideration. Initially conceived by Director Harding as a counter to 'lies, distortions and exaggerations' in the post-truth era, its remit was eventually extended to issues and controversies for which the provision of reality-checking background information could be useful to citizens, who could then say, 'Here are the facts, now I can make a judgment.'

Finally, our main informant stressed, as a general policy objective for reporting the 2017 campaign, 'listening to the audience'. It was to be approached in a spirit of 'give us your questions', and, using them as a 'starting point', we'll 'try to explain' what the election is about. Admittedly difficult to discern at times, polling data could be consulted for guidance. Young people were a sector of the audience, whose needs and concerns the BBC wished particularly to address this campaign time round. For example, an hour and a half programme, Newsbeat:

the Final Debate, involving a 100 young-person studio audience closely questioning party spokespersons, was transmitted on Radio 1, Radio 1Xtra, 5 Live, Radio Manchester, the News Channel and late night on BBC1.

TAKING STOCK AND LOOKING AHEAD

On balance, the above record seems to reflect a re-dedication of public service journalism at the BBC. It also points to four main sources of influence on the Corporation's campaign coverage policy in 2017:

- post mortem reflections on past campaign coverage experience
- readings of likely and actual campaign dynamics, emanating from major party strategies and events and from salient issues to be reported and debated
- impressions of citizen/audience needs to be understood and met
- revisiting and freshly interpreting the meaning and application of public service journalism.

Nevertheless, several challenges and issues arise from this review for policy attention before and during the next election campaign:

Journalistic norms. BBC political news is expected by the Corporation's executives, regulators and outside parties, commentators and critics to be presented with 'due impartiality'. There are dangers, however, that its elevation above all other considerations may result in what Krugman (2016) termed a 'false equivalency' between well-founded and patently unfounded claims and become a recipe for voter confusion over what to believe—as allegedly was the case at times during the Brexit Referendum campaign (Starkey 2017). Desirable would be continual reflection on the rationale for the impartiality norm and its relationship to other valid journalistic norms such as holding advocates to account for the accuracy of their claims and subjecting them to other evidence and analysis germane to the states of affairs concerned. Perhaps impartiality should not be regarded as a be-all end but rather as an important means to other ends, i.e. to ensure that (a) significant political advocates are not unfairly disadvantaged by the coverage of themselves and their opponents and (b) individual citizens are not propagandized by one dominant viewpoint but are offered bases for making informed choices on issues that matter for themselves and society at large.

Debates. As Blumler et al. (2017) state:

> Debate is not only good for democracy but a necessary
> condition...Given that citizens benefit from media exposure
> to politicians who are given time to set out serious
> political arguments and are faced by meaningful live
> challenge from skeptics and opponents, televised debates
> should not be regarded as an added extra within important
> democratic processes like election campaigns.

It follows that, instead of engaging in prolonged negotiations and bargains with the main political parties over whether to arrange televised debates in the next election campaign, how many, when in the schedules, with what participants, and whether potential Prime Ministers should go head-to-head, the BBC should throw its full weight behind the institutionalization of broadcast campaign debates, for the organization and terms of which an independent body would be responsible.

The political interview. This has been a long-standing staple of campaign coverage and is regarded as helpful by many viewers. BBC news people have sometimes regarded it as a 'problem', however, because in their eyes politicians have become so practiced in evasive responses to questions. The risk is that the interview comes across as a 'game', in which either the interviewer or the interviewee wins and the former tries to trip up the latter. An adversarial model tends to dominate (see examples on p.55), and in consequence politicians may be wary of requests to be interviewed unless acceptance of them would suit their own tactical objectives. Perhaps interviewers should occasionally remind themselves—and be reminded by their superiors—that in democratic terms their work should serve a dual purpose: not only to challenge and probe but also to clarify what politicians stand for and why.

Disconnect from citizens' concerns and experience. Our senior informant recognized this as 'a big challenge for the next five years'. As he went on:

> The news still feels top down. We're fundamentally choosing.
> We're still the keeper of the news...We do have to wrestle
> with the problem that Jon Snow recently identified... illustrated
> graphically by our failure to deal with the issues highlighted
> by the Grenfell Towers fire... To some extent there will always
> be a disconnect. But we must work hard to reduce it and to
> bring ourselves closer to the audience.

There was little time available in the interview to explore the efforts that such a commendable determination might entail. At the time the informant mainly reiterated the points mentioned above (see p.59) about needs to gear political coverage so far as possible to issues and concerns uppermost for audience members and to develop ways of ascertaining those. At bottom, however, the root of the problem may lie more in structure than in practice—in, that is, the decided Westminster bias of British political journalism. It is noteworthy in this connection that at its Millbank base the BBC employs a Political Editor, a Deputy Political Editor, an Assistant Political Editor and a large number of political correspondents and producers. From a 'top-down' perspective, journalists' forays beyond Westminster precincts might sometimes seem to resemble colonial explorers going out to meet the natives! Perhaps the BBC should consider appointing one or more *political correspondents,* nationally and locally, who would be specifically assigned to undertake grassroots political reporting.

Building understanding of what BBC journalists do. Recognition of this as a future need came up when we asked our interviewee whether policy for coverage of the 2017 campaign had taken any account of the fact that lots of criticisms had been leveled at the BBC for its coverage of the Brexit Referendum campaign. The gist of his response was that much of the criticism had been ill-informed. A need for greater transparency over what BBC journalists do followed: 'We have to be much clearer in showing how we work.' Again there was insufficient time to explore the implications of this. One of them might be to accept that the vital principle of editorial autonomy is not necessarily threatened by disclosure of how journalists go about their business, including even the trade-offs involved in certain reporting decisions. Secondly, transparency projects should be predominantly descriptive rather than PR-promotional. Thirdly, avoiding vague generalities such as 'we'll keep you informed' and 'we're on your side', the BBC should articulate more fully and concretely the purposes that the BBC intends and strives to pursue in its election campaign coverage.

CONCLUSION: A PERSONAL PHILOSOPHIC WORD

A democratic society is necessarily diverse. To be sustained, communication within it must be based on some degree of mutual respect. That is what justifies pluralist politics, bans on hate speech, criticisms of manipulative elements in campaign strategies, and exposures of fake news.

Attainment of these ends will always be imperfect. But, whatever its limitations, a public service-striving BBC is a welcome instrument in the cause of their realization.

Acknowledgements I am immensely grateful to: the informants who openly provided such informative insights into BBC policy making; Chris Anderson for his astute involvement in the interviews and comments on chapter drafts; Stephen Coleman for the inspiring creativity of his analysis of political communication processes in the time I have been privileged to know him.

REFERENCES

Blumler, J. G., & Esser, F. (2018). Mediatization as a combination of push and pull forces: Examples during the 2015 UK general election campaign. *Journalism: Theory, Practice and Policy*.
Blumler, J. G., & Gurevitch, M. (1995). *The crisis of public communication*. London: Routledge.
Blumler, J. G., Gurevitch, M., & Ives, J. (1978). *The challenge of election broadcasting*. Leeds: Leeds University Press.
Blumler, J. G., Coleman, S., & Birchall, C. (2017). *Debating the TV debates: How voters viewed the Question Time Special*. London: Electoral Reform Society and University of Leeds.
Bull, P. E., & Elliott, J. (1998). Levels of threat: Means of assessing interviewer toughness. *Journal of Language and Social Psychology, 17*, 220–244.
Clayman, S. E., & Heritage, J. (2001). Questioning presidents: Journalistic deference and adversarialness in the press conferences of U.S. Presidents Eisenhower and Reagan. *Journal of Communication, 52*(4), 749–775.
Corner, J. (2017). Personal communication.
Cushion, S. (2017). Conventional wisdom distorted TV news coverage of campaign. In D. Thorsen, D. Jackson, & D. Lilleker (Eds.), *UK election analysis 2017: Media, voters and the campaign*. Bournemouth: Centre for the Study of Journalism, Culture and Community.
Deacon, D. (2017). Personal communication.
Deacon, D., Downey, J., Smith, D., Stanyer, J., & Wring, D. (2017). A tale of two leaders: News media coverage of the 2017 general election. In E. Thorsen, D. Jackson, & D. Lilleker (Eds.), *UK election analysis: Media, voters and the campaign*. Bournemouth: Centre for the Study of Journalism, Culture and Community.
Gandy, O. H., Jr. (1982). *Beyond agenda setting: Information subsidies and public policy*. Norwood, NJ: Ablex.
Gould, P. (1998). *The unfinished revolution: How the modernisers saved the Labour Party*. London: Little, Brown.

Krugman, P. (2016, September 26). The falsity of false equivalence. *New York Times.*

Starkey, S. (2017). Declining newspaper sales and the role of broadcast journalism in the 2017 general election. In E. Thorsen, D. Jackson, & D. Lilleker (Eds.), *UK election analysis: Media, voters and the campaign.* Bournemouth: Centre for the Study of Journalism, Culture and Community.

Swanson, D., & Mancini, P. (1996). *Politics, media and modern democracy: An international study of innovations in electoral campaigning and their consequences.* Westport, CT and London: Praeger.

Voltmer, K., & Brants, K. (2011). A question of control: Journalists and politicians in political broadcast interviews. In K. Brants & K. Voltmer (Eds.), *Political communication in postmodern democracy: Challenging the primacy of politics.* London: Palgrave Macmillan.

Wheeler, M. (2017). The use and abuse of the vox pop in the 2017 UK General Election television news coverage. In E. Thorsen, D. Jackson, & D. Lilleker (Eds.), *UK election analysis: Media, voters and the campaign.* Bournemouth: Centre for the Study of Journalism Culture and Community.

Election Night: The View from Sky News

Isla Glaister

INTRODUCTION

UK elections generally produce clear winners and losers but 2017 was arguably one of those rare occasions when the winners 'lost' and the losers 'won'. The Conservatives took the most seats but lost their Commons majority. Their leader, Theresa May, lost her credibility and her authority over her party. In contrast, Jeremy Corbyn lost the election but, with his party's surprise tally of seats, he won an internal battle about Labour's ideological direction. It was a similar story in Scotland where Nicola Sturgeon and the SNP won again but the real victory was Conservative Ruth Davidson's defeat of an IndyRef2. The unequivocal losers were the Liberal Democrats and UKIP. Both parties lost a considerable amount of money in lost deposits and, in the end, their leaders too. The only obvious winner was the DUP which not only won the most seats in Northern Ireland but also influence over the UK's Brexit negotiations. In just a few hours overnight British politics turned on its axis. From the unexpected exit poll, to the results that proved it right, and the efforts of politicians to control the narrative, it all unfolded on live television. The prospect of a hung parliament raised questions about

I. Glaister (✉)
Sky News, London, UK
e-mail: Isla.Glaister@sky.uk

© The Author(s) 2019
D. Wring et al. (eds.), *Political Communication in Britain*,
https://doi.org/10.1007/978-3-030-00822-2_5

the legitimacy of a future government, the party leaders themselves and Britain's approach to Brexit. Politicians were quick to use their broadcast interviews to put their case to each other and the nation. Below is the story of election night on Sky News.

COUNTDOWN TO THE EXIT POLL

It is 20:20 on the 8 June, an hour before polls close, and Conservative headquarters believe the party has increased its majority. One source tells Sky's presenter Adam Boulton they expect a seventy-seat advantage in the new Parliament. Another one tells Sky's presenter Kay Burley, covering the Prime Minister's count in Maidenhead, the majority will be sixty-six seats and there will be a new Cabinet in place by lunchtime on Friday, with Damian Green replacing Philip Hammond as Chancellor. Both predictions are somewhat short of the landslide suggested by the polls at the start of the campaign. Nevertheless, if correct, Theresa May would still claim a legitimate and substantial mandate to lead the Brexit negotiations beginning in eleven days.

Like other broadcasters, Sky News has spent six weeks pondering the potential outcomes and planning a results programme capable of covering them effectively. The editorial team has developed a database, commissioned graphics, chosen where to deploy cameras and correspondents and booked guests to appear through the night. The Conservative predictions are our first indication of what story we might be telling and whether we have the tools to do so. The backbone of our coverage is the 'Sky 250', a digital camera project that enables us to broadcast live pictures from 250 constituency counts and declarations on television, on mobile and online. I was largely responsible for selecting the locations and did so for their relevance to the story in terms of marginality, geography, declaration time, and the personalities involved. I am confident we are in the right places but the exit poll will provide the next clue.

For me that comes, not at ten o'clock when polls close, but at 21:42. On election night itself, my role is to analyze the results as they come in, alongside our psephologist Professor Michael Thrasher, and to guide Sky News's coverage accordingly. This means I am one of a small editorial team who sees the exit poll figures before they are broadcast, a practice begun in 2010 when Sky News joined the BBC and ITV in commissioning a national exit poll. There are strict protocols around this because security is paramount and the numbers must remain secret until polls close. Even the programme's main presenter, Adam Boulton, does not know the exit poll forecast before he sees it on screen, along with the viewers, at ten o'clock. The numbers are phoned through to a secure room but I also receive them by encrypted email. The attachments include the headline seat projections as well as a set of data tables.

If the exit poll is correct, and it invariably is, then there has been an extraordinary reversal of fortune for the two main party leaders. It predicts that the Conservatives will win 314 seats and Labour 266. The Liberal Democrats will inch up to 14 seats and the SNP will be reduced from 56 to 34 seats. Just five weeks earlier, both Conservative and Labour sources thought Theresa May would increase her majority to 100 seats. Instead, these figures suggest the voters have wiped it out altogether and returned a hung parliament. The projection looks more like the one expected in 2015 and nothing like the one suggested an hour and twenty minutes earlier by Conservative headquarters. It is a good thing Sky News had planned for, and rehearsed, a hung parliament as one of the potential scenarios that also included overall majorities for both Conservative and Labour.

SHAPING THE BROADCAST NARRATIVE

So, where had it gone wrong for Theresa May? Some clues are to be found in the data tables. They suggest the Conservatives had limited success with their strategy of attracting former UKIP voters in seats that voted to leave the EU. Instead, Remain-voting London appears to have taken its revenge, with the data suggesting a number of ministers and high-profile personalities could lose their seats. Among them are Gavin Barwell in Croydon Central, Jane Ellison in Battersea, and even the arch Brexiteer himself, Iain Duncan Smith is in a close fight in Chingford & Woodford Green. Other Conservatives in trouble outside of London include the Home Secretary Amber Rudd in Hastings & Rye. Nicky Morgan's seat of Loughborough is also close and it has something in common with a number of other constituencies forecast to fall to Labour—a large student population. Perhaps Jeremy Corbyn had managed to motivate younger people to the ballot box, after all. Even Canterbury, Conservative controlled for more than 100 years, is said to be tight. As is Sheffield Hallam, the seat of the former Liberal Democrat leader Nick Clegg. Looking through the data, it seems Theresa May's hopes of governing could hinge on Scotland. A number of SNP-held constituencies are too close to call and, if they lose them all, the party could finish with as few as 21 seats. They might also lose their Westminster leader, Angus Robertson, and former leader Alex Salmond.

Sky's representative on the exit poll team is Professor Michael Thrasher and at ten o'clock, in his interview with Adam Boulton, he adds two more crucial pieces of information. The team believe turnout is high and that both Labour and the Conservatives have increased their vote in all the English regions, but critically Labour's vote is up more. As he speaks, viewers are watching pictures of Newcastle and Sunderland racing to be the first to declare. Behind the cameras, Sky News journalists are now racing to respond to the exit poll and to get reaction from the parties.

A correspondent and a crew are dispatched to Hastings. It was a 'Sky 250' seat but, if the Home Secretary is in trouble, then the programme will need an 'Outside Broadcast' presence there. Sky's results screen presenter Ed Conway prepares a graphic, originally built for 2015 but far more relevant for the story of 2017. The 'coalition builder' allows him to demonstrate the various ways a government could be formed based on the exit poll forecast. It features a potentially pivotal role for the DUP which, at quarter past ten, gets an earlier than scripted mention on the programme.

Labour's media operation is also reverting to its 2015 election night strategy. The party had expected the 2015 election result to prompt a battle for legitimacy and intended to argue that Prime Minister David Cameron had lost his majority and should resign, like Edward Heath in 1974 (Cowley and Kavanagh 2015: 214–216). In the end, Labour's poor performance made that script redundant. Two years later though, just minutes after the exit poll is broadcast, Emily Thornberry tells Sky's presenter Sophy Ridge that Theresa May "should consider her position". Almost simultaneously, a senior Labour source tells Sky's Senior Political Correspondent Jason Farrell: "She's the one who said if she lost six seats she wouldn't be Prime Minister." It is a phrase the party's representatives would repeat many times during the night as they argued Theresa May had set her own benchmark for failure and had effectively lost the election.

The Conservative response is much less unified. Official campaign sources cast doubt on the exit poll and say the results of individual contests will make a difference. Other Conservatives, though, start questioning aspects of the campaign and the Prime Minister's leadership.

Then her main rival, Boris Johnson, cancels a series of interviews, raising suspicions he could be preparing a challenge. Within fifteen minutes of polls closing, and without a single result declared, the balance of power in British politics has shifted and Theresa May's job looks in jeopardy. The talk now is of coalitions, not majorities, and the Liberal Democrats make it clear they will not be part of one. If the exit poll is right the party might not have enough seats to matter anyway. In classic expectation management mode, a spokesman says: "we're just looking to hold seats". It is a similar response from the SNP who argue that 34 seats would be considered a landslide if the party had not won 56 two years before.

EARLY RESULTS: POLITICIANS REACT

The first test of the exit poll arrives in the form of provisional turn-out numbers. The earliest ones are for the Newcastle and Sunderland constituencies and all show an increase on 2015. The student areas of Newcastle are up the most, Central by ten points and East by 14 points. It is the first results though that will provide a better clue and, as Big Ben chimes eleven o'clock, Newcastle Central declares.

There are two winners—the counting staff, who have ended Houghton & Sunderland South's reign as the first to declare at every election since 1992, and Labour's Chi Onwurah.[1] It is a safe Labour seat so the result is unsurprising, but the detail is interesting. Both the Labour and Conservative votes are up, but Labour's vote is up by more. Turnout has increased and the UKIP vote appears to have split. It is a similar story to the exit poll with one important caveat. The Conservatives have performed slightly better, and Labour slightly worse, than the exit poll suggested. The pattern is repeated in the next two seats to declare, Houghton & Sunderland South and Sunderland Central, both in the North East of England.

Conservative sources use this as evidence the exit poll is wrong and tell Sky's Political Editor Faisal Islam "things will look different by 3am". However, the unease about Theresa May's position is becoming clear. Ministers are now using interviews to dissuade their colleagues from

---

[1] The House of Commons library has recorded Newcastle-upon-Tyne Central's declaration time as 23:01 and Houghton & Sunderland South's as 23:10. Houghton & Sunderland South still holds the record for the fastest general election night count, 42 minutes and 46 seconds, which it set in 2005.

supporting a leadership challenge. The message from James Brokenshire, David Gauke and others is that the Brexit negotiations begin in eleven days and it would be a mistake to start "navel gazing". Nevertheless, the odds on Boris Johnson becoming the next Prime Minister have just fallen from 25-1 to 5-1.[2] The leadership question provides more ammunition for Labour in the battle for legitimacy. John McDonnell suggests his party is ready to form a minority government, if necessary.

As midnight approaches, the first seat outside the north east of England declares. The Conservatives hold Swindon North but the result makes sober reading for Tories hoping the exit poll had under-estimated their chances. There is a swing of 3.7% from Conservative to Labour, almost twice what the exit poll predicted. The UKIP vote has fallen almost 13 points, but Labour's is up by 11 points and the Conservative's by just 3 points. The belief of the Conservative campaign team that they could "hoover-up" UKIP votes in Brexit-voting constituencies looks increasingly misplaced.

At Theresa May's count in Maidenhead, a senior Conservative tells Kay Burley they are "still smiling" and that the final outcome might not be as bad as the exit poll suggests. The Darlington declaration half an hour later indicates otherwise. It is the first result from a seat where the UKIP vote in 2015 was more than the gap between Labour and the Conservatives. The party's hope of a large majority depended on gaining Labour seats like this. Just three weeks earlier, a Conservative campaign source had said Darlington was "in the bag". Instead, the party manages a swing from Labour of a mere 0.2%. Labour's winner, Jenny Chapman, says she is so shocked to win she has not prepared a speech. If the Tories had failed in Darlington, then other seats on their Brexit hit list, like Bishop Auckland, Middlesbrough South, Wakefield and Mansfield might be out of reach as well.

In Darlington, the two main parties polled 94% of the vote. Every other party to stand lost their deposit. In fact, in all the constituencies to declare so far, the Labour and Conservative votes had totaled more than 80%. Shares like these are reminiscent of the 1970s.[3] Conservative

[2]The odds quoted are from Sky Bet. Other bookmakers will have had slightly different prices, but none was very different.

[3]In 2017, the final combined vote share for the Conservatives and Labour was 82%. Records from the House of Commons Library show this was the highest two-party vote share since 1970, when the combined Labour and Conservative vote share was 89%.

pre-election confidence had been built on the belief their vote would increase. Perhaps, they had not considered that the decline of the minor parties could benefit Labour too. In the studio with Sophy Ridge, the academic and UKIP specialist, Matthew Goodwin concedes he did not see it coming either. Professor Goodwin had said he would eat his latest book if Labour got 38% of the vote. He says he also assumed UKIP voters would support the Conservatives but, if not, the party can forget about winning seats in the industrial north. Off camera, pro-Remain politicians are now reminding people that Theresa May had framed this as the 'Brexit election'. On camera, UKIP's Patrick O'Flynn accuses the Prime Minister of putting a so-called "clean Brexit in jeopardy". A third battle to control the election night narrative has begun—about the nature of Brexit.

The panic is now starting to show among Conservatives. There is talk of another vote and a suggestion the party could have a new leader by Christmas. Anna Soubry, whose seat in Broxtowe is said to be too close to call, will soon say publicly that Theresa May should go. Not one of the top four contenders for the leadership has yet been seen on camera, although one of them, Amber Rudd, has more pressing concerns. She arrives at the count in Hastings & Rye as the returning officer tells a Sky News producer that the result is so close there could be a recount. It is another small victory for the exit poll.

In contrast, Labour moderates, who had been so critical of Jeremy Corbyn during the campaign, are now tentatively congratulating him. From Manchester, Lucy Powell tells Adam Boulton "the exit poll is incredible" and "you just have to take your hat off to Jeremy". Outside Jeremy Corbyn's house, a Labour aide says the mood is "cautious" but then lists a series of seats the Party thinks it will gain. It includes Nick Clegg's seat of Sheffield Hallam. Votes from friendly Conservatives had saved him in 2015 but now it seems the former Deputy Prime Minister might finally have paid a personal price for his U-turn on tuition fees. Shortly afterwards, students with Sky's Senior Correspondent Ashish Joshi at the Isle of Wight Festival start chanting Jeremy Corbyn's name.

Three hours after the exit poll, and with less than fifteen results declared, the DUP effectively begin their coalition negotiations. Wanting an early voice in the conversation about who gets to govern, a spokesman tells Faisal Islam the DUP will not support Jeremy Corbyn, but would consider working with the Conservatives. Whether that makes a difference will depend on how many seats the Conservatives can win. Results from London and Scotland will be crucial. The one o'clock hour brings the first declarations from both.

TOWARDS THE HUNG PARLIAMENT

It also brings the first Labour gain—Rutherglen & Hamilton West from the SNP. As the exit poll suggested, the nationalist vote is down significantly but while Labour have taken the seat, the Conservative vote has advanced the most. The result shows a bigger swing from the SNP to the Conservatives than forecast by the detailed exit poll figures. Arguably, Labour activists have the Scottish Conservative leader, Ruth Davidson, not Jeremy Corbyn, to thank for their wafer-thin majority of 265.

While Conservative votes are helping Labour over the line in Scotland, the party is missing its own targets elsewhere. Wrexham was 25th on the Conservative target list, but Labour retain it, despite the absence of a UKIP candidate.[4] In Cardiff, Carwyn Jones, Labour's leader in Wales, looks stunned. There is a similar look on Conservative faces in London but for a different reason. The first seat to declare in the capital is another Tory target, Tooting. Labour's Rosena Allin-Khan takes it with almost 60% of the vote and a swing from the Conservatives of more than ten percent. Sky's team of psephologists say, if the result was repeated elsewhere in the capital, Labour would gain 11 seats from the Conservatives, including Battersea, Croydon Central and Kensington. The Liberal Democrats would also gain Kingston & Surbiton, Sutton & Cheam and Twickenham. On cue, Sky's producer at the Battersea count says Labour believe they have won there. Before Battersea declares, there is a scare for a more senior government minister. The Education Secretary Justine Greening clings on in Putney but her 10,000 majority is reduced to just 1,500. It is another double-digit swing to Labour in the capital.

In Scotland, though, Conservatives are celebrating their first gain of the night. The party has taken Angus from the SNP on a swing of 16%. Similar performances in other Scottish constituencies could give them an extra 12 seats. Our analysis shows the Conservatives are doing better in constituencies that voted 'No' during the 2014 independence referendum. Perhaps winning that debate in Scotland can compensate the

---

[4] The order of target seats in this chapter is based on where it ranks in the swing required for a party to gain. It does not necessarily reflect internal party target lists.

Conservatives for the 'revenge of the Remainers' in London. It certainly does not look like Brexit-voting England will help the Conservatives. The party is doing better in Leave supporting areas but not well enough to gain seats. Conservative sources now say they do not even think they will win the City of Chester, despite Labour's tiny 93-vote majority and the absence of a UKIP candidate. At the other end of the Tory target list is the Labour Deputy Leader's seat of West Bromwich East. At one thirty in the morning Tom Watson is re-elected comfortably. In his speech, he repeats what is now becoming a mantra for Labour politicians: "she said if we lose six seats Jeremy Corbyn will be Prime Minister and we are going to hold her to that." The smiles and celebrations are those of victory but, even with the expected gains in London, Labour is still on course to finish second in terms of seats. Whether they can hold Theresa May to her word will depend on the final arithmetic.

In timely fashion, as Labour hold both Hartlepool and Wolverhampton North East, Ed Conway presents his 'battleground' screen. Column after column of constituencies that the Conservatives had hoped would turn blue remain resolutely Labour red. In the context of this result the missed gains are as important as the losses. Theresa May set the benchmark for success so high that Tory backbenchers now consider anything less than a majority of 50 seats as failure. Losing ministers is considered a disaster and the first one goes at 2 a.m.

After hours of speculation, Jane Ellison's 8,000 majority is wiped out in Battersea by another ten-point swing to Labour. It is Labour's first gain in London and it is followed moments later by a 12-point swing in Ealing Central & Acton. Rupa Huq's once ultra-marginal seat now has a sizeable Labour majority. The scale of the Conservative's troubles in Remain-voting areas is becoming clear. Earlier in the night, Conservative sources had scoffed at the exit poll's prediction that Canterbury would be close. Now, the returning officer announces a recount. Conservative headquarters finally admit they have given up hope of achieving an overall majority.

Despite being silent and absent since ten o'clock Boris Johnson has been a significant presence in the coverage so far. The man rumoured to be plotting a leadership challenge makes his first appearance at 02:07 as he arrives at the count location in Uxbridge, which he shares with the Shadow Chancellor John McDonnell. He says nothing on the way in and his body language gives little away. At the same time, Jeremy Corbyn emerges from his home in Islington to chants of "Oh Jeremy Corbyn!".

The flash photography is worthy of a rock star and that is the reception he gets when he arrives at his count. Labour activists line up to applaud him inside as they did Tony Blair into Labour headquarters after his 1997 landslide. Looking slightly overwhelmed and waving to the crowd the Labour leader misdirects a 'high five' and instead makes contact with Emily Thornberry's chest. It is one of the images of the night. Back in Uxbridge reporters are asking John McDonnell if Labour can form a government. He says they will do so "at the earliest opportunity."

That opportunity looks increasingly dependent on results in Scotland. As John McDonnell is speaking the Conservatives gain two more seats from the SNP. The party jumps from third to first in Ochil & South Perthshire and defeats the SNP's Westminster leader Angus Robertson with a 14% swing in Moray. There is now something for the Conservatives to celebrate in England too. The party makes its first gain south of the border, taking Southport from the Liberal Democrats. The news is enough to entice Theresa May from her home but there is no fanfare departure for the Conservative leader, just the broadcasters' helicopter following her car to the Maidenhead count. While viewers watch her journey, Adam Boulton interviews another leading contender for her job, the Brexit Secretary David Davis. He clearly has not spoken recently to Conservative headquarters because he is still arguing that the exit poll could be wrong. When asked about Theresa May's future, rather inconveniently, he loses sound.

CONTRASTING FORTUNES: THE LEADERS' STORIES

There is now enough hard data from constituencies to produce the first Sky News forecast. Professor Thrasher predicts the Conservatives will be the largest party, with somewhere between 308 and 328 seats. He explains that the midpoint is 318, slightly higher than the exit poll suggested but there is still an outside chance of a small Conservative majority. The Party has missed opportunities to make gains in Wales and much will depend on its performance in Scotland. He also expects the Liberal Democrats to gain seats from the SNP. Seconds later they do just that as Jo Swinson wins back the Dunbartonshire East seat she lost in 2015.

Overall, though, the Liberal Democrat story is far from positive. The party's leader Tim Farron tried to position it as the natural home for Remain voters. He even included a promise of a second referendum in his party's manifesto. The psephology team's analysis reveals that strategy has failed. Based on the results declared so far, there is no correlation between change in the Liberal Democrat vote and places that overwhelmingly supported Remain. Instead, it is Labour that is attracting Remainers. Jeremy Corbyn's somewhat confused position on Brexit appears to be paying off on both sides of the divide. The 2010 U-turn on tuition fees also still appears to be affecting Liberal Democrat support among students. When he left his home, Tim Farron told reporters he could not confirm rumours that his predecessor, Nick Clegg, had lost in Sheffield Hallam. At 02:45 the seat that is home to students from two universities finally declares. Labour's Jared O'Mara has defeated the former Deputy Prime Minister. In his loser's speech Nick Clegg gives a powerful and prescient outline of the divisions in the country. He describes Britain as a nation polarised between left and right, between different regions and nations and between young and old. The results of the previous hours, and those still to come, illustrate his argument. Six minutes after one former Liberal Democrat leader leaves Parliament, a future one returns. Vince Cable is elected in Twickenham. His vote is up by 15 points and everyone else's is down. It is a rare Liberal Democrat victory outside of Scotland.

The two o'clock hour ends as it began with another Conservative minister losing their seat to Labour. This time it is the Paymaster General Ben Gummer in Ipswich. He had helped to write the Conservative manifesto but voters in his constituency are apparently unimpressed.

There appears to be an unwritten rule that the seat of a party leader, with the exception of the Greens, should declare between 3 a.m. and 4 a.m. It creates an hour of drama that showcases the power of television as a medium on such occasions. It also gives the team in the gallery some difficult choices about what to put to air next. The pictures tell the story better than any analyst or correspondent. On one side of the screen Jeremy Corbyn waits in Islington. He has been there for forty-five minutes basking in the adulation of his activists. On the other side, Maidenhead waits for Theresa May. Since she cast her vote on Thursday, the only sign of the Prime Minister has been the passage of her car through the darkness towards the count. Watching in the studio is Tony Blair's former Press Secretary, Alastair Campbell. His is the first Labour voice of the night to point out the party has now lost three elections in a row. Jeremy Corbyn increases his already enormous majority in Islington

North, getting the largest winning vote for any candidate there before.[5] He then utters those now familiar words about "six seats" and calls on Theresa May to resign.

Simultaneously, Kay Burley puts the same question to the Prime Minister who has just arrived in Maidenhead. Unsurprisingly, there is no answer. Standing next to Lord Buckethead, Theresa May looks disappointed, yet steely. The 'strong and stable' image of six weeks before is replaced by the now infamous 'grimace-grin' that was so evident at the Welsh manifesto launch when the wheels started to come off her campaign. Even in her own constituency there is a swing towards Labour. In fact, Maidenhead is one of the rare constituencies where the Conservative vote is down on 2015, albeit marginally. During the declaration a series of new results appear on the graphics at the bottom of the screen. Together they are a microcosm of the election. The Conservatives finally make a gain from their Brexit strategy, taking Middlesbrough South, the DUP gain Belfast South and Labour take Portsmouth South from the Tories. Confirmation that Labour has gained Canterbury appears on screen as Theresa May begins her speech. Her message is familiar: "the country needs stability" and "the Conservative Party will provide it" but her delivery is unsteady. At the end, her voice breaks with emotion. She walks off stage and quickly out of the back door. It is what pundits call a 'holding speech'. She does not address the questions raised about her future and it leaves a vacuum in the hours to come for others to debate whether she should stay or go.

It is Tim Farron's turn next and he narrowly survives a similar fate to Nick Clegg. The Liberal Democrat leader's majority in Westmorland & Lonsdale is reduced from almost 9,000 to 777. His speech is interrupted by the declaration in Boston & Skegness where another leader, UKIP's Paul Nuttall, is hearing his fate. Like the rest of his party's 378 candidates, he is defeated in emphatic style. He finishes third in the constituency known as the Brexit capital of the UK. He is, though, one of only 41 UKIP candidates to save their deposit (House of Commons 2017: 62–63). In 2015, UKIP were second in 120 constituencies. Two years later, they are second in none (ibid.: 60–62). Minutes after he leaves the Boston count, Paul Nuttall cancels a news conference

---

[5] In 2017, Jeremy Corbyn gets 73% of the vote in Islington North, the highest since the constituency was established in 1885. The previous highest was 69.3% in 1997, also achieved by Jeremy Corbyn as a Labour candidate.

he planned to hold in London later that day. It will now take place in Boston, fuelling speculation he has decided to quit.

In the past half hour, the SNP has lost another four seats in Scotland with the Conservatives, Labour and the Liberal Democrats sharing the spoils. Sky's producer in Aberdeen now confirms Alex Salmond's defeat in Gordon, which was forecast by the exit poll. Nicola Sturgeon's night has arguably been no better than Theresa May's but the SNP leader handles it differently. In bullish mood, she talks to the media in Glasgow, reminding them that her party has won the election in Scotland. Asked about IndyRef2, she says it was clearly a factor but she needs time to reflect. The real purpose of her foray into the spotlight is to make it clear that the SNP will take part in an "anti-Tory, progressive coalition", if Jeremy Corbyn asks and the arithmetic makes it possible. For all the troubles of Theresa May, the battle about who gets to govern is still the dominant narrative.

COALITION PROSPECTS: WHO WILL GOVERN?

There are now 479 results of 650 declared and it looks increasingly likely the Conservatives will fall short of a majority. However, the election in Northern Ireland is over and the DUP has ten seats with which to bargain for a place in coalition. The party's leader, Arlene Foster, makes her pitch to Adam Boulton. While viewers watch pictures of Theresa May's car making the next leg of its journey to London, she outlines a shopping list of DUP desires. At the top of it is "no hard border between Northern Ireland and the rest of the UK". Her words are a taster of the negotiations to come in the following days.

At 03:57 Professor Thrasher updates the Sky News forecast and calls the election as a hung parliament. The Conservatives will be the largest party on between 315 and 325 seats, with the upper limit one seat short of an overall majority. Whether the DUP's ten seats will be enough to support Theresa May will now depend on the scale of the losses in London and the gains in Scotland. With a hint of irony, at 04:00, the Conservatives gain Stirling from the SNP, putting them ahead of Labour in the popular vote for the first time.

The tight contests will now decide it and there are many of them. Vince Cable reveals that, in Richmond Park, there are less than 100 votes between the Conservative Zac Goldsmith and the Liberal Democrat Sarah Olney. There are recounts in Ashfield and Crewe & Nantwich, a second one in Hastings & Rye and a third in Fife North East. The list of Labour gains is also expanding from Reading East and Plymouth Sutton & Devonport to Colne Valley where the winning candidate Thelma Walker begins her speech with: "Wow". The Conservatives gain Mansfield from Labour and shortly after Stoke-on-Trent South. These are both extraordinary results and a reminder for the Conservatives of what might have been.

The Prime Minister is now at party headquarters. A source says when she arrived she conceded it had been a "difficult night" and spoke to staff for ten minutes, thanking them for their hard work. He denies what many are now speculating, that Theresa May is taking advice on whether to resign. It is a question that Ruth Davidson sidesteps too when asked by Adam Boulton. Her gushingly cheerful demeanor is such a contrast to her party leader. As she declares the death of IndyRef2, the Conservatives make another crucial gain from the SNP. Banff & Buchan is the eleventh Tory seat in Scotland, matching the total reached in 1992.[6] Next to contribute to the Conservative cause is Hastings & Rye. Amber Rudd finally defeats her Labour challenger and the leader of the council by a mere 346 votes. The Home Secretary makes another 'holding speech' focusing mainly on local issues.

At 04:56 the Sky News forecast narrows further, this time with seat projections for both parties. The Conservatives are expected to finish with between 315 and 321 seats. The Conservative midpoint is once again 318. Labour lies in the range of 260 and 266 seats. If Jeremy Corbyn achieves the forecast, he will become the most successful Labour leader since Tony Blair, securing the party's first net gain in seats since 1997. His former critics acknowledge his feat. Through almost gritted teeth, Yvette Cooper says she "applauds" him. From Ilford North, Wes Streeting, who looks stunned that he is still an MP, tells Adam Boulton: "it would be pretty churlish for me to come on television and say, after all these Labour gains, that Jeremy should start packing his bags." Labour might have lost another election but Jeremy Corbyn has temporarily won the argument about the direction of the party's future.

Theresa May's future remains a mystery. After an hour and twenty minutes inside Conservative headquarters with her advisers Nick Timothy and Fiona Hill, she leaves for Downing Street. Again she

[6]The final total of Conservative seats in Scotland is 12, the largest number since 1983 when the party won 21 seats.

gives no answer when asked if she is stepping down. Correspondents from a plethora of news organizations are now outside Number Ten. Sky's Senior Political Correspondent Beth Rigby is among them and says a number of senior Conservatives are now telling her the Prime Minister should resign, arguing she ran a campaign based on getting a personal mandate and failed. Iain Duncan Smith, the leading Brexiteer who has just been re-elected in Chingford & Wood Green, disagrees. He wants her to stay. Taking control of all three narratives, he says the Conservatives should form a government, with the DUP if necessary; and a leadership election would be "catastrophic" so close to the beginning of the Brexit negotiations. The anti-European Tories give Theresa May their backing because nothing can put Brexit in jeopardy.

The issue of who gets to govern is now largely resolved. Labour hold Southampton Test, making a Conservative majority now impossible. The country will have only its third coalition since the Second World War, but its second in a decade. For all the celebrations, Labour will not have enough seats to do business with other parties. The only realistic coalition scenario is one between the Conservatives and the DUP. Ironically, even Sinn Fein can lend a helping hand because they will not take the seven seats they have won.

It is 06:00 and the front door of number 10 Downing Street is a constant on-screen presence. Outside, Beth Rigby is told the Prime Minister is alone and writing a statement to make later in the morning. Its content will depend on what party colleagues are telling her. Senior ministers are said to be frantically sending WhatsApp and text messages to find out how many of their colleagues will support the leader. The 1922 committee and the Chief Whip, Gavin Williamson, are also talking to MPs. Theresa May's former press adviser Katie Perrior, who resigned shortly before the election, diverts the blame from her former boss to the people around her. Responsibility for the result lies with Nick Timothy and Fiona Hill, she says, before sounding a warning about underestimating Boris Johnson. Finally, there is some action at the front door of Number 10. David Davis is on his way inside. He seems not hear journalists' questions about the Prime Minister's future.

In Brighton, another female party leader is getting a resounding reception. Caroline Lucas is re-elected in Brighton Pavillion as the only Green MP. She joins a number of Remainers who have said they will use their place in Parliament to push for a vote on the final Brexit deal.

There are now just nine seats left to declare and most are said to be close. They could either bolster the Conservative total or hinder the party's coalition hopes. One of them is Kensington where, despite being long held by the Tories in London, there is now a recount. One of the features of the 2017 election is the increase in the number of constituencies settled by small margins. In the end, 31 seats were won with majorities of less than one percent (House of Commons 2017: 67–68). The smallest is Fife North East where the fourth recount has just finished and the SNP have held off the Liberal Democrat challenge by just 2 votes. Another to make the top ten of close finishes is Richmond Park where, at 07:06, Zac Goldsmith is re-elected with a majority of 45. It is a rare victory for the Conservatives in London. Perhaps, in the context of what unfolded overnight, it is fitting that the final seat to declare is another one in London. The staff in Kensington are so exhausted that after three recounts they take a break. The result finally comes at 21:03 on Friday, nearly twenty-four hours after polls closed. It is another Labour gain in a Remain voting seat in the capital and a swing away from the Conservatives of more than ten percent.

In the end, the exit poll that some Conservatives had dismissed at ten o'clock proved to be remarkably accurate. The final figures of Conservative 318, Labour 262, Liberal Democrat 12, SNP 35 and others 23 were extremely close to the original forecast. The seat projections also foresaw the unlikely loss of constituencies like Canterbury and Kensington and politicians like Nick Clegg and Alex Salmond.

Final Thoughts

The exit poll was, indeed, sensational but the night that followed was truly extraordinary. The drama of it was worthy of award-winning theatre and I was privileged to have both a front row seat and a role backstage. Immersed in the data and challenging the politician's spin, I helped tell viewers the story of the most memorable reversal of electoral fortunes in decades. I will forever be reminded that I did not select Canterbury for the 'Sky 250' but few would have thought it would play such a part in the story. However, Sky did broadcast live declarations from 56 of the 70 seats that changed hands, capturing and sharing those moments of history with its viewers and readers. Their votes had helped to shift the balance of power in British politics and alter the dynamics of the Brexit negotiations to come. Few politicians had seen it coming, particularly those in the Conservative campaign. On the evening of Friday 9 June, shortly after Kensington declared, I came across the Conservative's former Chairman, Sir Eric Pickles, near Sky's studios in Westminster. "We didn't pick it", he said. "I spent plenty of time on the doorstep campaigning and our vote was up. What we didn't realise was that their's was too."

References

Cowley, P., & Kavanagh, D. (2015). Different scripts required: Election night. *The British general election of 2015* (pp. 214–216). Basingstoke: Palgrave Macmillan.

House of Commons. (2017). *General election 2017: Results and analysis* (Briefing paper CBP 7979). London: House of Commons Library.

The Agenda-Setting Role of Newspapers in the UK 2017 Elections

Angela Phillips

INTRODUCTION

The story of the 2017 election has been constructed as one of declining newspaper influence and a surge in youth engagement on the back of successful social media campaigning. This was often seen as the election that broke the hegemony of the mainstream media and relegated the newspaper barons and the BBC to a back seat. But a closer reading of the evidence tells a somewhat different story. Elections are not won or lost by the media but when the media captures the public mood it can provide the drumbeat which encourages people to believe that their side is winning and that leads to increased participation (Dvir-Gvirsman et al. 2015). On the other hand, a campaign that relies mainly on attacking the opposition, without also providing positive reasons to vote, often backfires, as the campaign against London Mayor Sadiq Khan did in 2016 (Media Reform Coalition 2016).

The vote for Brexit in 2016 was clinched by a higher than usual turnout in areas with a largely white population and lower levels of education

A. Phillips (✉)
Goldsmiths, University of London, London, UK
e-mail: A.Phillips@gold.ac.uk

© The Author(s) 2019
D. Wring et al. (eds.), *Political Communication in Britain*,
https://doi.org/10.1007/978-3-030-00822-2_6

(Ashcroft 2017). Those marginalised voters who, the previous year, chose to vote Brexit in order to Take Back Control, were expected to provide Theresa May with a Brexit dividend. But only one in six (17%) of previously Labour-voting Leave voters switched to the Conservatives (Burn-Murdoch et al. 2017). Many of them failed to vote at all. At the same time a significant number of Remain voting 35–44 year olds switched from Conservative to boost the Labour vote (Ashcroft 2017).

I will argue that, although it is likely that the Labour-supporting Momentum organisation had an influence via social media, among younger voters, the mainstream Conservative leaning press, which in turn sets the agenda for television news, was still of critical importance both in terms of what it did, but perhaps more important, what it didn't do. It could not turn the rather stiff and anxious figure of Theresa May into a popular leader and it failed to provide unconditional support to her for a critical period in the lead-up to the election. Given the agenda-setting role that the newspapers play on the television news agenda (Cushion et al. 2016) this also impacted the way that television covered the debate. Given that television is still the major source of news information in the UK, this was a significant factor. This failure to connect does not suggest that the power of the mainstream media has been over-turned. It seems more likely that, given an un-popular election, a lack-lustre leader, and a population divided by attitudes to Europe rather than just by class or party, it failed to produce the necessary mood music.

THE NEWS MEDIA CONTEXT

The circulation of newspapers in the UK and elsewhere has declined sharply over the last twenty years (Ofcom 2017a) alongside their advertising income (Enders Analysis 2016). It is the role of social media, as both an amplifier and an agenda-setter, that has come to dominate discussions of the election coverage. Much has been made about the arrival of new digital news challengers, the most significant of which, *The Canary*, challenging from the left of the political spectrum and *Breitbart*, from the right, are now each accessed by two percent of the UK audience at least once a week (Newman et al. 2017). This is largely through the use of highly polarised material circulated via social media (Newman et al. 2017). However these numbers are dwarfed by the reach of the mainstream press online. Research by Curran et al. (2013)

suggests that traditional news brands maintain their hegemony across digital platforms (directly, via search and in social media) and that newspapers (for want of a better word) have a greater impact than that suggested by their own audience figures. Indeed successive years of analysis from the National Readership Survey (NRS 2017) suggest that the readership of the newspaper brands is increasing, rather than declining.

Figures for 2016, gave a monthly audience of 29 million to the *Daily Mail*, 26.2 to the *Sun*, 25.8 to the *Mirror* and 22.7 million to the *Guardian*. These figures cannot easily be compared to daily print readership and in some cases might only represent a single article over the month in question, rather than a daily news habit. They also include overseas audiences, which in the case of the *Mail Online* and *theguardian.com* are considerable, nevertheless they suggest that the newspapers, far from retreating in the face of an advancing web and social media presence, are alongside the broadcasters, dominating the web news space. In December 2017, according to figures on their pages, the *Mail* had 13 million Facebook followers while the *Guardian* had nearly 7 million Twitter followers. By comparison, in the same month the *Canary* was followed by 155,561 people on Facebook and *Breitbart London* had 64,564 followers.

In the UK, the cross platform audience figures for the newspapers are still lower than those of the broadcasters, in particular the BBC. According to analysis by the Reuters Institute for the Study of Journalism, it is the television news that dominates news consumption both on and off line (Newman et al. 2017). More than half the population claimed to have accessed BBC TV or radio news in 2016, at least three times per week. Ofcom figures put that higher, finding that 73% of those questioned used BBC One for news; and of that group, 85% did so regularly. That compares to 68% of the total digital audience accessing the *Mail Online*/the *Daily Mail* and 64% accessing the *Sun* online in April 2017 (Ofcom 2017a).

Research by Stephen Cushion and colleagues into the 2015 election (Cushion et al. 2016) found that not only did the newspapers have a formidable web presence, they also had a clear agenda-setting role in relation to the broadcasters. Stories considered important by the newspapers, would also be covered by the broadcasters, usually with a similar angle. Further research by Justin Schlosberg for the Media Reform Coalition found that News UK media are particularly influential in this respect (Schlosberg 2017). Given that the two largest circulating newspapers online (*The Mail* and *The Sun*) lean towards the Conservative Party in their coverage, this agenda-setting relationship tends to amplify stories favouring the Conservatives, in spite of regulation requiring fairness and impartiality.

The BBC regularly reports newspaper election coverage on and offline. In the week of the launch of Labour's election manifesto the introduction to this press summary read: "*Labour's draft manifesto is widely discussed, with the Daily Mail summing it up as 'Corbyn's fantasy land'*" (BBC Staff 2017). This was followed by a list of negative comments, with more positive comments from the *Guardian* and *Mirror* tacked onto the end for balance. Arguably the *Guardian's* decision to back Corbyn and the manifesto, might have been a more interesting lead but clearly an editorial decision was taken to weight the article towards the biggest group by, circulation and influence, rather than according to the news value of the content. This may have been seen as balance, but it is a form of balance that merely reproduces the hegemony of the right-wing press.

Research by the Media Reform Coalition into the BBC newspaper reviews found that during the election period: "the BBC gave between 69 and 95% more attention to the Conservative Party compared to what would be considered a balanced proportion, using 2015 election voting as a reference" (Media Reform Coalition 2017). I will argue that the link with broadcasting, as well as the dominance of the mainstream press online, was still of key importance in the 2017 elections, in spite of the arrival of new entrants into the news field and the rising importance of social media.

SOCIAL MEDIA, FAKE NEWS AND BOTS

Those using social media for news were most likely to be in the youngest age group. Forty percent of 16–24 year olds find news on social media compared to 24% using online content direct from broadcasters and 15% using online content direct from newspapers (Ofcom 2017a). Evidence suggests that those who do access political messages online are more likely to engage with them than if they had seen similar messages on TV (Conroy et al. 2012; Boulianne 2015), and that those seeing Facebook messages encouraging them to vote, are more likely to do so (Bond et al. 2012). However figures for news consumption across all age groups found that only 27% said that they used Facebook for news whereas 56% use the BBC online services (Ofcom 2017a). Ofcom also found that in the 65 plus age group fewer than eight percent used any form of online or social media sites for news. So although much larger numbers may have been targeted by political parties, or their surrogates, via social media advertising, only a minority deliberately seek news via social media.

There is no way of predicting whether the higher news consumption via social media amongst the youngest age group is a long-term trend or merely a generational factor (Elvestad and Phillips 2018b). Ofcom figures indicate that time spent on social media starts to decline quite rapidly as young people move into their mid-twenties (Ofcom 2017a: 36). People also tend to be more interested in news as they get older (Buckingham 2000; Marchi 2012) and the Ofcom figures suggest that those in the higher social groups are both more likely to use social media for news and to go directly to a website or app of a news provider, so it is likely that a significant proportion of social media users in the 35–44 age group, which was most likely to have switched to Labour, are also using mainstream media to access or verifying news (Ofcom 2017a: 37). For older voters, a combination of social media, plus mainstream media, is more likely than the use of social media alone for news consumption. This is an important factor because social media tends to provide information that is polarised but often unenlightening (Conroy et al. 2012).

The role of social media in election campaigning has been the subject of a large quantity of research, mainly in the United States (Boulianne 2015). While this body of work is indeed useful, there is increasing evidence that differences in media systems and political systems are also relevant to the way in which news is both disseminated and accessed (Elvestad and Phillips 2018a). A team from the Computation Propaganda Project at the Oxford Internet Institute has been examining social media, the use of automated Twitter accounts (bots) and the circulation of fake news across a number of countries during elections. They found significant differences between the United States, Germany, France and the UK. In the UK 11.4% of the relevant content shared on social media was identified as fake news (similar quantities were found during the German elections). This compares to 5.1 and 7.6% in two French elections and 33% of shared material in swing state of Michigan during the US 2016 elections (Kaminska et al. 2017). This research also found that more than fifty percent of election-related material, circulating on social media in the UK in the 2017 election period, came from professional journalism sources.

An analysis by the *Press Gazette* of the top 100 most shared stories on the BuzzSumo database (which provides data for advertisers) confirms the presence of a high proportion of professional journalism during the election campaign. Using the search term "general election", *Press Gazette* found that left-leaning news media were largely responsible for shared stories online, while new entrants, *The Canary*, *Skwawkbox* and the *London Economic*, were responsible for six of the most shared posts (Mayhew 2017). During the referendum campaign, the most shared story, according to BuzzSumo, came from the tabloid *Daily Express* (Waterson 2016). In the USA professional journalism was no more likely to be shared than fake news stories.

In the UK a little more than 11% of shared stories came from civil society organisations and private blogs. The Oxford Institute research also found that, although a far higher volume of pro-Labour material was shared during the election, a similar percentage of pro-Conservative and pro-Labour Tweets (15 and 16% respectively) were automatically generated by Twitter bots (Kaminska et al. 2017). Twitter bot activity during the European Referendum was analysed by a team at City University who found that the majority of automated activity came from outside the United Kingdom (Bastos and Mercea 2017). However the researchers also found that the bots were mainly engaged in re-Tweeting hyper-partisan material and that there was little evidence of linking to fake news sites. The researchers concluded that the activity of the botnet examined was relatively minor compared to the over-all conversation during the Referendum campaign (Bastos and Mercea 2017).

Perhaps the most striking thing about this research is the change in the political direction of Twitter posts. In June 2016, during the campaign on the European referendum, 54% of tweets circulating were pro-Leave, including those generated by the heavily partisan, Conservative-leaning, popular press. Only 20% were pro-Remain. One year later, the majority of tweets circulating at the start of the campaign were also strongly pro-Conservative but this changed towards the end of the 2017 campaign when the majority became strongly pro-Labour (Kaminska et al. 2017). This suggests that the direction of political activity on social media had changed markedly over the year and over the period of the election campaign. While there is clear and growing evidence of organised activity by political parties and campaigning organisations on social media during both the European Referendum and the 2017 election, it seems likely that majority of social media activity was organic. In other words it was driven by individuals, choosing to share material, rather than by fake news factories or automated bots emanating from outside the country. The question that then arises is what happened to so completely change the mood?

NEWSPAPERS, POLLS AND THE 2017 ELECTION

A series of polls by Survation, the polling organisation which most closely predicted the final result, noted that the Conservative lead over Labour started at 11% when the election was called in April and rose to a high of 18% the day before the official release of the Labour Party manifesto (Lyons-Lowe 2017). But by the end of the campaign the polls were level-pegging. I will argue that the change in mood was a response to changing events and the way they were reflected in the mainstream press (Fig. 1).

The newspaper election campaign was largely negative. In the first week, analysis by Loughborough University, (Deacon et al. 2017), weighted according to circulation (see Fig. 2), found that the Conservatives attracted slightly more positive than negative coverage

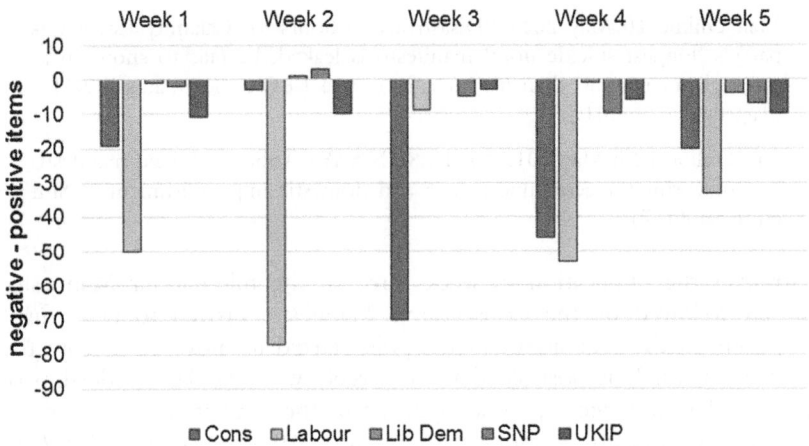

Fig. 1 Evaluations by week in newspapers (unweighted) (*Source* Deacon et al. [2017])

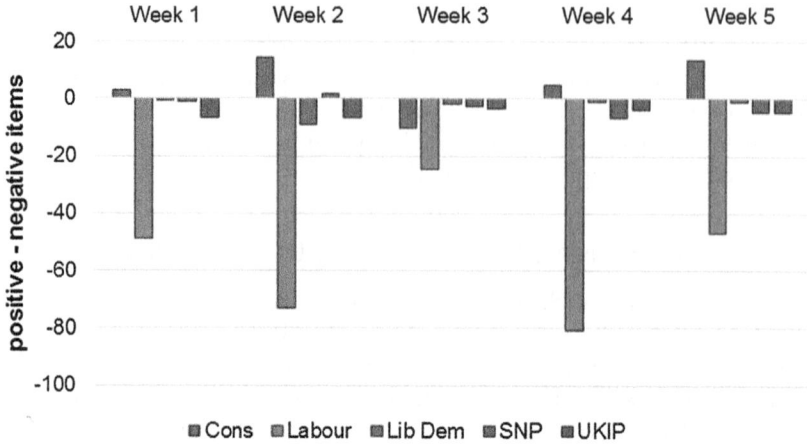

Fig. 2   Evaluations by week in newspapers (weighted)

while at that stage of the campaign, the newspaper coverage of Labour was almost entirely negative. In the second week, the focus of the two largest circulation newspapers (in print and online), was on leaked information about the Labour Party manifesto, which attracted such headlines as:

> Mail Online 10 May 2017 "Disastrous 14 hours for Calamity Corbyn as party's 'longest suicide note' manifesto is leaked, he fails to show up at poster launch... and then his car runs over a BBC cameraman's FOOT." (Tapsfield et al. 2017)

> Sun Online 12th May 2017 "THE SUN SAYS: Labour's leaked manifesto is a blueprint for economic failure and domestic impoverishment." (Sun editorial 2017)

However the publication in week three of the full Labour Manifesto, closely followed by the Conservative Manifesto, proved to be a turning point in the campaign and the polls started to move away from the Conservatives. It is possible that the largely working-class readership of the *Sun* had not been quite as opposed to the Labour manifesto as the editorial anticipated. A *Sun* splash on May 10 said: '*BACK TO THE 1970S, Leaked Labour manifesto shows Jeremy Corbyn wants to re-national-ise Britain's railways, energy and postal service in the most Left-wing election pledge for decades'* (Newton-Dunn 2017). The assumption of the editors was that readers would feel as horrified as they did by Labour's promise to nationalise the railways. However a YouGov poll that week found that sixty percent favoured nationalisation of the railways, 65% would have liked the Royal Mail to be re-nationalised and 59% thought that the water companies should be nationalised too (Smith 2017).

But the biggest shift in emphasis was not about the coverage of the Labour manifesto. It was when the Conservative Manifesto was announced on May 18, that the newspapers' coverage of May turned decisively negative. The change reflected consternation about the Conservative's flagship policy on social care, which was seen as an attack on those older, low-income voters, whose only asset was the house they lived in. These are people who are likely still to be reading the Conservative-leaning newspapers, in particular the *Daily Mail,* and the editors clearly had no desire to offend them. In the un-weighted balance of coverage, the negative stories about the manifesto were almost as numerous as the negative stories about the Labour Party had been the previous week. Even the weighted coverage, adjusted for the far higher circulation of the Conservative leaning press, was negative towards May in the third week and perhaps more important for Corbyn, the number of negative stories about Labour shrank as the press turned on the Tories.

Two days after the manifesto launch, this was the lead in the *Mail Online, 21 May 2017, "The Dementia tax backlash: Tories' lead slips by 5% after manifesto pledge to make more elderly pay for care"* (Walters 2017). By May 22, four days after the launch of the Conservative manifesto and coinciding with a terrorist attack in Manchester, the percentage poll lead had halved to nine percent. Then as the campaign entered its final week, May decided not to take part in a televised leaders debate and once again the *Mail Online* pulled no punches (1 June 2017): *"Fresh polls crunch fuels Tory nerves as Theresa May pleads with voters to have 'faith' in her despite backlash over skipping BBC election debate".* Her poll lead dribbled down to a low of 1.1% on 5 June, three days before the election on June 8 (Lyons-Lowe 2017).

As the election drew closer, the Conservative Press came back into line, but their messages leaned heavily on attacking Corbyn, rather than supporting May. At the same time, Corbyn's presence on TV, addressing huge rallies across the country, was providing a counterpoint to the press attacks.

Formerly wavering Labour voters were now seeing the Labour leader in the context that he had chosen, rather than only seeing him filtered through the lens of a largely hostile press.

During the 2017 election, older, television-watching voters, who had been previous Labour voters, but had been suspicious of Corbyn, were, for the first time in the two years of his leadership, able to make their own judgements because they were seeing him and his supporters every night on their television news. These were the people that May needed to win over in order to increase her majority. On the basis of voting patterns in the Referendum and polling in the lead-up to the election, that should have happened, but it didn't. Or rather it didn't do so in the numbers she had anticipated.

The significance of television is not the main focus of this paper but it is not possible to look at any section of the media in isolation and, arguably television, regulated to ensure that the major parties had equal airtime, and impacted as it is by the agenda-setting press, had a key role in relation to other news platforms. Differences between the UK and the USA are instructive in helping to understand the role of television. International comparative research from Aalberg and Curran (2012) found that in the USA people in the lowest income groups and with the lowest levels of education, were significantly less likely to be informed about news than those in higher income brackets or with higher levels of education. In Europe education is of far less significance. People across education and income groups tend to be reasonably well informed. The researchers attributed this difference to the much higher levels of television news consumption in Europe, where television is regulated and news is provided throughout the evening. In the US only a third of those with low levels of education watched national news broadcasts. In the UK three quarters of this group engaged with TV news.

Given this relatively high level of television news consumption, in particular in the Brexit supporting, older age-groups (Ofcom 2017b), the difference between the referendum and the 2017 election, requires explanation. During the referendum campaign, the BBC took a neutral stance between Remain and Leave but in doing so they focussed almost entirely on the different wings of the Conservative Party. Indeed the Conservatives were given three times as much airtime as the Labour Party and discussion amongst Remain politicians focussed on the future of the City of London rather than the likely impact on jobs in manufacturing (Phillips 2016, forthcoming). This left an open goal for pro-Leave messages organised as a counter-hegemonic attack on the Liberal elite and circulated via social media. Social media thrives on precisely the kind of simple "team building" messages (Conroy et al. 2012; Hasell and Weeks 2016) that attack a perceived enemy. Arguably, as the 2017 election campaign progressed, the confusion of the Conservative supporting press, and the lack of a simple counter-hegemonic narrative to circulate online, meant that the social media space was left to the Labour party and Corbyn's supporters.

CONCLUSION

Social media is best used for circulating simple, emotive messages (Conroy et al. 2012; Hasell and Weeks 2016). During the 2016 Referendum, the Leave campaign, spearheaded by the tabloid press (which had been campaigning to leave the European Union for many years), had the momentum. Their Leave messages were simple and compelling. In the 2017 election campaign, Prime Minister May had chosen the slogan "Strong and Stable" however the Conservative campaign messages that were coming out, also amplified by the press, suggested confusion and muddle. Muddled messages don't travel well in social media and it was the counter-hegemonic messages coming from the Left (both mainstream and non-mainstream), helped along by Corbyn's increasing presence on television, that made the running.

Given the partisan nature of social media (Hasell and Weeks 2016) those who were already very committed to Labour and Corbyn, would have been more likely to see social media messaging from the left-leaning blogs being circulated amongst friends and people with similar concerns. The use of social media is also connected with a greater interest in political activity and voting, so that younger voters might have been encouraged to vote whereas in the past they abstained (Boulianne 2011; Bond et al. 2012). It seems unlikely however that messages emanating from left-wing blogs would have penetrated the social media bubbles of those 35–44 year olds who had previously voted Conservative and who switched in this election, or those older Labour supporters, who had deserted Ed Miliband in the 2015 election and had considered voting Tory in the early stages of this campaign. On the whole, social media operates to confirm pre-existing biases rather than to persuade or inform (Conroy et al. 2012; Elvestad and Phillips 2018a). While those who had voted Labour in the past, or who follow broadly liberal causes, would be likely to have been targeted by automated Labour Party messages (Kaminska et al. 2017), these groups would also have been likely to be watching television and aware of the key events of the campaign.

Conversely, the group that May most needed to appeal to in order to consolidate her early lead, was the working-class voters who had most strongly supported Leave in the referendum. According to YouGov figures, 30% of those who voted for the UK Independence Party (UKIP) and 21% of previous Labour supporters, who voted to leave Europe, stayed at home in 2017 (Curtis and Smith 2017). Looking at the overall picture of media influence in the 2017 election, the temporary withdrawal of press support for the Conservatives, in the third week of the campaign, may have had a negative influence on the campaign because it sent out a confused message to those ex-Labour voters who had come out in 2016 to vote Remain. Labour supporters, having responded to the apparently anti-elitist messages of the Leave campaign, now found that they were being asked to support a Government offering nothing more exciting than "strength and stability". The lack of any clear counter-hegemonic messages can be seen in the failure of Conservative supporting social media posts to be widely shared.

Given the inter-connected nature of media platforms and the difficulty of measuring media influence, it is hard to argue that any particular media platform had a key influence for any groups of voters, however it is possible to make a case the other way around. Given the key role of the popular press in propagating pro-Leave messages in the referendum it seems unlikely that their influence would simply have vanished in a year. The more likely explanation is that the Conservative Press fatally damaged the Conservative campaign by attacking May's manifesto. This does not imply that the power of the press has waned. Merely that it was used to different, and rather unexpected ends.

REFERENCES

Aalberg, T., & Curran, J. (2012). *How media inform democracy: A comparative approach*. London: Routledge.

Ashcroft, L. (2017). How did this result happen? My post-vote survey. Lord Ashcroft Polls. http://lordashcroftpolls.com/2017/06/result-happen-post-vote-survey/. Accessed November 23, 2017.

Bastos, M. D., & Mercea, D. (2017). The Brexit botnet and user-generated hyperpartisan news. *Social Science Computer Review*. http://journals.sagepub.com/doi/10.1177/0894439317734157.

BBC Staff. (2017, May 12). The papers—Newspaper headlines: Labour manifesto in the spotlight. *BBC News*. http://www.bbc.co.uk/news/blogs-the-papers-39892048.

Bond, R. M., Fariss, C. J., Jones, J. J., Kramer, A. D. I., Marlow, C., & Settle, J. E. (2012). A 61-million-person experiment in social influence and political mobilization. *Nature, 489*(7415), 295–298. https://doi.org/10.1038/nature11421.

Boulianne, S. (2011). Stimulating or reinforcing political interest: Using panel data to examine reciprocal effects between news media and political interest. *Political Communication, 28*(2), 147–162. https://doi.org/10.1080/10584609.2010.540305.

Boulianne, S. (2015). Social media use and participation: A meta-analysis of current research. *Information, Communication & Society, 18*(5), 524–538. https://doi.org/10.1080/1369118X.2015.1008542.

Buckingham, D. (2000). *Making of citizens: Young people, news and politics.* London: Routledge.

Burn-Murdoch, J., Ehrenberg-Shannon, B., Wisniewska, A., & Rai, A. (2017). Election 2017: How the UK voted in 7 charts. *The Financial Times.*

Conroy, M., Feezell, J. T., & Guerrero, M. (2012). Facebook and political engagement: A study of online political group membership and offline political engagement. *Computers in Human Behavior, 28*(5), 1535–1546.

Curran, J., Coen, S., Aalberg, T., Hayashi, K., Jones, P. K., Splendore, S., et al. (2013). Internet revolution revisited: A comparative study of online news. *Media, Culture and Society, 35*(7), 880–897. https://doi.org/10.1177/0163443713499393.

Curtis, S., & Smith, M. (2017). How did 2015 voters cast their ballot at the 2017 general election? *YouGov.* https://yougov.co.uk/news/2017/06/22/how-did-2015-voters-cast-their-ballot-2017-general/.

Cushion, S., Kilby, A., Thomas, R., Morani, M., & Sambrook, R. (2016). Newspapers, impartiality and television news. *Journalism Studies*, 1–20. https://doi.org/10.1080/1461670X.2016.1171163.

Deacon, D., Downey, J., Smith, D., Stanyer, J., & Wring, D. (2017). *Media coverage of the 2017 general election campaign (report 4).* Loughborough: Loughborough University Centre for Research in Communication and Culture. http://blog.lboro.ac.uk/crcc/general-election/. Accessed November 30, 2017.

Dvir-Gvirsman, S., Garrett, R. K., & Tsfati, Y. (2015). Why do partisan audience participate? Perceived public opinion as the mediating mechanism. *Communication Research*, 0093650215593145. https://doi.org/10.1177/0093650215593145.

Elvestad, E., & Phillips, A. (2018a). *Misunderstanding news audiences: Seven myths of the social media era.* London: Routledge.

Elvestad, E., & Phillips, A. (2018b). The net generation will revolutionise the way we relate to news. In E. Elvestad & A. Phillips (Eds.), *Misunderstanding news audiences, seven myths of the social media era*. London: Routledge.

Enders Analysis. (2016, February). *UK advertising expenditure forecast 2016–2018*. London: Enders. http://www.endersanalysis.com/content/publication/uk-advertising-expenditure-forecast-2016-2018.

Hasell, A., & Weeks, B. E. (2016). Partisan provocation: The role of partisan news use and emotional responses in political information sharing in social media. *Human Communication Research, 42*, 641–661. https://doi.org/10.1111/hcre.12092.

Kaminska, M., Gallacher, J. D., Kollanyi, B., Yasseri, T., & Howard. P. (2017). Social media and news sources during the 2017 UK general elections. Computation Propaganda Project, Oxford. http://comprop.oii.ox.ac.uk/wp-content/uploads/sites/89/2017/06/Social-Media-and-News-Sources-during-the-2017-UK-General-Election.pdf. Accessed November 23, 2017.

Lyons-Lowe, D. (2017). Conservative lead over Labour has dropped 16 points in a month—What's going on? *Survation*. http://survation.com/conservative-lead-labour-dropped-16-points-month-whats-going/.

Marchi, R. (2012). With Facebook, blogs and fake news, teens reject journalistic "objectivity". *Journal of Communication Inquiry, 36*(3), 246–262. https://doi.org/10.11770/96859912458700.

Mayhew, F. (2017). General election: Only five of the top 100 most shared stories on social media were pro-Tory. *Press Gazette*. http://www.pressgazette.co.uk/general-election-only-five-out-of-top-100-most-shared-stories-on-social-media-were-pro-tory/.

Media Reform Coalition. (2016). The bias of objectivity: The evening standard not so neutral after all. *Media Reform Coalition*. http://www.mediareform.org.uk/blog/bias-objectivity-evening-standard-not-neutral-mayoral-race-editor-claimed.

Media Reform Coalition. (2017). What the BBC has to say about the papers. *Media Reform Coalition*. http://www.mediareform.org.uk/blog/bbc-say-papers. Accessed December 1, 2017.

National Readership Survey. (2017). *National Readership Survey data in 2017*. http://www.nrs.co.uk/nrs-data-in-2017/. Accessed December 5, 2017.

Newman, N., Fletcher, R., Kalogeropoulos, A., Levy, D., & Nielsen, R. K. (2017). *Reuters Institute digital news report 2017*. Oxford: Reuters Institute.

Newton-Dunn, T. (2017). BACK TO THE 1970S, Leaked Labour manifesto shows Jeremy Corbyn wants to re-nationalise Britain's railways, energy and postal service in the most left-wing election pledge for decades. *The Sun*. https://www.thesun.co.uk/news/3531585/corbyn-pledges-to-scrap-university-tuition-fees-re-nationalise-britains-railways-and-inject-6billion-a-year-extra-to-nhs-in-leaked-manifesto/. Accessed December 1, 2017.

Ofcom. (2017a). *News consumption in the UK: 2016.* London: Ofcom. https://www.ofcom.org.uk/__data/assets/pdf_file/0017/103625/news-consumption-uk-2016.pdf.

Ofcom. (2017b). *Adults media use and attitudes.* London: Ofcom. https://www.ofcom.org.uk/__data/assets/pdf_file/0020/102755/adults-media-use-attitudes-2017.pdf.

Phillips, A. (2016). How the BBC's obsession with balance took Labour off air ahead of Brexit. *The Conversation.* http://theconversation.com/how-the-bbcs-obsession-with-balance-took-labour-off-air-ahead-of-brexit-62393. Accessed December 1, 2017.

Phillips, A. (forthcoming). The British right wing mainstream and the European referendum. In A. Nadler & A. J. Bauer (Eds.), *News on the Right.* Oxford University Press.

Scholsberg, J. (2017). *21st Century Fox/Sky merger inquiry: Submission to the Competition and Markets Authority on plurality.* London: Media Reform Coalition and Avaaz. http://www.mediareform.org.uk/wp-content/uploads/2017/10/CMA-plurality-submission-FINAL-CORRECTED-26-October.pdf. Accessed December 1, 2017.

Smith, M. (2017). Nationalisation vs privatisation: The public view. *YouGov.* https://yougov.co.uk/news/2017/05/19/nationalisation-vs-privatisation-public-view/. Accessed December 1, 2017.

Sun editorial. (2017). Labour's leaked manifesto is a blueprint for economic failure and domestic impoverishment. *Sun Online.* https://www.thesun.co.uk/news/3542134/the-sun-says-labours-leaked-manifesto-is-a-blueprint-for-economic-failure-and-domestic-impoverishment/. Accessed December 1, 2017.

Tapsfield, T. (2017). Fresh polls crunch fuels Tory nerves as Theresa May pleads with voters to have "faith" in her despite backlash over skipping BBC election debate. *Mail Online.* http://www.dailymail.co.uk/news/article-4558536/Jeremy-Corbyn-decides-BBC-election-debate.html. Accessed December 1, 2017.

Tapsfield, J., Fergusen, K., & Sculthorpe, D. (2017). Disastrous 14 hours for Calamity Corbyn as party's "longest suicide note" manifesto is leaked, he fails to show up at poster launch... and then his car runs over a BBC cameraman's FOOT. *Mail Online.* http://www.dailymail.co.uk/news/article-4493596/Labour-s-manifesto-Britain-1970s.html. Accessed December 1, 2017.

Walters, T. (2017). The dementia tax backlash: Tories' lead slips by 5% after manifesto pledge to make more elderly pay for care. *Mail Online.* http://www.dailymail.co.uk/news/article-4525918/Tories-lead-slips-5-care-manifesto-pledge.html#ixzz50lng1wDa. Accessed December 1, 2017.

Waterson, J. (2016). Britain has no fake news industry because our partisan newspapers already do that job. *BuzzFeed.* https://www.buzzfeed.com/jimwaterson/fake-news-sites-cant-compete-with-britains-partisan-newspape?utm_term=.ayEqPYOJ0#.pfb8Dqk4L. Accessed December 1, 2017.

Alternative Agendas or More of the Same? Online News Coverage of the 2017 UK Election

Emily Harmer and Rosalynd Southern

INTRODUCTION

The results of the snap election have led to some debate that the influence of the press on the political process is declining. Coupled with the proliferation of new digital news platforms and outlets, this election was an interesting one in which to analyse online election news in the UK context. Much of the empirical literature about election coverage focuses on traditional broadcast and print media, particularly in the UK context, due to the continued influence and agenda-setting functions of these news forms. The literature that does address online news of election campaigns is somewhat scarce, despite that fact that audience studies have shown that voters are increasingly accessing digital news. Online news is increasingly important for a younger audience (Dennis and

E. Harmer (✉) · R. Southern
University of Liverpool, Liverpool, UK
e-mail: E.Harmer@liverpool.ac.uk

R. Southern
e-mail: R.Southern@liverpool.ac.uk

© The Author(s) 2019   99
D. Wring et al. (eds.), *Political Communication in Britain*,
https://doi.org/10.1007/978-3-030-00822-2_7

Sampaio-Dias 2017) and the introduction of a number of digital-born sites like *BuzzFeed* with its own way of combing entertainment and news highlight the importance of analysing the extent to which online news may offer new ways of reporting and scrutinising politics. This chapter will assess to what extent online news differs from mainstream press and broadcast coverage by focusing on three important areas; the issue agenda, which candidates are most prominent, and the way women are represented in the coverage. These three aspects of the coverage shape the way politics is presented to the audience, constructing an understanding of which policy areas are most important, whose voices should be listened to and whether the political sphere is inclusive (or not). We will firstly set out some results from a content analysis of five online news sites. We discuss the overall issue agenda and most prominent campaigners featured in online news before setting out some differences between outlets. The chapter then goes on to discuss the gendered nature of the campaign coverage in more detail. This is especially important since women have traditionally struggled to be adequately represented in broadcast and print coverage and it would be telling if this pattern continues online.

We will argue that despite the overwhelming potential for online news to provide a unique issue agenda and to give space to a more diverse range of voices, looking at the online news that is actually consumed in the UK demonstrates that this potential is largely neglected and in fact these online outlets reflect a very similar set of priorities to their broadcast and print rivals and partners.

ELECTION NEWS

It is important to analyse news coverage of elections because they represent key moments in which politics and politicians are most visible and when citizens need reliable information about politics. Elections are therefore important moments when it might be possible to assess the quality of political news provided to ordinary voters (Cushion 2012). The conventional wisdom about election news coverage is that it has become increasingly focused on reporting the tactics and strategies employed by political parties, more focused on the personalities and characteristics of politicians, in particular party leaders, at the expense of other interested parties and moving towards comment or interpretation rather than just reporting factually (Cushion 2012). As a result empirical studies of recent elections have showed that substantive policy issues have been squeezed out by a focus on the political process and campaigning activities of the major parties (Cappella and Jamieson 1997; Cushion et al. 2006; Deacon et al. 2006). There has also been scholarly interest in the extent to which political news is becoming more personalized or candidate-centred (rather than party or policy-centred). This change has been attributed to two interrelated factors, firstly the weakening of traditional party allegiances amongst voters and secondly, the changing media environment (Van Aelst et al. 2011). Election news also tends to be dominated by a narrow range of voices, so that non-political actors and women are often marginal to the campaign and its coverage (Ross et al. 2013). We are particularly interested in the extent to which these patterns are also reflected in online news.

The content analysis assessed the top four most viewed online news outlets according to the *Reuters Institute Digital News Report* (Newman et al. 2017). Of these, three were online versions of legacy media outlets—the *Mail Online, The Guardian* and the *BBC News* website. The other one was a so-called 'digital-born' site, meaning that it originated online and there is no offline version—the *Huffington Post*. Since we were interested in whether digital-born sites in particular might reflect different issue agendas, we also included the next most highly ranked digital-born sites, the UK version of *BuzzFeed*. The political partisanship of these sites is very different to those displayed by the majority of the mainstream press. *The Guardian* and *Huffington Post* represent a centre-left perspective whilst similar conclusions have been drawn about *BuzzFeed*. The BBC website reflects its efforts to maintain due impartiality across its broadcast outputs. The only overtly-right-wing news source represented here is *Mail Online*. This alone might lead to assumptions that the online news agenda would offer an alternative set of priorities. We selected up to ten most prominent news stories on each website's news page every weekday between 4 May 2017 (the official start of the campaign) and 7 June 2017 (the day before polling day). This gave us five weeks of coverage and resulted in 1001 news items.

ONLINE NEWS: ISSUE AND PERSONALITIES

The results of this study demonstrate that clearly, despite the proliferation of ways to gain access to the news, when you examine the online news that most UK citizens say they consume then the issue agenda and sources they call upon remains remarkably consistent to those of main-stream print and broadcasters. Our study showed that the five news out-lets tended to focus on the electoral process itself, accounting for almost 43% of the themes recorded (Table 1). This was by far the most promi-nent theme and indicates the appeal of the 'horse race' for online news. Although other studies of press and broadcasting indicated a decline in process coverage in comparison to previous elections (Deacon et al. 2017), online news outlets in 2017 continued to place a lot of emphasis on the day-to-day politics of the campaign. Process was the top theme for all outlets.

Perhaps unsurprisingly, Brexit was the most salient substantive issue in the coverage. Brexit was either the second or third most prominent issue across all outlets, with the exception of the *Huffington Post* (where Brexit did not feature in the top 10 at all, perhaps surprisingly). However, despite this being undoubtedly the issue of the day and with many trying to frame this as the 'Brexit election', the depth of coverage about Brexit differed across online outlets. In order to determine the extent to which Brexit was discussed in a substantial way or was just a background issue we measured whether each item referred to it all, if it was mentioned in an incidental way (fewer than three separate sentences) or whether there was a substantial reference. This measure is different to the theme cate-gory discussed in Table 1 because it captures mentions of Brexit when it is alluded to in relation to other themes, such as immigration for exam-ple, rather than when it is the overall theme of the article. Overall, 60% of stories about the election failed to mention Brexit at all, and around a quarter mentioned it in passing, usually as an accompanying point to

Table 1 Top ten most prominent themes, 4 May–7 June 2017

Theme	Percentage
Electoral process	42.6
Brexit	7.2
Media	5.9
Social security	4.6
Health/NHS	4.5
Crime/law and order	3.3
Standards/corruption	3.3
Taxation	3.2
Immigration	2.9
Defence/military	2.7

other main themes such as the economy (Table 2). Overall, only 16% of stories, gave substantial discussion to Brexit as an issue. Again, there were differences here between the online-only outlets and the other outlets. The digital-born outlets featured substantially lower levels of Brexit coverage than the other outlets. The *Huffington Post* mentioned Brexit substantially at half the rate the *Guardian* did. This might be an indication that although digital-born news outlets reflect the mainstream agenda in some ways, this is not always the case when dealing with specific issues. This also suggests that these more recently established news sources are less concerned with the substantive questions of the day, preferring to cover process and cover media reaction to process even more than their offline counterparts. This finding is also striking given the fact that digital-born sites appeal to younger voters who voted in higher numbers to remain in the EU than their older counterparts.

Returning to Table 1, the third most prominent theme was 'media' which we differentiated from political process coverage. In fact, for the digital-born outlets, media was the second most salient theme. In this case, *BuzzFeed* and *Huffington Post* seemed particularly interested in responding to what legacy media were reporting, featuring an abundance of stories about accusations of media bias, or stories assessing the public reaction to key election moments such as the *BBC* Leader's Question Time specials or various interviews containing gaffes by politicians. One example of this would be BuzzFeed's article explaining 'how TV broadcasters are scrambling to cover the snap election' (BuzzFeed, May 9). Some items took the form of a series of tweets highlighting certain voters' views that coverage had been biased or unfair and as kind of 'virtual vox-pop'. These were particularly common after the televised leaders' debates.

Beyond this, the other substantive issues which were covered with most frequency were social security, the NHS and taxation. These issues were largely discussed in the articles covering manifesto launches.

Table 2   Extent of Brexit coverage per outlet

	BBC	Daily Mail	Guardian	BuzzFeed	Huffington Post	All
Not mentioned	59.9	69.5	40.5	66.7	63.6	59.7
Mentioned incidentally	20.4	14.4	38.3	21.3	25.9	24.7
Mentioned substantially	19.7	16.0	21.2	12.0	10.5	15.6

The prominence of health and social security can largely be attributed to the Conservatives' poorly received 'dementia tax' policy and the U-turn which followed. There was also much focus on Labour's proposal to increase tax on those earning over £80,000. Law and order stories were prominent, mainly as a result of the Manchester and London Bridge terror attacks. There are some other notable differences between the digital born sites and those websites with a print or broadcast counterparts. On issues that could broadly be considered to be 'left-wing' or 'right-wing', these mapped onto the expected outlets. *The Guardian* gave greater focus to social security, public services and health and was the only outlet to feature education in its top ten themes. *Mail Online* on the other hand, was more focused on taxation, crime, defence and immigration. The BBC website reflected a mixture of these two agendas, with health, crime, immigration and social security all being prominent themes for them. The digital-born outlets appeared to give more prominence to progressive issues. *BuzzFeed* was the only outlet to have LGBTQI+ issues and ethnic minority issues in their top ten, and the *Huffington Post* was the only outlet to emphasis women's issues in their top ten.

A similar story can be told about which political actors received most prominent in the online news. Again, although there were a few small differences across the different websites, there were very few differences to those actors who captured the attention of the mainstream press and broadcast media (see Deacon et al. 2017). The Conservatives and Labour sources dominated the coverage (Fig. 1). The Conservatives were slightly ahead in terms of the proportion of coverage, on 27.5% compared to 25.3% for Labour, perhaps reflecting a small incumbency effect. This may be partly due to the Conservatives mishandling of the campaign after May seemed to attempt to reverse one of her own manifesto pledges after it was dubbed 'the dementia tax'. The smaller parties gained much less coverage which lends some weight to the assertion that this election indicated a return to two-party politics—at least as far as online news coverage is concerned.

The two most prominent individual campaigners were the only realistic candidates for Prime Minister, Theresa May and Jeremy Corbyn (Table 2). They appeared almost as frequently as each other, with May appearing in 37.3% of news items and Corbyn in 36.4%. This illustrates the highly presidential nature of the campaign in online news, and reflects May's attempts to frame the campaign as a choice between herself and Corbyn. May and Corbyn were the top two actors for every

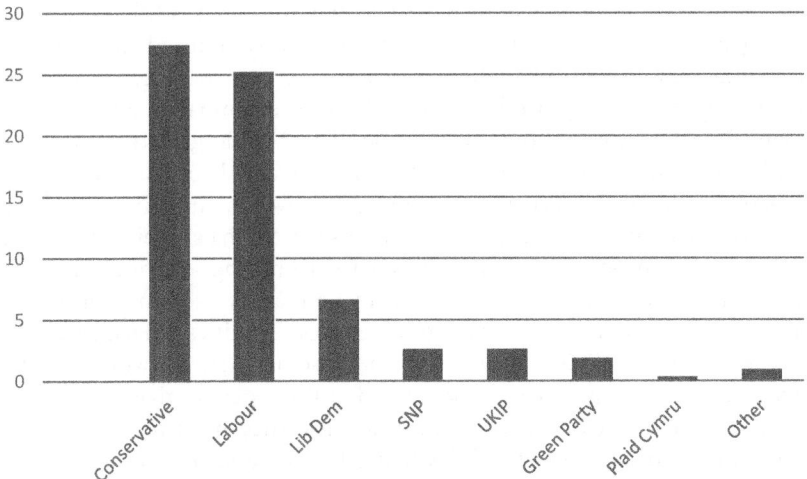

Fig. 1 Appearance of politicians by party (percentages), 4 May–7 June 2017

outlet. There were however some differences in the extent to which these leaders featured on each website. *Mail Online* included May in 49% of all election items, compared to just 27% of items in the *Guardian*. Coverage of Corbyn followed a similar pattern, he appeared in 54% of items on the *Mail Online* compared to 24% in the *Guardian*. Although we did not formally measure the extent to which they received favourable coverage, a qualitative reading of the tone of the coverage makes it clear that the prominent focus on Corbyn in the *Mail Online* was largely negative, much like its print counterpart (Deacon et al. 2017). The partisanship of these sites might explain this tendency as the *Mail Online* was particularly keen to contrast the perceived competence of May against Corbyn whilst *The Guardian* might have chosen to downplay the leaders due to their recent lack of support for Corbyn after his two Labour leadership elections.

Beyond this, there was still a heavy focus on party leaders. Tim Farron, Liberal Democrat leader was the third most salient actor for each outlet except the *Daily Mail* and SNP leader Nicola Sturgeon also appeared frequently. Paul Nuttall, the leader of the UK Independence Party was in the top ten for three out of five outlets, as was Caroline Lucas, the co-leader of the Green Party. With very few exceptions leaders, former leaders and those occupying the Great Offices of State and their Shadows made up the vast majority of top ten individual actors overall as well as within the different outlets. Given the extent to which these people were deployed prominently on the campaign trail by their political parties, this is no great surprise. These findings show a striking similar to those observed in mainstream print and broadcast news (see Deacon et al. 2017). What is strikingly, however is that six out of the ten most prominent individual campaigners were female, which given the over-representation of men in politics is worth noting. Previous research clearly demonstrates that women tend to be marginalised in mainstream press and broadcast news coverage of electoral politics (Harmer 2017; Ross et al. 2013). This is problematic because in order for women to be taken seriously as political actors, and for their perspectives and views to be considered relevant to political debates, they need to be included in the public discussion of politics that takes place in media coverage of elections. Our analysis of online coverage shows that women were marginalized and portrayed in stereotypical ways, which demonstrates once again that although online news has the potential to offer alternative perspectives on the election, this potential was largely unrealised.

GENDERED ELECTION COVERAGE

Despite the fact that six out of the ten of the most prominent campaigners were women, the other main way in which online news coverage was strikingly similar to the mainstream press and broadcast coverage, was the way in which women were portrayed. Given that this was the first election in thirty years since the UK has had a female Prime Minister along with the presence of numerous female party leaders, cabinet and shadow-cabinet members, this election had the potential for increasing the prominence of female voices. However, in practice online news consistently preferred male subjects and sources much like its broadcasts and print rivals (see Deacon et al. 2017).

From the very beginning of the campaign, May sought to present herself as a strong and competent leader. She light-heartedly evoked her colleague Ken Clarke's description of her as a 'bloody difficult woman' suggesting this would be crucial in securing a good deal in the negotiations and perhaps attempting to emulate Hillary Clinton's repurposing of Donald Trump's 'Nasty Woman' jibe. As previously discussed, 2017 was a highly presidential campaign (Table 1) in digital news. In the online coverage, it proved to be difficult for any women who were not politicians (and particularly leaders) to gain a voice. Women accounted for just 36.8% of all individuals featured in the news coverage (Harmer and Southern 2018). This is particularly striking as the most prominent politician in this coverage was the Prime Minister (who appeared in 37.3% of all items in our study). It is notable that despite May's presence, women still did not receive parity with their male counterparts.

Although there were several women who were not party leaders who gained some prominence in the campaign—particularly Amber Rudd, Diane Abbott and Emily Thornberry—the traditional struggle for women to be heard seemed to be exacerbated by this highly presidential campaign. For parties with female leaders (or joint leaders) such as the Conservatives, Scottish National Party, Plaid Cymru and the Green Party, female voices were well-represented even if they were the same voices (Harmer and Southern 2018). Labour Party sources instead tended to be dominated by men (mainly their leader Jeremy Corbyn, again reflecting the presidential nature of the campaign) however, they managed better female representation, as evidenced by Table 3 when compared to other parties with male leaders—UKIP and the Liberal Democrats had the fewest women campaigners in online news (Harmer and Southern 2018).

Women in non-political roles were very marginal in the coverage. Despite the presence of a reasonable volume of voices from other media and online platforms in online news coverage, just 29.7% of media sources and 20.8% of bloggers referred to were female (Harmer and Southern 2018). Even female citizens, potentially the easiest group to

Table 3 Top ten most prominent campaigners, 4 May–7 June 2017

Actor	Percentage
Theresa May	37.3
Jeremy Corbyn	36.4
Tim Farron	9.9
Nicola Sturgeon	5.2
John McDonnell	4.6
Amber Rudd	4.4
Paul Nuttall	4.1
Diane Abbott	3.6
Emily Thornberry	3.1
Caroline Lucas	2.8

represent, accounted for just 39% of all citizens featured in our study of online news, even though one of the most prominent ordinary person in the campaign was a woman called Brenda, who spoke for a nation when she declared 'Not another one!' (BBC, April 19) when asked for her reaction on BBC news.

Most strikingly of all, every individual pollster or other kind of expert who received any mention or reference in the online news sources assess here was male. This dearth of women's expertise is also reflected in the authorship of online news items. Just 31.8% of all items with a single author were authored by women. This shows, similar to studies of mainstream broadcast and print news coverage, that online political news is still dominated by male sources, authors and experts (Harmer and Southern 2018). If we compare these figures with data from Deacon et al. (2017) who analysed print and broadcast news, it becomes clear that in some ways online news may actually marginalise women even more. For example, their study showed that just more than 10% of experts featured were women. Given the increasing levels of online news consumption, this marginalization of female political expertise in the coverage is dispiriting. Ignoring women as experts not only limits perspectives and the range of ideas that are considered relevant to the political sphere, but furthermore serves to reinforce the male dominance of politics, and impoverish our understanding of the political process.

Given the number of high profile female politicians, it is also important to note that tone of the campaign was somewhat mixed in terms of gendered coverage. From the very start, May chose to run on a highly personalised campaign. The Conservatives once again deployed the services of Lynton Crosby, whose penchant for repeating short soundbites at every appearance throughout the campaign ('long-term economic plan' in 2015) had served them so well in 2015. In a speech in Bristol on May 2, May asked '…who will lead Britain through Brexit and beyond? Will it be me and my team showing the strong and stable leadership that our country needs? Or will it be Jeremy Corbyn at the head of a coalition of chaos?' (Conservative Press 2017). 'Strong and stable' became a common refrain over the subsequent weeks. However, it soon became clear that this time the approach might have proved to be counterproductive. May's repetition of the 'strong and stable' mantra played into the impression that she was wooden or even robotic. The phrase was much lampooned in the online coverage. BuzzFeed published five articles mocking the phrase including a quiz asking 'How Strong and Stable

Are You Actually?' (BuzzFeed, May 11) and another listing all the occasions she had said it in the past few days (BuzzFeed, April 28). May's efforts to portray herself as a strong leader is at odds with traditional gender stereotypes that code women as weak and emotional might help to explain why this tactic backfired (Harmer and Southern 2018).

The Conservative campaign became characterised by its highly controlled, overly safe approach. As the campaign wore on, the narrative began to focus on Theresa May seemingly hiding from the electorate and avoiding real voters. A walk about in Cornish Fishing Village was cut short once May had been photographed quickly eating some chips, and a visit to Scotland where May was seen knocking on a handful of unanswered doors before leaving, was roundly derided. This impression was reflected in the online coverage with *BuzzFeed* running a piece titled 'People are Getting Fed Up with Theresa May's Campaign Being So Stage Managed' (BuzzFeed, May 2 (a)) decrying the fact that journalists had been locked in a separate room and that activists had been bussed in from 50 miles away for the official campaign launch. Perhaps more problematically for May, this campaigning style was thrown into even greater relief by the seeming authenticity and numerous personal appearances by Jeremy Corbyn on the campaign trail. His apparent ease in talking to ordinary people as well as holding well-attended rallies and speaking at music festivals only served to highlight the aloof and cautious approach taken by May. In another widely commented-on campaign moment, May was unable to think of anything 'naughty' she had done in response to her interviewer Julie Etchingham of ITV except running through a wheat field when she was young. This provoked an amused reaction from many quarters including in the online coverage. *BuzzFeed* (BuzzFeed, June 8) ran an article outlining the best social media reactions and a common theme was Theresa May's 'square' personality in comparison to Corbyn's 'cooler' or more personable one. For instance, May was mocked for her wheat field comments and for apparently not knowing what chips are called.

The perception of May as someone hiding from the electorate and having a cold personality was furthermore cemented over her handling of the BBC leader's debate. Such debates are masculinised rituals that often result in highly gendered evaluations of candidate performances (Harmer et al. 2017) so it might not be surprising that she was reluctant to participate. May insisted she would not take part in the televised leader's debates and chose to send Home Secretary Amber Rudd in her place.

This led to accusations from the press that May was attempting to hide her defective personality from the electorate and that she was incapable of debating with the other leaders (Huffington Post, May 31, 2017). The weakness was highlighted further when Rudd was widely received as having performed well, despite the death of her father just a few days earlier. When news of the bereavement emerged, May was heavily criticised. The Conservative-friendly *Mail Online* (Mail Online, June 1) avoided direct criticism of May instead praising Rudd for her being 'tough'. However, they included quotes from a Labour source stating that May's absence showed she was unable to 'stand up for herself'. The best-rated comments under the *Mail Online* article were scathing. Some of the criticism was implicitly gendered including one calling her 'heartless, self-centred, arrogant and nasty piece of work' and questioning whether it is possible to 'call yourself strong if you send a bereaved colleague to do your job?'. Another criticised her for lacking 'compassion'. The assumption being that women ought to be caring and compassionate, demonstrating once again the gendered nature of expectations about political leaders (Campus 2013). These more subtle forms of gendered coverage aside, although much of the coverage was personally critical of May and her performance there was actually very little overtly sexist or misogynistic coverage of the Prime Minister in the five online news outlets included in this study.

Other prominent female politicians on the other hand, were not so lucky. Diane Abbott came in for scathing coverage due to a gaffe she made in an interview with LBC radio. In the interview, she was asked about a manifesto promise on police funding and firstly gave an incorrect figure, then could not remember it at all, leading to an uncomfortably long silence. This prompted a savage response in the online press. *BuzzFeed* declared it 'The most cringeworthy interview ever' and suggested that to compare it to a car crash was 'unfair to car crashes' (*BuzzFeed*, May 2 (b)). The *Huffington Post* moreover suggested that the interview has 'reduced her credibility' (May 2, 2017). Ross (2017) argues that the term 'car-crash' was almost exclusively reserved for discussing poor interview by women during the campaign, "implying a biological predisposition for incompetence" (Ross 2017: 80) even when other figures like Philip Hammond and Boris Johnson made arguably worse mistakes. The right leaning *Mail Online* was even more brutal, declaring that Abbott was like a 'frog man wading into cow manure' (*Mail Online*, May 2), but even the left-leaning *Guardian* stated that she had 'embarrass[ed] herself' (*Guardian*, May 2). Of the coverage analysed here, only the BBC (BBC News, May 2) used a more muted tone, stating that Abbott 'misspoke' and 'gets her figures muddled'.

Interview gaffes then became a narrative around Abbott, the *Mail Online* followed up the initial piece with several other items about slip-ups during interviews: 'ANOTHER toe curling TV meltdown' (Mail Online, June 5). The criticism became deafening and eventually she stood down from her prominent role in the last days of the campaign, citing ill-health (Independent, June 7). It is furthermore notable that both Philip Hammond and Jeremy Corbyn had their own 'brain fades' (to use a phrase coined by Natalie Bennett, the erstwhile Leader of the Green Party, who forgot her own figures on a radio interview during the 2015 election). These received much less coverage than Abbott's mistake and the tone was indeed different. Corbyn received some criticism for the prickly *Woman's Hour* interview where he also forgot figures on funding childcare, but the tone was more neutral. BuzzFeed ran the headline 'Jeremy Corbyn forgot how much Labour's childcare policy would cost' (BuzzFeed, May 30). This is in marked contrast to the 'most cringeworthy interview ever' for Abbott, even though the mistakes were comparable. Chancellor of the Exchequer Philip Hammond got his figures for HS2 wrong by £20 billion, whilst this was picked up by the press (Mirror, May 17), our sample of online news contained just two articles specifically about Philip Hammond the day after he made this gaffe and neither mentioned it (Huffington Post, May 17; Mail Online, May 17).

Research has shown that campaign coverage can be fraught with danger for women candidates, particularly those in leadership positions. The main risk is reinforcing stereotypical assumptions about the incompatibility between traditional understandings of femininity and conventional ideals of politics. Female politicians are often viewed as more compassionate, honest and warmer than men, whilst men are viewed as more competent, decisive and stronger leaders (Dolan and Lynch 2013; Kahn 1996). These differences are problematic because stereotypically masculine traits are more highly valued by the electorate (Huddy and Terkildsen 1993), which goes some way to explain the continued over-representation of men in politics. Therefore if women are already perceived to lack political competence, the consequences of reinforcing that assumption can be damaging. It is also important to consider that the harsh treatment of Abbott stems not only from her gendered identity, but also from the fact that she is the most prominent black woman in British politics. Ward's (2016) analysis of US congressional candidates indicates that women of colour receive more negative coverage than white women or men of colour. She also finds minority women are less visible than their white female counterparts, and when they do receive coverage, it is twice as likely to explicitly foreground their gender. Gabriel (2017) argues that Abbott has often received coverage that emphasises her ethnicity as well as her sex and was subjected to more intense scrutiny than other candidates in similar roles. It is perhaps surprising that even considering the fact that women politicians have gained considerably prominence in the online coverage of this election that gendered coverage persists, albeit in rather subtle ways. It is also striking that since women politicians have managed to gain visibility, non-political women such as experts, ordinary citizens and pollsters struggled to receive similar levels of attention.

Conclusion

The 2017 election campaign was highly unusual in many ways. It was the first election after the historic referendum decision in 2016; the first election since 1987 to be called and contested by a female Prime Minister, and public opinion appeared to be strongly in favour of returning an increased majority for the Conservative Party for the first time in decades. In practice, the campaign was widely perceived to be a disaster for May and a triumph for Corbyn's Labour party even though the actual results suggested otherwise. Our findings suggest that the online reporting of the campaign was highly presidential, with May and Corbyn dominating the coverage. The other most prominent campaigners were the leaders of other political parties or member of the Cabinet and Shadow Cabinet. Analysis of press and broadcasting revealed very similar trends (see Deacon et al. 2017). The issue agenda was also similar to that of the legacy media, although our findings show that online news featured a higher proportion of news about the political process than offline rivals. This was especially the case with the digital born sites who devoted a lot of coverage to the role of media in the campaign. Our analysis of the gendered dynamics of the campaign coverage show that once again online news is dominated by men, despite the fact that the Prime Minister is female. Our qualitative analysis of the portrayal of women shows that whilst May received some very subtle gendered coverage which constructed her as weak and robotic, other prominent women like

Diane Abbott received much more overtly sexist coverage questioning her competence, demonstrating another way in which online news follows similar trends to its mainstream competitors.

This chapter has demonstrated that despite some small differences, UK online news coverage of the election shared many similarities with broadcast and press coverage. Previous research has noted that much of the content on online newspapers and websites of broadcasters tends to repackage their original content for the online environment (Quant 2008), and this is particularly the case for the *Mail Online*, which might go some way to explaining the continuity of the mainstream news agenda online. With the advent of digital-born news providers we wanted to assess to what extent these newsmakers are following the mainstream agenda, or whether they are exhibiting a different range of stories. Our study did not include any of the new highly partisan outlets like *Breitbart* or *The Canary* that receive high volumes of shares on social media from their political supporters, but clearly going forward it would be useful to analyse such media alongside the mainstream journalism that already receives academic attention.

It is striking then, that our study demonstrates that online news sites reported the election in a very conventional way. The issues they covered were predictable and the range of voices included was typically narrow. Much has been said about the potential decline in influence of the British press and the importance of paying more attention to online news but if our results tell us anything, then it is that when the online news that British citizens claim to consume is analysed, there are remarkable similarities to the mainstream broadcast and press agendas.

References

Barnicoat, B. (2017, May 11). How strong and stable are you actually? *BuzzFeed*. https://www.buzzfeed.com/beckybarnicoat/what-percent-strong-and-stable-are-you?utm_term=.klB6xWpqY0#.wc2P2zVNGx. Accessed December 20, 2017.

BBC. (2017, April 17). *BBC News*. http://www.bbc.co.uk/news/av/uk-politics-39631693/views-from-bristol-after-snap-election-announcement. Accessed April 17, 2017.

Bennett, O. (2017, May 17). *Theresa May refuses to confirm Philip Hammond will stay as chancellor after the election*. http://www.huffingtonpost.co.uk/entry/theresa-may-philip-hammond_uk_591c2c41e4b0a7458fa4689c. Accessed May 17, 2017.

Buchanan, R. (2017, May 2). *Here's Diane Abbott's absolute car crash of an interview about hiring more police officers.* https://www.buzzfeed.com/rose-buchanan/unfair-to-carcrashes?utm_term=.vekDOo5zj7#.vf2wgO2bY9. Accessed May 2, 2017.

Burrows, T. (2017, June 1). *'Unflappable and stoic'. Home Secretary Amber Rudd is praised for appearing on TV debate just THREE DAYS after her father died.* http://www.dailymail.co.uk/news/article-4560926/Amber-Rudd-appeared-debate-despite-death-father.html. Accessed June 1, 2017.

Campus, D. (2013). *Women political leaders and the media.* Basingstoke: Palgrave Macmillan.

Cappella, J. N., & Jamieson, K. H. (1997). *Spiral of cynicism.* New York: Oxford University Press.

Conservative Press. (2017, May 2). *Conservative Press.* http://press.conservatives.com/post/160443296880/theresa-may-speech-in-bristol-2nd-may. Accessed December 20, 2017.

Crace, J. (2017, May 2). *Diane Abbott has several numbers on police costs—Sadly they are all wrong.* https://www.theguardian.com/politics/2017/may/02/diane-abbott-has-several-numbers-on-police-costs-sadly-they-are-all-wrong. Accessed May 2, 2017.

Cushion, S. (2012). *The democratic value of news: Why public service media matter.* Basingstoke: Palgrave Macmillan.

Cushion, S., Franklin, B., & Court, G. (2006). Citizens, readers and local newspaper coverage of the 2005 general election. *Javnost: The Public, 13*(1), 41–60.

Deacon, D., Wring, D., & Golding, P. (2006). Same campaign, differing agendas: Analysing news media coverage of the 2005 general election. *British Politics, 1*(2), 222–256.

Deacon, D., Downey, J., Smith, D., Stanyer, J., & Wring, D. (2017). *Media coverage of the 2017 general election campaign report 4.* Loughborough: Loughborough University Centre for Research in Communication and Culture.

Dennis, J., & Sampaio-Dias, S. (2017). Not just swearing and loathing on the internet: Analysing BuzzFeed and VICE during #GE2017. In E. Thorsen, D. Jackson, & D. Lilleker (Eds.), *UK election analysis 2017: Media, voters and the campaign.* Bournemouth: Centre for the Study of Journalism, Culture and Community Bournemouth University.

Dolan, K., & Lynch, T. (2013). It takes a survey: Understanding gender stereotypes, abstract attitudes, and voting for women candidates. *American Politics Research, 42*(4), 656–676.

Edds, R. (2017, June 8). 52 genuinely funny tweets that made the election just about bearable. *BuzzFeed.* https://www.buzzfeed.com/robinedds/election-tweets-that-are-guaranteed-to-make-you-laugh?utm_term=.jyoV58BMYo#.osAQm0Gw3P. Accessed June 8, 2017.

Gabriel, D. (2017). The othering and objectification of Diane Abbott MP. In E. Thorsen, D. Jackson, & D. Lilleker (Eds.), *UK election analysis 2017: Media, voters and the campaign*. Bournemouth: Centre for the Study of Journalism, Culture and Community Bournemouth University.

Harmer, E. (2017). Pink buses, leaders' wives and "the most dangerous woman in Britain": Women, the press and politics in the 2015 election. In D. Wring, R. Mortimore, & S. Atkinson (Eds.), *Political communication in Britain: Polling, campaigning and media in the 2015 general election*. London: Palgrave Macmillan.

Harmer, E., & Southern, R. (2018). More stable than strong: Women's representation, voters and issues at the 2017 general election. *Parliamentary Affairs, 71*, 237–254.

Harmer, E., Savigny, H., & Ward, O. (2017). 'Are you tough enough?' Performing gender in the UK leadership debates 2015. *Media, Culture and Society, 39*(7), 960–975.

Huddy, L., & Terkildsen, N. (1993). The consequences of gender stereotyping for women candidates at different levels and types of office. *Political Research Quarterly, 46*(3), 503–525.

Kahn, K. F. (1996). *The political consequences of being a woman: How stereotypes influence the conduct and consequences of political campaigns*. New York: Columbia University Press.

Letts, Q. (2017, May 2). Eek. She was like a frogman wading into cow manure. http://www.dailymail.co.uk/news/article-4467502/QUENTIN-LETTS-Diane-Abbott-s-awful-day.html. Accessed May 2, 2017.

Newman, N., Fletcher, R., Kalogeropoulos, A., Levy, D., & Nielson, R. K. (2017). *Reuters Institute digital news report 2017*. Oxford: Reuters Institute for the Study of Journalism.

Quandt, T. (2008). (No) News on the World Wide Web? A comparative content analysis of online news in Europe and the United States. *Journalism Studies, 9*(5), 717–738.

Ross, K. (2017). It's the way I tell 'em: Car crash politics and the gendered turn. In E. Thorsen, D. Jackson, & D. Lilleker (Eds.), *UK election analysis 2017: Media, voters and the campaign*. Bournemouth: Centre for the Study of Journalism, Culture and Community Bournemouth University.

Ross, K., Evans, E., Harrison, L., Shears, M., & Wadia, K. (2013). The gender of news and news of gender: A study of sex, politics, and press coverage of 2010 British general election. *International Journal of Press/Politics, 18*(1), 3–20.

Simons, N. (2017, May 2). *Diane Abbott told 'Hughley embarrassing' LBC interview 'reduces her credibility'*. http://www.huffingtonpost.co.uk/entry/diane-abbott-told-hugely-embarrassing-lbc-interview-reduces-her-credibility_uk_590868d4e4b02655f8404172. Accessed May 2, 2017.

Simons, N. (2017, May 31). The best thing Jeremy Corbyn did in the BBC debate was turn up. *Huffington Post*. http://www.huffingtonpost.co.uk/ned-simons/bbc-debate-jeremy-corbyn_b_16901094.html. Accessed May 31, 2017.

Smith, M. (2017, May 17). Tory Philip Hammond skewered in BBC interview as he gets his figures in a major muddle. *Daily Mirror*. http://www.mirror.co.uk/news/politics/tory-philip-hammond-skewered-bbc-10438641. Accessed May 20, 2017.

Smith, P. (2017, April 28). The 57 times Theresa May has said "strong and stable leadership" so far since she called the election. *BuzzFeed*. https://www.buzzfeed.com/patricksmith/here-are-57-times-theresa-may-has-said-strong-and-stable?utm_term=.ldJ2JjXyG4#.dukyVb0YjQ. Accessed December 20, 2017.

Spence, A. (2017, May 2). People are getting fed up with Theresa May's campaign being so stage-managed. *BuzzFeed*. https://www.buzzfeed.com/alexspence/theresa-mays-aides-insist-shes-not-just-meeting-tory?utm_term=.olr8Jl9Kx7#.snQBOzNoWn. Accessed December 20, 2017.

Stevens, J. (2017, May 17). May will drop pledge not to raise income tax, VAT or national insurance after David Cameron's vow was dubbed 'dumbest economic policy possible'. *Mail Online*. http://www.dailymail.co.uk/news/article-4516590/Theresa-scrap-David-Cameron-s-tax-lock-promise.html. Accessed May 17, 2017.

Tapsfield, J., Robertson A., & Groves, J. (2017, June 5). *Diane Abbott goes underground: Corbyn's terror supremo ducks out of big radio debate, claiming to be 'sick' after yet ANOTHER toe-curling TV meltdown—But is then spotted out and about on the tube*. http://www.dailymail.co.uk/news/article-4574822/Diane-Abbott-embarrasses-new-TV-interview.html. Accessed December 20, 2017.

Van Aelst, P., Sheafer, T., & Stanyer, J. (2011). The personalization of mediated political communication: A review of concepts, operationalizations and key findings. *Journalism, 13*(2), 203–220.

Ward, O. (2016). Seeing double: Race, gender, and coverage of minority women's campaigns for the U.S. House of Representatives. *Politics and Gender, 12*, 317–343.

Waterson, J. (2017, May 30). *Jeremy Corbyn forgot how much Labour's childcare policy would cost*. https://www.buzzfeed.com/jimwaterson/jeremy-corbyn-forgot-how-much-labours-childcare-policy?utm_term=.eqDp8OzKQa#.ciMN5mvoP7. Accessed May 30, 2017.

Alternative Media: A New Factor in Electoral Politics?

Craig Gent and Michael Walker

Novara Media emerged from the direct action wing of the UK student movement in 2013 off the back of the Novara FM radio show and podcast, founded in 2011 and broadcast live on the London arts radio station Resonance FM. In 2015 our election liveblog attracted 5500 readers; in the build-up our most popular election-related article was '9 Anarchist-Friendly Reasons to Vote in 2015', attracting a modest 3700 readers. During the 2017 election campaign novaramedia.com received a quarter of a million hits, our videos were viewed 2.3 million times on Facebook alone, and on election day we reached 1.2 million people on the platform. What changed?

On one hand, it has become clear that since the dawn of 'web 2.0'— the participatory web—changes to online news and comment publishing have impacted on traditional, 'mainstream' outlets which had previously relied on offline broadcast and circulation, as well as the 'read-only' logic of the early web. Lower costs of entry combined with the modest levelling of the playing field brought by social media platforms have meant major legacy media organisations have been forced to compete with the

C. Gent · M. Walker (✉)
Novara Media, London, UK

© The Author(s) 2019
D. Wring et al. (eds.), *Political Communication in Britain*,
https://doi.org/10.1007/978-3-030-00822-2_8

likes of BuzzFeed and the Huffington Post since the latter part of the 2000s.

Yet any explanation of the role of specifically online media in the 2017 general election must also consider the political juncture we find ourselves in. The technologies and social media platforms which enabled Novara Media and other left-wing outlets to reach large audiences in 2017 were mostly around in 2015. Yet it was only in this last election that "newspapers lost their monopoly on the political news agenda" (Waterson 2017). The difference in this election was a candidate who simultaneously prompted print journalists' ire whilst generating enthusiasm and interest amongst online journalists. Crucially, Jeremy Corbyn's ability to gain a foothold within internet culture created an online environment conducive to new and not-so-new media platforms reaching unprecedented audiences with no significant financial capital outlay.

MEDIA FOR A DIFFERENT POLITICS

Novara Media was founded in 2013 as a multimedia platform for political journalism. Across our audio, video, articles and events operations, we have sought to fulfill a dual purpose: to enable left-wing working class and social justice movements to speak to themselves, and to extend radical left-wing ideas to people who might not encounter them otherwise.

Publishing alongside the strap-line 'media for a different politics', we have always eschewed the idea that journalists can take a disinterested "view from nowhere" (see Rosen 2010) and have sought to imbue our journalism with political honesty, integrity and passion. Our editors and presenters are encouraged to be honest about their political positions, which have always been as varied as our audience, but our perspectives have historically been broadly libertarian socialist in character and our output has contributed to the notion of 'fully automated luxury communism' (Merchant 2015), a political vision which advocates a transition to a post-work society where abundance is held in common. Although some of our team had been members of political parties, our output was never particularly supportive of any party, although during the #GreenSurge of the 2015 election some qualified exceptions were made for the Greens. Meanwhile the Labour party had never been much of a feature of our coverage, except when noting its growing irrelevance and the general trend of 'pasokification' afflicting social democratic parties across Europe.[1]

A significant change of political direction was brought about by the groundswell surrounding Jeremy Corbyn's first election to the leadership of the Labour party. Historically, like many on the 'far left', the attitude towards Labour of those editing, producing and writing for Novara Media had generally veered between sceptical and hostile—but certainly not hopeful. However, unlike the bulk of the Labour apparatus, Corbyn and his primary allies John McDonnell and Diane Abbott had been seen as friends of Britain's extra-parliamentary left. Far from being just a small handful of many forgettable Labour backbenchers, Corbyn, McDonnell and Abbott (alongside the Green party's Caroline Lucas) were familiar faces from the picket lines, demonstrations and university occupations where Novara Media's own team had come to know one another.

The shift in editorial direction was complemented by technological changes which helped us find a larger audience. In particular, Facebook began to invest more heavily in its native video hosting, which meant our videos were now beginning to see a greater reach than any other form of content. Having already established ourselves as a multimedia project, Facebook's algorithmic changes boosted the branch of Novara Media which would most closely following Labour developments, reinforcing our growing image as a 'pro-Corbyn' outlet among supporters and detractors alike.

THE 'MAINSTREAM MEDIA' AND ITS DISCONTENTS

As our coverage and political sympathies gravitated towards the Labour party for the first time, most of Britain's media decisively turned away. A study conducted by researchers at LSE confirmed what many on the political left had suspected, finding coverage concerning Corbyn was

---

[1] 'Pasokification', a term which in the UK originated on Novara Media, refers to the process by which formerly dominant social democratic parties are outflanked from the left by particularly insurgent anti-austerity parliamentary parties. The term originally referred do the near electoral elimination of the Greek party Pasok by Syriza, but has also been used to speculate on Podemos's once-anticipated 'sorpasso' (surpassing) of PSOE in Spain, and to describe the rise of an anti-austerity oriented SNP against Labour in Scotland. For further information see: Doran (2013, 2015) and Chakrabortty (2015).

disproportionately negative, and, while acknowledging the democratic importance of media scrutiny, deemed the print media to have regularly strayed beyond its purview as 'watchdog' to an 'attackdog' position (Cammaerts et al. 2017).

In our own experience, feedback from our new readers, viewers and listeners in the two years leading up to the 2017 election consistently referred to disillusionment with formerly preferred outlets. In our case this was most commonly the *Guardian* (indeed an excerpt from Alex Nunns' book *The Candidate*, 'How the Guardian Changed Tack on Corbyn - Despite Its Readers', remains one of our most popular longer pieces), though others such as The Canary have purposefully set out to capture readers of tabloids such as *The Sun*, the *Daily Express* and the *Star* (Real Media 2016). In short, there existed a growing frustration at what Corbyn supporters saw as the inability or unwillingness of the so-called 'mainstream media' (or 'MSM'—a term we have never much liked) to understand either their motivations or Corbyn's own positions, which provided a ready audience for media outlets who were willing to give a sympathetic hearing to some of the basic propositions of the Corbyn project.

The rejection of Corbyn by mainstream outlets also had the effect that Labour's new leadership were willing to give interviews to alternative outlets like our own. Corbyn and his team were immediately amenable us, agreeing to an interview in July 2015 during his leadership campaign (in which he predicted "things are not going to be the same in 2020"). Unlike establishment outlets which quizzed him on what we saw as sensationalist irrelevancies such as whether he was really "friends" with Hamas (obviously not), our interview took him at his word and scrutinised his programme from the left. Where the BBC saw him as a hippie radical, we still wanted to be convinced this career politician (from *the Labour party*) was worth our critical support. A fruitful and mutually-respectful relationship emerged, Corbyn providing a further interview during the week of mass resignations from his shadow cabinet in June 2016 (and appearing onstage in a live episode of The Fix, our weekly webcast TV programme, at The World Transformed festival in 2017), and John McDonnell providing one interview during July 2016's 'coup' against Corbyn's leadership and another during Labour's 2017 conference.

Corbyn's receptiveness to non-traditional media was continued into the general election campaign, sitting down to video interviews with *NME*, VICE's i-D platform with grime artist JME, the UNILAD Facebook page, and a special edition of YouTube channel COPA90's 'Fifa and Chill' series. Each tapping into different 'youth' demographics (broadly construed), the interviews demonstrated a keen ear for the groundswell emerging around Corbyn's candidacy on social media and within online culture. The consistent willingness of Corbyn to engage with online media was in sharp contrast with his predecessor. A lifetime of grassroots activism gave his presence on alternative outlets a certain naturalness, unlike Ed Miliband's hastily organised 2015 interview for Russell Brand's YouTube channel. While the capacity of social media platforms to 'level the playing field' between traditional and 'alternative' media is commonly overstated given disparities in financial war chests between these groups of outlets, Corbyn's open approach to non-traditional outlets reflected the populist ambitions of the Corbyn campaign—in particular his 'man of the people' image—and was vindicated in their organic reach across social networks.

SNAP ELECTION

On Tuesday 18th April Theresa May called for a snap election, arguing the need for a stronger mandate (and more seats) from the British public to steer the country through its Brexit negotiations. Following a flurry of messages over the Novara Media Slack channel, we arranged a meeting for 20th April to discuss our approach.

As our audience would expect, our first impulse was to launch into a conversation about the upcoming campaign alongside our predictions, hopes and fears. In-keeping with major events in the news cycle, this would usually have demanded an in-depth discussion on our flagship podcast NovaraFM, however as the show is broadcast live on FM radio we would be restricted to a policy of impartiality for the duration of the election campaign in line with Ofcom rules. This wouldn't be a problem, except that Novara Media is a *political* media project with specific ambitions and convictions; as such it would be unthinkable that we would spend an entire election campaign without intervening in the campaign in a partisan way. As such, NovaraFM shows relating to the election were necessarily broad and conducted in a more disinterested manner than usual, while our in-house podcasting capacity was put into use exploring the ideas we had to refrain from promoting on-air. A newer podcast, TyskySour, became particularly useful in this regard. When the

Labour manifesto 'For the Many, Not the Few' was launched, swathes of left activists began to get excited about some of the headline policies. On NovaraFM we hosted a discussion on 'The Meaning of Manifestos', using the opportunity to take a political but more historical and intellectual look at the political manifesto as a form and tool. Naturally we wanted listeners to draw their own conclusions but it was necessary for us to be restrained when it came to making comparisons with the Labour and Conservative manifestos. By contrast, the same week TyskySour hosted a parallel discussion playfully entitled 'The Manifesto - It's Beautiful'.

However, Novara Media's critical support for Labour at the election was not a given. Having never supported a party at a general election before (besides wishing the Greens well), and with a minority of Novara's editors registered as supporters or members of the Labour party, it was not immediately clear to us—nor our audience—how we would proceed. Alongside the slogan 'media for a different politics', Novara's other tagline has always been 'no future, utopia now'. Perhaps reflective of an initial anarchist commitment developed against the backdrop of austerity Britain, 'no future, utopia now' has served to capture an enduring sense of indignance and righteousness (despite, and especially living through, times of crisis) that we have sought to convey in our output. So to be put in a situation of 'possible future, utopia pending' in 2017 presented a dilemma. Our response was to record a special podcast featuring a candid discussion in which three of Novara's senior editors asked whether they should 'Vote Labour?'. Reflecting the range of views held within the team and to an extent across our audience, the discussion was a nuanced exploration of the intricacies of advocating for a Labour vote. It was to be a turning point our organisation's discourse both in terms of its ambitions and how we relate to our audience. 'Vote Labour?' became our most-listened podcast of the general election; narrowly followed by the final podcast of the campaign, TyskySour's 'Last Lap 'Til Socialism'.

If our podcast operation sought to box clever in generating critical enthusiasm for Corbyn's prospects of winning by triangulating between excitement and more distanced analysis, our videos and articles during the campaign period showed the strategy on a larger scale. Most of our videos are presenter-led in terms of their content, whilst articles are commissioned based on pitches or editorial initiative. As such, the content of video series such as 'IMO Bastani' and 'OMFG Sarkar' reflect the interests and views of the presenters (senior editors Aaron Bastani and Ash Sarkar, respectively) whereas articles are almost always authored by contributors external to the Novara team.[2]

As the format is well-suited to 'snap reaction' style content, our videos closely followed the campaign itself, responding to news item stories as they developed and intervening where we could, particularly on issues where we felt most fluent: the housing crisis; young people (as a generation rather than demographic); the Conservatives' record since 2010, particularly against their campaign slogan 'strong and stable leadership in the national interest'; the crapulent moronism of the Liberal Democrats, a strong feeling among the post-2010 student generation; and the idea of socialism more broadly. Aside from surprise hit 'Cafe Corbyn', a short video focusing on a Corbyn-loving Finsbury Park cafe owner, our most popular videos were an interview discussing Corbyn with hip-hop artist and activist Lowkey, and two IMO Bastani videos, 'Do not vote for the Lib Dems' and 'Tories are not stable or secure'. The reactive style of the videos served us beyond just their immediate reach, with our senior editors becoming repeat commentators on Sky News and BBC radio.

Meanwhile our articles operation generally solicited pieces from contributors external to the organisation, and as such sought to reflect some of the differences and debates present across our audience, as well as approaching election topics from a less direct angle. Naturally, during a general election campaign everything becomes framed in terms of the various offers and records of the main political parties, but with videos generally being responsive to the election new cycle, and knowing we did not have the resources to provide the immediate written commentary on breaking stories that could be done faster by traditional outlets, we chose a more issues-focused arc for articles coverage to push discussion on core election concerns—austerity, the Conservatives' record, the security conversation emerging from the Manchester Arena and London Bridge terror attacks—as well as maintaining normal service covering topics such as the French election, labour disputes and migrant struggles.

For Novara Media the election campaign culminated in #ElectionSESH, an eight hour live Facebook broadcast on the night of polling day.[3] Although Facebook Live had been launched in summer

---

[2] IMO meaning 'in my opinion', 'OMFG' meaning 'oh my fucking god'.

[3] 'Sesh' meaning session; a long time spent with friends, usually drinking.

2015, it took until the turn of 2017 for it to be developed for profes-sional broadcasts with multiple cameras and computers. As far as we are aware we were the first outlet of our kind to use this technology in the UK, which became a key fixture of our general election coverage.

Featuring six Novara members and fifteen guests, mostly young free-lance journalists, but also YouTube personalities, authors, political advi-sors, and the freshly re-elected MP Chris Williamson (via weblink), the #ElectionSESH broadcast attracted 90,000 viewers and became a pole of attraction for left-leaning activists and journalists on election night. Having been recognised as one of the outlets who broadly 'pre-dicted' the outcome, #ElectionSESH was later featured in a profile of Novara Media by the BBC Media Show. But beyond simply provid-ing another outlet for rolling results coverage, the space opened up by #ElectionSESH allowed us to return to many of the points of discussion we had highlighted in the course of the campaign, as well as relate to the results on a political and personal level as well as a journalistic one. While sympathetic broadcasters would have had to stifle smiles come the exit poll, our editors were let off the reins to reflect and acknowledge the excitement felt by so much of our audience. Even as a media project, Novara Media is fundamentally concerned with radical political change; we don't profess any 'view from nowhere'—any other response would have been unthinkable.

An Alternative Media Ecology

Novara Media had slowly built up a committed audience that had largely travelled a similar journey from movement to party and appreciated our ongoing analysis of the tensions and strategies this 'institutional turn' would involve. As Corbyn's leadership increased political engagement and the popularity of left-wing ideas, our following and sphere of influ-ence steadily increased—a process accelerated once the general election was called. However, whilst our reach was on a steady upward curve, the reach of new sites such as The Canary and Evolve Politics had positively exploded.

Since their launch in the early months of Corbyn's leadership, The Canary and Evolve Politics had been building a huge reach by hammer-ing the Conservatives, the 'mainstream media' and the Labour right in tabloid style hit-pieces. Matt Turner, editor at Evolve Politics, told us articles which achieved the most reach were those which attacked media bias, Tory hypocrisy, or which covered animal rights. During the election campaign it was the impact of the latter theme, ignored by the press (and even ourselves at Novara), that was most surprising. Evolve's article 'Theresa May's Tory manifesto SCRAPS THE BAN on elephant ivory sales after bowing to millionaire antique lobbyists' clocked 115,000 views. The piece targeted Lady Victoria Borwick, MP for Kensington, due to her role as president of the British Antique Dealers' Association. Borwick went on to lose her seat by a mere 20 votes. Evolve's most viewed video targeted May's plans to lift the ban on foxhunting. Remarkably simple, the video consisted of footage of a fox sat on a person's lap with text overlaid asking "Are you seriously going to vote for a person that wants to bring back fox hunting?". At the time of writing it had been shared 73,000 times and clocked 4.5 million views.

Whilst a focus on animals spoke to the Conservatives' image as the 'nasty party', a crowd-sourced video of campaign events threw the spotlight on the perceived arrogance and shiftiness of the Conservative campaign. In a two-minute video posted by the Evolve Politics Facebook page, the Home Secretary Amber Rudd was shown appearing to shut down the speech of an opposing candidate at a hustings event in Hastings. The clip, shot on a mobile phone by an audience member, begins with independent candidate Nicolas Wilson criticising weapons sales by the Conservative government to Saudi Arabia. Amber Rudd is seen passing a note to the chair, who then asks Mr. Wilson to refrain from this line of argument before attempting to physically take the microphone from him. The video racked up 3.6 million views and was shared 79,000 times.

A brand new platform, Double Down News launched on 19th May 2017 with a four-minute video of UK hip hop artist Lowkey speaking about his support for Jeremy Corbyn. Edited down from 30 minutes of raw footage and backed with emotive music, Lowkey describes the victories of the Labour movement and their repeal under Margaret Thatcher. Lowkey, who came to prominence with music protesting the Iraq war, then describes Corbyn's break with establishment foreign policy and explains why the media get it wrong when they describe him as soft on defence. Closing with a passionate call to register to vote and vote Labour, the video was shared 81,000 times and received 4 million views.

The platform's second video was a call for unity by comedian Guz Khan in the wake of the Manchester Arena bombing. Khan's video called out the divisive rhetoric of figures like Mail Online columnist Katie

Hopkins. It also made direct reference to the general election by drawing a connection between British foreign policy and global terrorism, before highlighting Corbyn's consistent opposition to military interventions in the Middle East. The video was shared 134,000 times and received over 8 million views. Double Down News would release two more videos before the election's close, one a critique of media bias by popular YouTube personality Rants n Bants, the other a short interview with John McDonnell. In total, Double Down News's four videos received 16 million views.

Conclusion: Disruptive Media?

Platforms like Evolve Politics and Double Down News worked in a similar way to traditional partisan media during the general election. Like *The Sun* or *Daily Mail*, their coverage responded to events during the election campaign and framed them in such a way to highlight the strengths of their favoured party and the weakness of their opponents. Just as the establishment media amplified Diane Abbott's disastrous interview on police funding to highlight Labour's perceived fiscal irresponsibility, Evolve Politics amplified Amber Rudd's behaviour at local hustings to highlight perceived Conservative duplicity. However, the analogy between the right-leaning press and online left media shouldn't be taken too far. The *Daily Mail*, which devoted its first 13 pages to attacking Labour the day before the election, has a turnover of £574 million. Evolve Politics, Double Down News and Novara Media are all staffed by part-timers or volunteers.

Beyond turnover and the amount of reach outlets are able to buy, the differences in resources available to online-only left media and the print media is felt in how content is produced and distributed. For publications like the *Sun* or *Daily Mail*, election coverage is a top-down affair, and once proprietors and editors agree their favoured outcome scores of reporters can be instructed to build a narrative which fits the paper's line. In contrast, the impact of online left publications had a more organic relationship with their particular readerships. Not only was the reach of any content they produced dependent on the enthusiasm of social media users, many of the most popular articles and videos were drawn from people who did not consider themselves journalists. One example is the Rudd video, shot on a smartphone and reproduced by Evolve Politics.

Even more striking was an article titled 'This Facebook comment about the general election is going viral' published by The London Economic, which reproduced a Facebook post by Chris Renwick arguing the media opposed Corbyn only because he threatened their vested interests. Contacting Renwick for this chapter, he told us he has no connection with journalism and runs a fashion label with his girlfriend. According to BuzzFeed's Jim Waterson (2017), the reproduction of Renwick's post became the most shared article of the general election, read by over 4 million people.

Thus, the strength of left-wing online media during the general election was effectively a consequence of crowd-enabled collective action. Left-wing outlets were able to tap into the widespread energy generated online by Labour's general election campaign and achieve unprecedented levels of reach for progressive, activist media. This obviously depended on there being a candidate who inspired enthusiasm among social media users, both in person and policy (according to BuzzFeed [Phillips and Waterson 2017], the Labour manifesto was the most shared election-related text in the week of its launch), and who was receptive to the advantages of courting alternative media outlets, especially in the context of a left populist programme.

But it was also made possible by a matured online media environment. Far from every online outlet still being 'new media' and every web-based journalist being a 'blogger', we are now at least ten years into a changed media ecology where any almost any outlet is reliant on its online presence and platforms which bring its content into closer relation with that of other outlets than ever before. While many establishment journalists lament the seemingly unending proliferation of both social media and alternative media sites—including what former BBC political editor Nick Robinson (2017) called the "guerilla war" being waged on 'mainstream' outlets by activist outlets, including Novara Media—many others see it as an overdue corrective to a media environment with high costs of entry and a limited range of perspectives on offer.

The panic over social media effect on political journalism—in particular the liberal establishment's over-egged concern over alternative outlets peddling 'fake news'—deserves attention, as we have given it elsewhere (Gent 2017), because it is not going away. But neither is the new online media ecology, in all its variation. This is the media reality now. At the 2017 general election, Corbyn's team knew that.

REFERENCES

Cammaerts, B., DeCillia, B., Magalhães, J., Jimenez-Martínez, C. (2017). *Journalistic representations of Jeremy Corbyn in the British press: From watchdog to attackdog.* Media@LSE Report. https://www.lse.ac.uk/media@lse/research/pdf/JeremyCorbyn/Cobyn-Report-FINAL.pdf. Accessed January 21, 2018.

Chakrabortty, A. (2015, January 27). What Greek politics teaches the Labour party: There is an alternative. *The Guardian.* https://www.theguardian.com/commentisfree/2015/jan/27/uk-austerity-greece-parallels-labour-toxic-eliteness. Accessed January 21, 2018.

Doran, J. (2013, September 15). Liquidating Labour. *Novara Media.* http://novaramedia.com/2013/09/15/liquidating-labour/. Accessed January 21, 2018.

Doran, J. (2015, January 28). 5 things you need to know about Pasokification. *Novara Media.* http://novaramedia.com/2015/01/28/5-things-you-need-to-know-about-pasokification/. Accessed January 21, 2018.

Gent, C. (2017, January 13). Truth and politics. *Jacobin.* https://jacobinmag.com/2017/01/trump-fake-news-russia-leaks-cnn-buzzfeed. Accessed January 21, 2018.

Merchant, B. (2015, March 18). Fully automated luxury communism. *The Guardian.* https://www.theguardian.com/sustainable-business/2015/mar/18/fully-automated-luxury-communism-robots-employment. Accessed January 21, 2018.

Phillips, T., & Waterson, J. (2017, May 21). People on Facebook really like sharing Labour's manifesto. *BuzzFeed.* https://www.buzzfeed.com/tomphillips/people-on-facebook-really-like-sharing-labours-manifesto?utm_term=.tyQXr9GdO#.ifwpXax3J. Accessed January 21, 2018.

Real Media. (2016). *Kerry-Anne Mendoza—The future of new media.* https://www.youtube.com/watch?v=fufz-3xlv2c. Accessed January 21, 2018.

Robinson, N. (2017, September 27). If mainstream news wants to win back trust, it cannot silence dissident voices. *The Guardian.* https://www.theguardian.com/commentisfree/2017/sep/27/mainstream-news-win-back-trust-dissident-voices. Accessed January 21, 2018.

Rosen, J. (2010, November 10). The view from Nowhere: Questions and answers. *PressThink.* http://pressthink.org/2010/11/the-view-from-nowhere-questions-and-answers/. Accessed January 21, 2018.

Waterson, J. (2017, June 18). This was the election where newspapers lost their monopoly on the political news agenda. *BuzzFeed.* https://www.buzzfeed.com/jimwaterson/how-newspapers-lost-their-monopoly-on-the-political-agenda?utm_term=.qylVZ46x9#.oxMnE3ow0. Accessed January 21, 2018.

PART II

Campaigns

'Strong and Stable' to 'Weak and Wobbly': The Conservative Election Campaign

Anthony Ridge-Newman

INTRODUCTION: STUDYING THE TORY CAMPAIGN 2017

The British Conservative Party's 2017 general election effort, under the leadership of Theresa May, resulted in a loss of 22 seats in England and 3 seats in Wales, totalling a loss of 25 seats across England and Wales. However, this poor result for the Conservatives is juxtaposed against the Scottish Conservatives' 12 seat increase north of the border, suggesting divergent trends and political drivers in different parts of Britain. Overall, the Tories suffered a loss of 13 seats in the House of Commons, which resulted in a minority Conservative government (BBC 2017a). Although Theresa May is presented as having won the election by some, the overall outcome of the 2017 campaign is largely deemed to have been a failure for the Conservatives—especially in England and Wales, which is the focus of this study.

When compared to the two previous elections in 2010 and 2015, the 2017 Tory campaign had notable similarities in some areas and diverged in others. This chapter aims to analyse comparatively the Conservative

A. Ridge-Newman (✉)
Liverpool Hope University, Liverpool, UK
e-mail: ridgena@hope.ac.uk

© The Author(s) 2019
D. Wring et al. (eds.), *Political Communication in Britain*,
https://doi.org/10.1007/978-3-030-00822-2_9

131

Party's communications and campaign strategies in the election against characteristics of the Tory campaigns in 2010 and 2015, based on findings from corresponding studies. The Conservatives' campaign strategies in the earlier general elections, under the leadership of David Cameron, progressively developed in line with some of the wider trends observed in digital technologies and political communication (Ridge-Newman 2014; Ridge-Newman and Mitchell 2016). Unlike in 2017, the party also made significant electoral progress in both 2010 and 2015. These elections were characterised by a mix of sometimes competing mediated political elements like citizen-initiated campaigning (Gibson 2015) and the personalization of the campaigns (Holtz-Bacha et al. 2014), including, to some extent, the presidentialization of party leaders (Langer 2011).

Gibson suggests that citizen-initiated campaigning is a form of political engagement, particularly suited to the use of digital technologies, which 'challenges the dominant professionalized model of campaign management by devolving power over core tasks to the grassroots' (2015: 183). In contrast, Karvonen defines personalization as 'the notion that individual political actors have become more prominent at the expense of parties and collective identities' (2009: 4). Holtz-Bacha et al. (2014) argue that personalization is a multifaceted concept and researchers should be clear about the focus of a given study in terms of the type of personalization applicable to the specifics of the factors of interest. Therefore, in relation to this chapter, particular attention is given to mediated Conservative Party leadership in the context of its elections campaigns of 2010, 2015 and 2017. In this sense, the concept of presidentialization is a useful tool when comparing the party's campaign approaches and, specifically, the roles played by the Conservative Party's leaders: David Cameron in 2010 and 2015; and Theresa May in 2017.

In this chapter, presidentialization is defined as a case of personalization in which the leader of a party becomes more prominent than the party and other key party figures during an election campaign (Foley 2000; Poguntke and Webb 2005). The concepts of citizen-initiated campaigning and presidentialization in isolation appear as opposing and contradictory trends. However, Chadwick's hybrid media logic (2017) helps explain how the new media environment contributes to unpredictable and chaotic relationships between political actors, like the elites and grassroots, as they compete through mediated forms of politics.

CONTEXTUALIZING THE CONSERVATIVES
AND GENERAL ELECTION 2017

Pierre Bourdieu described elections as a 'sublimated form of civil war' (1991: 181). In the post-Brexit context it seems the UK has split into two camps that have been at war since the EU referendum 2016. The reproduction of this in the tumultuous Brexit-driven intra Conservative Party dynamics between the Leave (Eurosceptic) and Remain (Europhile) factions has been no exception (Ridge-Newman 2018a, b). However, the outcome of the 2017 election seems to have been most impacted by the Conservative's lacklustre campaign. The focus on Theresa May as the apparent winner of the election represents an over-simplistic reading of the result and is also an example of how presidentialization can work its way into everyday contexts. One of the first problems with this kind of reductive representation of an election result is that Britain's parliamentary and party-based electoral system has traditionally denoted that it is the party, in this case the Conservatives, not the leader that ultimately wins or loses an election. However, with an observable trend towards personalization (Bennet 2012) and presidentialization (Poguntke and Webb 2015) in British politics, election campaigns and political parties are perhaps increasingly appearing that way.

Following the 2015 general election, the Conservative Party, branded by the leadership of David Cameron (Ridge-Newman and Mitchell 2016), made electoral advances that allowed the party to shake off the shackles of coalition government with the Liberal Democrats. 2015 saw the first clear Conservative majority since John Major's premiership in the 1990s. However, Theresa May's snap election resulted in the Conservatives losing a majority in Parliament. May attempted to cling onto power through forming a minority government, which, in keeping with the party's much derided 'strong and stable' campaign slogan, she claimed would offer 'certainty'. However, following the election, television news networks suggested the opposite was the case in reporting that financial indicators had reacted negatively to the 'uncertainty' of a minority Tory administration in negotiations with Northern Ireland's controversial Democratic Unionist Party (DUP) (Bloomberg 2017). The subsequent partnership demonstrated its precarious stability during later Brexit negotiations (Ridge-Newman 2018a). Furthermore, TV news largely framed the outcome of the election around notions of crisis and uncertainty (Sky News 2017); and May's role in the Conservative Party and EU Brexit negotiations as significantly weakened (EuroNews 2017).

Prior to the election, Jeremy Corbyn's leadership of the Labour Party had been ridiculed across public discourse, largely in the press and, in contrast, Theresa May had been riding high on largely positive coverage and polls. One month before election day, the Tories achieved a 22-point lead ahead of Labour, according to an ICM poll (Tapsfield 2017). Within the next three weeks, the Conservative lead would diminish dramatically (Helm and Savage 2017). One week before the election, an article in *The Times* newspaper reported a noticeable switch in the party's strategy. It noted that the party's campaign rhetoric and communications began to place the Conservative Party in the foreground and Theresa May less so (Fisher 2017a). This suggests a transition from a more presidentialized campaign model, focused on the leader, as was the case with David Cameron in the 2010 (Ridge-Newman 2014) and 2015 elections (Ridge-Newman and Mitchell 2016), to a more traditional party-focused campaign in order to limit the damage done by Theresa May's rapidly declining popularity. Another example of the party's selective approach to the use of a presidentialized campaign model was in arenas in which the absence of the Conservative Party leader was highly salient. For example, the Home Secretary Amber Rudd was the only non-leader representing a UK wide party in the BBC's 2017 election leaders debate (BBC 2017b).

The significant gap between Theresa May's perceived popularity prior to the election and the Conservatives poor electoral performance begs the key question relating to the Conservatives' 2017 campaign: what happened? How did the Conservatives transition from a period of stability to an unstable governing position? The obvious and popular answer is that Theresa May's campaign style and approach were uninspiring and inadequate. May herself confessed to being a poor campaigner and took the unprecedented decision to apologise explicitly, admitting the campaign was too presidential (Buchan 2017). The campaign is also thought to have been constructed by Theresa May and the Conservative Party upon poor advisory counsel at the core of Theresa May's team. Conflicted sentiments from within the Conservative Party in the run-up to the impending Tory electoral shock can be summed up in the following ConservativeHome editorial: 'The Tory campaign has been forced off-track. It began with a core offer of "strong and stable government". The social care fiasco brought that claim into disrepute' (Tory Diary 2017).

The calling of a snap election nods to an element of hubris on behalf of those advising Theresa May. Perhaps driven by not wanting to repeat Gordon Brown's approach prior to the 2010 general election in which he delayed calling an election and was forced to fight the campaign when his approval rating was much lower. That said, May's post-Brexit premiership has operated under different and somewhat extraordinary rules of the political game (Ridge-Newman 2018a).

The loss of a majority was a colossal embarrassment and disaster for the Conservative Party, particularly because it significantly weakened the party's governing position and negotiating strength in relation to Brexit. These considerations were also mixed with the unfavourable intra party dynamics in which the Leave versus Remain wings within the party were poised for a Conservative civil war (Ridge-Newman 2018b). Furthermore, the snap election was accompanied by a sense in the country and the wider party that a general election amid important Brexit negotiations was unnecessary and perhaps even unhelpful. Given repeated major electoral events following the general election in 2010 (cumulatively these were the 2011 alternative vote referendum; 2014 European Parliament election and Scottish independence referendum; 2015 general election; and 2016 European Union referendum) the prominence and importance of the 2017 election was accompanied by a degree of election fatigue from some and annoyance across the Conservative rank and file. It served to fuel tensions in the party and weaken the hand of Theresa May and her Government in terms of Brexit negotiations with the European Union and, consequently, the UK parliaments and devolved assemblies.

Deeper analysis of the election demonstrates just how complex British elections have become, especially in the post-EU Referendum context. It is on this basis that the analysis of the Conservative Party's 2017 election campaign effort should be understood. A key question for further study should be, given the party's history for unceremoniously disposing of supposedly toxic or ineffectual leaders, would Theresa May have survived as leader of the party with such longevity in a similar electoral scenario outside of a Brexit context? Given the analysis below, which represents aspects of the immediate aftermath of the 2017 election result, it seems the answer is likely to be no. Indeed, immediately following the election, ConservativeHome issued a survey with a clear question that asked whether Theresa May should resign (ConservativeHome 2017a). Two days later, the blog's editor Paul Goodman reported that many Conservative MPs believed Theresa May should make way for another leader prior to the next election and ConservativeHome agreed (Goodman 2017a). The same day, Nick Timothy and Fiona Hill, May's joint chiefs of staff, resigned, the public announcement of which was made via the ConservativeHome blog (Timothy 2017). Yet with the backdrop of Brexit, May has ridden some political highs and significant lows in a precariously fragile electoral framework to maintain her place as the Brexit premier longer than many of her most ardent of supporters could have predicted. It demonstrates the political peculiarity that has been injected to the heart of British politics since the European Union Referendum of 2016.

Two weeks after the election, Goodman's analysis (2017b) had turned its focus from Theresa May's leadership and condemnation of the party's manifesto to criticisms of the party's campaigning mechanisms. In the same post, ConservativeHome compared the election results of the last three general elections in which the Tories held: (a) 306 seats and 36% vote share in 2010; (b) 330 seats and 37% vote share in 2015; (c) 317 seats and 42% vote share in 2017. It, therefore, suggested that Theresa May and the party's manifesto achieved significantly higher overall approval among voters in the 2017 election than the party achieved under David Cameron in the previous two elections. The blog post recognises that the Conservative lead in the polls declined following the launch of the party manifesto, with blame placed on its social care 'debacle' otherwise known as the 'dementia tax' (Asthana and Elgot 2017). However, given that the increased vote share resulted in far fewer seats in 2017, ConservativeHome began to place blame on the Conservatives' campaign organization, strategy, and, in particular, its approach to targeting voters in key marginal seats. For example, the post cites data from a Lord Ashcroft poll suggesting that Labour attracted the 18–34-year olds, women and 2016 EU referendum Remainer voting groups. It seems blame for the outcome of the election began to shift towards Conservative Campaign Headquarters (CCHQ) for having not led a tighter target seat strategy. In June 2017, ConservativeHome published further evidence of this in a series of testimonies from campaign participants with one provocative piece entitled: 'How good Tory candidates in Wales were betrayed by a dire central campaign' (Baines 2017). Others feature below in some more in-depth analyses of key elements in the 2017 Tory campaign.

THE TORY CENTRAL MESSAGE

During the Conservatives' 2017 general election campaign, the central message of 'strong and stable' leadership was repeated incessantly. Like brand Cameron in 2010, the Conservative Party strategy centred on Theresa May as the primary brand, with her face and name featuring on most party communication. Ultimately, in addition to a number of political communication blunders, this proved to be a significant miscalculation. In the first few hours and days following the indecisive election result, May's so-called strong and stable leadership looked like metaphorical rhetoric as she was described 'weak and wobbly'; 'robotic'; the 'zombie prime minister'; and a 'dead woman walking' (Ridge-Newman 2017). Evidence from a ConservativeHome post suggests that the Conservative campaign was being viewed as 'repetitive', 'dull', 'robotic', more tightly 'stage managed' and avoidant of potentially hostile journalism than usual—and thus a lacklustre and highly centralised campaign—as early as 10 May 2017 (Goodman 2017c). The post suggests that CCHQ press officers questioned journalists about their intended questions for Theresa May and that, unlike David Cameron who liked playing the media game, she found media engagement highly challenging.

In contrast to the approach of Cameron, May is thought to have relied on a small number of advisers. It, therefore, begs the question how well the advisers understood May's campaigning skills. The presidential strategy was suited to the media savvy Cameron. However, the apparent direct transfer of that approach to May was evidently a poor fit for someone who has a lack of aptitude and/or inclination to engage robustly and confidently within the hybrid media environment (Chadwick 2017).

Theresa May's high-profile appearance with husband Philip on the One Show (BBC One 2017a) gained mostly negative comments on the programme's Twitter posts about the episode (One Show 2017). It revealed how she was less comfortable in more intimate media settings and yet performed relatively confidently when challenged in the more familiar Dispatch Box style format of the Question Time election programme (BBC One 2017b). Given the lack of consistency vis-à-vis the leaders debates, May's role in the campaign was demonstrating inconsistent messages. One moment she appeared to be a presidential figure and the next moment a shrinking violet. Voters heard and read May's repetitive rhetorical strong and stable mantra yet witnessed simultaneously an unravelling of the campaign through inconsistent and poorly executed campaign strategy and organization. May's performances in front of the camera did not project the image her close-knit and centralised team aimed to portray.

LEADER'S BRAND AND CREDIBILITY IN 2017

Theresa May, the second woman to lead the Conservative Party and country, underwent inevitable media comparisons to the first, Margaret Thatcher. In a political marketing sense, the 'strong and stable' message was well suited to building a Thatcher-like, 'Iron Lady', personal brand. However, to gain traction in the wider populace, the product, in this case Theresa May, had to some extent live up to the image being created. This can be thought of as brand credibility, which has a close relationship to trustworthiness (Seiler and Kucza 2017). Steve Hilton, David Cameron's former director of strategy, appeared on Fox News stating the election was meant to be the 'Brexit election', but instead it became a referendum on May's ability to lead (Fox News 2017). It appears trust in May's premiership became a widely questioned, something Thatcher largely avoided until the end of her long and formidable premiership. Unlike Thatcher, the strength of May's leadership came into question early on and during her first electoral test as leader of the party. May's awkward U-turns on policy and manifesto commitments, like the 'Dementia Tax', is not reminiscent of the Iron Lady, or, indeed, 'strong and stable' leadership. Furthermore, in terms of credibility, May's apparent ineptitude in communicating convincingly via Twenty-First Century media was perhaps more important to the overall campaign narrative. It became a theme of media analysis and critique. For example, Michael Crick broadcast an entire feature questioning the Conservative's overly cautious media management, which, like the calling of the snap election, ultimately seems to have backfired (Channel 4 News 2017).

Engagement, credibility and trust can be closely related factors in this interactive digital age (Westerman et al. 2014), which, for the Conservatives, has been poorly understood and in decline since the party's early advances in engagement online in the 2010 election (Ridge-Newman 2014; Ridge-Newman and Mitchell 2016). In keeping with this theme, May's credibility as a strong and stable leader took a nosedive when media headlines and narratives became dominated by the Prime Minister's refusal to take part in any televised debates. May's notable absence left a silence that spoke volumes. In contrast to and at odds with an image of a strong and stable premier, May inadvertently communicated to the electorate that, in actuality, she was much more timid, unconfident and weak than she wanted voters to believe. Therefore, from the outset, the central campaign message became an oxymoron that could be flipped to 'weak and wobbly' rhetoric by opponents of the Conservative Party to undermine the Prime Minister's credibility (Ridge-Newman 2017). Furthermore, the overuse and repetitiveness of the phrase 'strong and stable' morphed into anti-Tory media witticism both on- and off- line, which appears to have spread virally via anti-Conservative citizen-initiated campaigning uses of social media (Gibson 2015).

Digital Campaigning in 2017

Anti-Conservative citizen-initiative campaigning seems to have played a significant role in the 2017 campaign insofar as, in this politically charged post-Brexit context, many personal social media pages that might have otherwise remained personal in an election period sprung into political action. Early indications suggest this was largely due to younger sections of the electorate, large numbers of whom were thought to have become more politically active having been inspired by Jeremy Corbyn (Ridge-Newman 2017). It appears that mass online support from Momentum, a left-wing political organization, played a significant role. This did not escape the attention of political commentators, some of whom suggested in this election social media activity replaced the role of the popular tabloid press in shaping the political mood (BBC Radio 4 2017). *The Times* acknowledged the role of Momentum and its use of social media to mobilise the youth vote in support of Corbyn (Fisher 2017b).

Since 2017, some key individuals within the Conservative hierarchy have recognised that the party has neglected areas of strategy and organization to the point that it might struggle to compete with Labour's new Momentum contingent in the future. In 2010, a strong Conservative youth wing was developing and the party began leading the way in terms of grassroots digital campaign innovations with citizen-initiated uses of Facebook helping to encourage mass youth activism on rallies and campaigns (Ridge-Newman 2014). However, by 2015, the party began centralizing and controlling its digital campaign operations to the point at which large swathes of earlier online initiatives and engagement from the youth ranks in the party seemed evermore redundant (Ridge-Newman and Mitchell 2016). The party's move towards digital centralization post-2010 together with the tightly controlled nature of the Tories 2017 campaign, which eschewed relationship building online seemed to create an uninspiring environment for younger Conservatives (Ridge-Newman and Mitchell 2016). As a result, Tory self-initiated activity this time was more muted than in 2010. In contrast, Corbyn inspired an online flurry of anti-Conservative activity that was more archetypally characteristic of the digital era in which the campaign was taking place; this effort helped to develop more trust for Labour's leadership than would have been thought possible before the 2017 election was called (Westerman et al. 2014). In comparison to David Cameron's innovative use of the interactive platforms of *WebCameron* and *Ask David* (Ridge-Newman 2014), Theresa May's leadership became reminiscent of that of the analogue political style of Gordon Brown and his awkward uses of YouTube during the run-up to the 2010 election (Klotz 2014).

The Conservatives' stilted 2017 style of campaigning online was also perhaps representative of the wider offline campaign. Compared to Corbyn's energetic and well attended rallies, May's events were reportedly tightly controlled and devoid of engaging with people (McFall 2017). The Conservatives' approach to trying to control the uncontrollable—specifically internet activity—appears to have peaked in 2017, when compared to the approaches taken in the 2010 and 2015 elections (Ridge-Newman 2014; Ridge-Newman and Mitchell 2016). In response to the realization the party was adventuring along a counter-cultural path, in its avoidance of digital engagement in 2017, the Conservatives relaunched its youth wing in March 2018, changing the name from 'Conservative Future' back to the 'Young Conservatives' (Yorke 2018), which was at its peak in the 1950s (Ridge-Newman 2016).

In 2015 and 2017, instead of encouraging Tory grassroots-initiated campaigning, the party's online operations were increasingly focused on Cambridge Analytica-style data-driven and highly centralised and targeted techniques (Ridge-Newman and Mitchell 2016). Questions about this type of campaigning had actually begun to be raised during the 2017 election campaign with an article in *The Times* reporting that 'parties may be breaking data laws to target voters' (Bridge et al. 2017). Following the eruption of the subsequent Facebook-Cambridge Analytica data story, the Tories' strategic digital rethink will undoubtedly involve a reassessment of where it should place its digital emphasis.

Politicians will be likely keen to ensure their uses of targeted data-driven strategies are developed using a transparent and ethically driven approach. Going forward it seems that all political parties would do well to invest in digital listening and engagement strategies (Crawford 2011), in which the then highly successful Scottish National Party were especially adept by 2015 (Ridge-Newman and Mitchell 2016). This approach avoids being over reliant on the one-way broadcast model of digital political marketing in which the key driver is to centrally control communication output (Gibson and Ward 2009).

INTRA PARTY CRITIQUE

The ConservativeHome blog has been described as a thorn in the side of the Conservative Party (Ridge-Newman 2014). Its prominence, autonomy and significant grassroots engagement allows it to support, criticise, lobby and steer the Conservatives in certain contexts. It provides a forum for both established and ordinary party participants to try and hold aspects of the party to account and drive transparency. The uninspiring 2017 Conservative election campaign was no exception. A week before election day, the blog published results of party members survey showing that the largest proportion of respondents gave a 5 out of 10 approval for the Conservative campaign. The blog's editor, Paul Goodman, argued that Theresa May's: (1) brand had been compromised; (2) campaign management appeared overly centralised; and (3) government focus was out of kilter with the wider party, because the wider party had not been duly consulted in the development of the 2017 manifesto (Goodman 2017d).

If members were frustrated with the party's electoral approach, influential opinion-formers expressed similar reservations. A month before the election, ConservativeHome executive editor Mark Wallace argued that the campaign was chaotic and overly centralised (Wallace 2017). For example, he suggests that candidate selection was less devolved to local Conservative associations than would ordinarily be the case. According to Wallace, the party had a candidate deficit. At short notice, there were too few candidates on the Conservative Party's List of Approved Candidates (known as the candidates list) willing to fight the election. It demonstrates the party's lack of preparation for a snap election and suggests May's close-knit team at Number 10 had not given much notice to CCHQ. Between 2010 and 2015, the party cut the candidate's list with a degree of brutality. CCHQ and the Candidates Team placed increasingly stringent practical demands on candidates that discriminated against those on the list who were not independently wealthy, able bodied, single, without childcare demands and/or able to cancel work commitments at short notice. It is suspected within the party that these measures were implemented as a management tactic to get candidates out campaigning. This was also evidence of a greater trend towards the centralization of party operation and an increasing professionalization at CCHQ (Ridge-Newman 2016). This was interpreted as something of a sinister trend by those within the organization in favour of greater internal Conservative party democracy (for example, see Stafford 2018). Wallace suggests that many candidates, former candidates and local associations were left feeling 'trampled', 'angry' and 'demoralised' (Wallace 2017). Far from an isolated view, this kind of criticism is shared by candidates, members and supporters who have frequently reported feeling used by a CCHQ that demonstrates its loyalties and gratitude to a small cohort favoured within the party ranks (Baines 2017).

One of the most compelling testimonies from the 2017 election published on ConservativeHome was by a grassroots activist, entitled: 'Teller's work wasted. Invaded privacy. Computers that spewed gibberish. How CCHQ bungled this election campaign' (McFall 2017). The activist Hamish McFall claimed that CCHQ, which he sarcastically describes as 'Big Brother', exhibited a lack of regard for how the voluntary party contributes to the local campaign—a consistent complaint of local volunteers since Cameron's ascendancy to the leadership in 2006. Some members complained that the party's continued heavy reliance on intrusive targeted telephone and literature-based campaigning might have actually irritated voters in 2017. This was, perhaps, related to the wider electoral fatigue that was evident within the Conservative Party. McFall also reported his concerns that the targeted canvass cards the party had been using since before the 2015 general election had become significantly longer and more detailed to the point they bordered on an invasion of voter privacy.

Hamish McFall is an example of a type of recalcitrant party participant who resists CCHQ's orders from on high and can now voice dissent through influential platforms like ConservativeHome. McFall further claimed that he defied the party instruction to local activists to refer to the local Conservative candidate as 'Theresa May's candidate' when canvassing on the doorstep, preferring to introduce his local representative as a Conservative instead. Actions like this signal a resistance within the Tory grassroots to the presidentialization trend in the Conservative Party. It is reminiscent of a phenomenon reported in some Tory constituency campaigns in 2010 whereby literature branded with David Cameron's face were considered by local activists to be less popular than those without (Ridge-Newman 2014). Generally, CCHQ seldom acknowledges the existence of this type of dissent. In contrast, via ConservativeHome, activists like McFall regularly identify areas in which CCHQ could improve campaign operations and the management of party activists. McFall suggests that CCHQ should better explain its requests to party volunteers—thereby respecting them as activists and candidates—not by simply giving orders, but through offering the rationales behind the requested tasks. Testimony of this kind is in keeping with accusations that CCHQ has been involved in a power grab. However, it seems the central organization's disregard for the voluntary party has led to a decline in the party's effectiveness and morale. The consequences of loyal activists feeling disenfranchised reinforces the membership's isolation from the party hierarchy, something that is unlikely to be improved if the primary relationship revolves around the central organization trying to control a voluntary base.

The resultant outcome of May's seemingly weak and wobbly leadership, three days after the election, is perhaps best summed up in a comment published by the influential Tory blog ConservativeHome stating: 'Conservative MPs do not believe that May can lead them into the next election. Nor, reluctantly, do we' (Goodman 2017a). The post-Brexit context is arguably the reason that Theresa May has maintained her premiership (Ridge-Newman 2018a). The awkward post-EU Referendum has led to a form of stasis in the party in which May's continuing premiership is the best solution to an unfavourable situation given her position between the rival Conservative Leave and Remain factions.

Conclusions

The Conservative Party's primary mistake was to risk its majority by calling a snap election in 2017. In the post-Brexit context, the party and its leader would have offered the UK greater strength, stability and leadership by seeking to maintain some sense of continuity until the Brexit negotiations had concluded. If this was the first error, the party's second mistake was to retain the kind of presidential model of campaigning so central to the party's 2010 and 2015 election strategies under David Cameron (Langer 2011). Theresa May's comparatively unknown and underdeveloped campaign skills were misjudged by key party strategists. Temporary popularity was mistaken for the ability to connect with the UK electorate, resulting in an incongruous campaign emphasis on the party leader. CCHQ's apparent contempt for party volunteers and its lack of relationship building strategies seemingly contributed to a decline in wider party engagement. This is counterproductive when competing with growing citizen-initiated campaigning in other parties (Gibson 2015).

The digital age and its communication technologies are well suited to a decentralised model of political campaign engagement that shares authority within a more party-focused campaign. Ironically, it was Jeremy Corbyn and Momentum that brought this to the attention of the Conservatives. Momentum's 2017 digital activity has catalysed a Tory rethink about how the party's organization can compete with such phenomena in the digital age. In the post-Brexit context, such discussions still remain relatively low down as priorities on the party's agenda. Sun Tzu's 'Art of War' famously advises never to underestimate your opponent. If the Conservatives' unpreparedness in terms of policies, presentation and communication of message is anything to go by, it seems the party underestimated its opponent in Jeremy Corbyn while overestimating Theresa May's strength as a leader (Ridge-Newman 2017). This was particularly embarrassing given the snap election was designed to exploit a considerable strategic advantage in terms of its timing and the element of surprise in calling it. Yet the initiative was lost when the plan backfired. It proved to be the party's third major error.

The Conservatives, and other parties behind the curve, would benefit from developing a deeper understanding of the fast-evolving political communication environment and hybrid media system in which they now operate (Chadwick 2017). Highly controlled and centralized campaigns like Theresa May's awkward and analogue performance in 2017 can create an anachronistic atmosphere, which discourages democratic interactivity on- and off- line, thereby undermining public credibility and trust (Seiler and Kucza 2017). The Conservative Party seems out of sync with recent technocultural trends that require the party to trust and empower its own increasingly disenfranchised membership and redevelop the type of campaign engagement environment that developed naturally at its grassroots in 2010 (Ridge-Newman 2014). Campaigns are likely to become increasingly real-time and digital: and fluid campaign strategies that embrace interactivity and relationship building will likely be increasingly significant to campaign successes in future general elections.

REFERENCES

Asthana, A., & Elgot, J. (2017, May 22). Theresa May ditches manifesto plan with "dementia tax" U-turn. *The Guardian*. https://www.theguardian.com/. Accessed May 31, 2018.

Baines, G. (2017, June 16). How good Tory candidates in Wales were betrayed by a dire central campaign. *ConservativeHome*. https://www.conservativehome.com/. Accessed June 1, 2018.

BBC. (2017a). Election results. *BBC News*. http://www.bbc.co.uk/news/election/. Accessed May 31, 2018.

BBC. (2017b, June 1). BBC debate: Rivals attack Theresa May over absence. *BBC News*. http://www.bbc.co.uk/news/election-2017-40105324. Accessed May 31, 2018.

BBC One. (2017a, May 9). *The one show*. https://www.bbc.co.uk/programmes/b08pl018. Accessed May 31, 2018.

BBC One. (2017b, June 3). *Corbyn vs May: Question time special, 2017 UK general election*. https://www.youtube.com/watch?v=QoJxzvMLsmo. Accessed May 31, 2018.

BBC Radio 4. (2017). *BBC Radio 4* broadcast, c. 8 June.

Bennett, W. L. (2012). The personalization of politics and political identity, social media, and changing patterns of participation. *The ANNALS of the American Academy of Political and Social Science, 644*(1), 20–39.

Bloomberg. (2017). *Bloomberg* TV news broadcast, c. 10 June.

Bourdieu, P. (1991). *Language and symbolic power* (J. B. Thompson, Ed.). Cambridge: Polity Press.

Bridge, M., Gibbons, K., & Zeffman, H. (2017, June 1). Parties may be breaking data laws to target voters. *The Times*. https://www.thetimes.co.uk/. Accessed June 1, 2018.

Buchan, L. (2017, October 4). Theresa May apologises for disappointing election campaign during Tory conference speech. *The Independent*. https://www.independent.co.uk/. Accessed June 2, 2018.

Chadwick, A. (2017). *The hybrid media system: Politics and power*. New York: Oxford University Press.

Channel 4 News. (2017). Michael Crick election report. *Channel 4 News*, c. 1 June.

ConservativeHome. (2017a, June 9). ConHome snap survey. Should the prime minister stay or go? *ConservativeHome.* http://www.conservativehome. com/. Accessed June 1, 2018.

Crawford, K. (2011). Listening, not lurking: The neglected form of participation. In H. Grief, L. Hjorth, & A. Lasén (Eds.), *Cultures of participation* (pp. 63–74). Berlin: Peter Lang.

EuroNews. (2017, June 9). UK election: What will a hung parliament mean for Brexit. *EuroNews.* http://www.euronews.com/2017/06/09/. Accessed May 31, 2018.

Fisher, L. (2017a, May 31). Enough about Theresa May—Let's talk about the Tories instead. *The Times.* https://www.thetimes.co.uk/. Accessed June 1, 2018.

Fisher, L. (2017b, June 2). Momentum runs clever campaign to get out the youth vote for Corbyn. *The Times.* https://www.thetimes.co.uk/. Accessed June 1, 2018.

Foley, M. (2000). *The British presidency.* Manchester: Manchester University Press.

Fox News. (2017). Steve Hilton interview. *Fox News* TV broadcast, c. 9 June.

Gibson, R. K. (2015). Party change, social media and the rise of "citizen-initiated" campaigning. *Party Politics, 21*(2), 183–197.

Gibson, R., & Ward, S. (2009). Parties in the digital age a review article. *Representation, 45*(1), 87–100.

Goodman, P. (2017a, June 11). Conservative MPs do not believe that May can lead them into the next election. Nor, reluctantly, do we. *ConservativeHome.* http://www.conservativehome.com/. Accessed June 15, 2017.

Goodman, P. (2017b, June 22). The crucial difference between a non-win this month and the win in 2015 was the failure of the Tory machine. *ConservativeHome.* http://www.conservativehome.com/. Accessed June 1, 2018.

Goodman, P. (2017c, May 10). No, this is not "the most controlled election campaign ever". But it is, perhaps, the most dull. *ConservativeHome.* http:// www.conservativehome.com/. Accessed June 1, 2018.

Goodman, P. (2017d, June 1). Our survey. The Conservative election campaign fails to enthuse party members. *ConservativeHome.* http://www.conservative-home.com/. Accessed May 31, 2018.

Helm, T., & Savage, M. (2017, May 27). Tory nerves fray as Jeremy Corbyn narrows Theresa May's lead in new poll. *The Observer.* https://www.the-guardian.com/. Accessed May 31, 2018.

Holtz-Bacha, C., Langer, A. I., & Merkle, S. (2014). The personalization of politics in comparative perspective: Campaign coverage in Germany and the United Kingdom. *European Journal of Communication, 29*(2), 153–170.

Karvonen, L. (2009). *The personalization of politics: A study of parliamentary democracies*. Colchester: ECPR Press.

Klotz, R. (2014). Sources and formats of campaign information on YouTube. In A. M. G. Solo (Ed.), *Political campaigning in the information age*. Hersey: IGI Global.

Langer, A. I. (2011). *The personalization of politics in the UK: Mediated leadership from Attlee to Cameron*. Manchester: Manchester University Press.

McFall, H. (2017, June 16). Tellers' work wasted. Invaded privacy. Computers that spewed gibberish. How CCHQ bungled this election campaign. *ConservativeHome*. http://www.conservativehome.com/. Accessed May 31, 2018.

One Show. (2017, May 9). Theresa May's [love] of [shoes] has inspired others to get into politics. *@BBCTheOneShow*. https://twitter.com/bbctheoneshow/. Accessed June 1, 2018.

Poguntke, T., & Webb, P. (Eds.). (2005). *The presidentialization of politics: A comparative study of modern democracies*. Oxford: Oxford University Press.

Poguntke, T., & Webb, P. (2015). Presidentialization and the politics of coalition: Lessons from Germany and Britain. *Italian Political Science Review/Rivista Italiana di Scienza Politica, 45*(3), 249–275.

Ridge-Newman, A. (2014). *Cameron's conservatives and the internet: Change, culture and Cyber Toryism*. Basingstoke: Palgrave Macmillan.

Ridge-Newman, A. (2016). *The Tories and television, 1951–1964: Broadcasting an elite*. London: Palgrave Macmillan.

Ridge-Newman, A. (2017). "Strong and stable" to "weak and wobbly": Tory campaign, media reaction and GE2017. In E. Thorsen, D. Jackson, & D. Lilleker (Eds.), *UK election analysis 2017: Media, voters and the campaign*. CSJCC: Bournemouth University.

Ridge-Newman, A. (2018a). The Conservative Party: Past, present and future. *Political Insight, 9*(1), 30–33.

Ridge-Newman, A. (2018b). Preface. In A. Ridge-Newman, F. Leon-Solis, & H. O'Donnell (Eds.), *Reporting the road to Brexit: International media and the EU referendum 2016*. London: Palgrave Macmillan.

Ridge-Newman, A., & Mitchell, M. (2016). Digital political marketing. In D. G. Lilleker & M. Pack (Eds.), *Political marketing and the 2015 UK general election* (pp. 99–116). London: Palgrave Macmillan.

Seiler, R., & Kucza, G. (2017). Source credibility model, source attractiveness model and match-up-hypothesis—An integrated model. *Economy and Business Journal, 11*(1), 1–15.

Sky News. (2017, June 9). *Sky News* TV.

Stafford, J. (2018). *Campaign for Conservative democracy blog*. http://copov.blogspot.com/. Accessed June 1, 2018.

Tapsfield, J. (2017, May 8). Tories open up RECORD 22 point lead over Labour in election poll after PM's assault on "meddling" Eurocrats. *Daily Mail.* http://www.dailymail.co.uk. Accessed May 31, 2018.

Timothy, N. (2017, June 10). Why I have resigned as the prime minister's adviser. *ConservativeHome.* http://www.conservativehome.com/. Accessed June 1, 2018.

Tory Diary. (2017, June 3). In these last few campaigning days, May must spell out what the choice means for your wallet, purse and savings. *ConservativeHome.* http://www.conservativehome.com/thetorydiary/2017/. Accessed May 31, 2018.

Wallace, M. (2017, May 9). Centralization and chaos—Inside the rush to select Conservative candidates in time for the election. *ConservativeHome.* http://www.conservativehome.com/. Accessed May 31, 2018.

Westerman, D., Spence, P. R., & van der Heide, B. (2014). Social media as information source: Recency of updates and credibility of information. *Journal of Computer-Mediated Communication, 19*(2), 171–183.

Yorke, H. (2018, March 16). Conservative youth wing relaunched in bid to win back millennials from Labour. *The Telegraph.* https://www.telegraph.co.uk/politics/. Accessed June 1, 2018.

The Labour Campaign

Greg Cook

The electoral cycle, rather like the economic one, is easier to recognize in hindsight than to understand or explain. There is and was no doubt however that, when she stood in Downing Street on April 18, 2017 to announce that a general election would be held on June 8, Theresa May was breaking it. Just two years into a parliament and with a working majority of MPs, there was no real precedent for a government putting itself at such unnecessary risk.

Of course the two years leading up to the announcement had been a traumatic and unprecedented prelude with the country split down the middle by a referendum, choosing against expectations to leave the European Union, and the Prime Minister who had triumphed at the polls in 2015 similarly against expectations being the first casualty of that choice. To add to the drama, Labour had twice elected Jeremy Corbyn as its leader despite his lack of support in the Parliamentary Labour Party and their vote of no confidence in his leadership in the wake of the referendum.

There might have been genuine reasons why any government in those circumstances might have sought a fresh mandate, but no one seriously believed this to be anything other than electoral opportunism.

G. Cook (✉)
Labour Party, London, UK
e-mail: greg_cook@labour.org.uk

© The Author(s) 2019
D. Wring et al. (eds.), *Political Communication in Britain*,
https://doi.org/10.1007/978-3-030-00822-2_10

In the Labour Party there had long been an expectation among some that May would be unable to resist the lure of an early election. In part this flowed from the natural assumption that any Prime Minister would want the personal endorsement of the electorate rather than wish to rely on a predecessor's legacy. In the main it was a recognition that Tory prospects might never be better.

By April 2017 the Conservatives' lead in the opinion polls averaged more than 20 percentage points. May's advantage as preferred Prime Minister was more than 25 points. Those polls indicated that barely more than half of Labour's 2015 voters were committed to voting Labour again. Following the EU Referendum result, support for UKIP in the opinion polls had roughly halved with the clear benefit to the Tories which it had always been assumed would be the result of their demise.

Not only was the polling picture bleak for Labour. Real elections were validating the story the polls told. In February, the Tories achieved the almost unheard of feat of gaining a seat from the main opposition as a government party which even Labour under Tony Blair had not managed during the extended honeymoon period which followed the 1997 election. The seemingly iron law of the electoral cycle that government parties will lose support in the mid-term was overturned as they gained the Copeland seat which although marginal had never previously been won by the Tories, and they did so without the assistance of an increase in Lib Dem or UKIP support. On the same day Labour held the Stoke-on-Trent Central constituency by just 2620 votes over UKIP.

Whatever the protestations of Mrs. May that she had no intention of cashing in on her popularity, the sceptics believed that naked political advantage would be hard to resist. Indeed, it might be reckless if she did not. The folklore persisted among many in Labour that had Gordon Brown called the election in October 2007 he would have won it and transformed his premiership (a belief that is probably less widely held now).

It did mean that some preparation had been done for a snap general election. Analysis had been prepared of potential key seats and the types of voters who would decide them. Practicalities like templates for leaflets and direct mail, email and Facebook advertising and the selections of voters that might receive them were prepared. Much of this of was simply updating the processes that had been painstakingly put in place prior to the 2015 election and whose successes and failures had been pored

over since, but many in the party had also been involved in the two leadership elections which Labour had held since that election in which new
techniques, particularly for communicating with young voters, had been
widely applied. The greatest transformation of all since 2015 was that
Labour had over half a million members, by far the largest number of
any party, many of whom were seasoned activists and enthusiastic supporters of Labour's new political prospectus.

The strategic mismatch at the heart of those preparations however was
that Labour was behind in the polls and any election would be likely to
result in a swing to the Tories and the loss of seats. The task, if the polls
were to be taken seriously, would be to ensure that Labour did not lose
seats in an early election, not preparing for government. A strategy to
gain seats from a position of 25% in the polls would lack credibility, but
were there not to be an early election there was plenty of time for the
polls to change.

So by April 18 there were rudimentary structures and processes in
place, to a great extent replicating those used in 2015, when Mrs. May
called that early election. There were though some hurdles to be overcome. One was money, particularly for a campaign that would last seven
weeks. Another was a lack of candidates. None had been selected in any
non-Labour seat, partly in the expectation of a boundary review being
implemented. That meant that over 400 candidates had to be put in
place over a period of a couple of weeks, the vast majority in seats which
no one at the time thought Labour had any serious prospect of winning.

One unique feature of the 2017 General Election campaign was that
it incorporated a set of May local elections, this particular cycle being
in the shire counties of England plus the whole of Scotland and Wales.
The opportunity for electors to have a dry run at voting in the middle
of a general election felt very odd, but the results did provide a wealth
of information on the mood of the electorate which turned out to be
much as the polls had suggested. The Projected National Vote Share
placed the Conservatives on 39% to Labour's 28%, which translated into
a general election equivalent would certainly have implied a Tory lead
of about 20 points. The results were so poor that had they stood alone
they might paradoxically have attracted more attention than they in fact
received. For a government two years into its term and a year after having ignominiously lost its leader to be ahead by any margin was extraordinary. The only example of any government winning the comparable
set of local elections was Labour in 1999 when the projected lead was

two percentage points and the contemporary lead in the opinion polls 15 points. Labour's net loss of seats in England and Wales was 378, and in England Labour's sole council win was in Durham County, with losses in Derbyshire and Nottinghamshire and a failure to gain in key authorities such as Lancashire and Northumberland. In Scotland, Labour again lost all its councils and fell into third place behind the Tories in votes. In the Tees Valley and the West Midlands, Tory metro-mayors were elected.

A strong argument could be made that these were Labour's worst set of local elections ever, certainly when in opposition. The share of the vote was below even that in Labour's local elections nadir (in opposition) in 1982 and in this case it was a period when minor parties were also weak. Even allowing for the much lower turnout and the concentration of these contests in Labour's weakest areas in England, they showed that the opinion polls were right. The collapse of the Tory lead which occurred between those local elections and the General Election in June can only have been the result of real changes in the electorate and its view of the parties.

In recent elections, manifestos have rarely been regarded as significant in themselves. While some academics continue to analyse their contents and relate their political positioning to electoral opinion, their chief function has been as the platform for the major broadcasters to present their balanced explanation of policies that have mostly been rehearsed over many months and years. In 2017 however many believe that they transformed the election.

Labour's manifesto had a seemingly inauspicious outing when it was leaked, almost a week in advance of its formal publication. While the process story that this generated was one of apparent incompetence, much of the coverage was of the content, and it also appeared to make little or no difference to the real analysis by the broadcasters and mainstream media when it was formally published a week later. So in effect Labour had two bites at the cherry, and the radicalism of many of the policies within it grabbed the attention and perhaps handed Labour the initiative in the campaign.

The reputation of the Labour manifesto, at the time and in hindsight, was undoubtedly boosted by the fiasco of the Tories' and the u-turn on their proposals for social care funding. Apart from the flaws in the policy itself the so-called "dementia tax" gained prominence partly because of the lack of pretty much anything else of interest within the Tory prospectus. Amazingly, the Tories even failed to cost their pledges which had the effect of enhancing the credibility of Labour's costing of its own manifesto, which many pundits and journalists had anticipated might itself prove fatal to Labour's prospects. Instead the fact that Labour had made the effort and the Tories hadn't neutered any possibility that they might lay a glove on the financial implications of Labour's proposals.

Tory candidates, and indeed those of all parties, duly reported back the backlash on the doorstep from the social care proposals, leading to May's modifying the policy, but some of us remain sceptical of the true significance of the policy itself and its supposed unpopularity. The evidence for it is almost wholly anecdotal, a source which in other respects became largely discredited as a result of this election. The idea that the dementia tax itself was the main reason why the Tory lead began to fall does not really stand up to scrutiny. As a theory it depends largely upon the notion that votes are won and lost in significant numbers by rational assessment of the pocket-book implications of different proposals which if it were true would lead to wildly erratic electoral trends. In any case, there was nothing in the polls to suggest that any particular group affected was behaving in any way differently before and after the policy was announced. The Tory share in the polls was barely affected, the change was the rise in Labour's. The group who were supposedly most sensitive to the issue, those over the age of 50, ended up voting disproportionately more Tory than they had ever done before according to Ipsos MORI.

Where the Tory manifesto and the dementia tax were really potent was in the intangible concept of campaign momentum. The whole episode transformed the perspective of the election by exposing Tory incompetence, lack of preparedness and weakness, which must have impinged upon May's personal reputation. Already in focus groups the "strong and stable government" mantra, which started out as at worst an inoffensive slogan, was being gently ridiculed because of the style of robotic repetition with which it was being conveyed. After the manifesto launch, the suspicion hardened that the mantra was covering a vacuum of purpose and thus feeding the idea that the whole election might be self-serving and indeed frivolous.

This may have added to the damage done by May's failure to engage properly in the process of the election, and in particular her shying away from televised debates. A leader with a clear message in an election that is both serious and necessary, like David Cameron in 2015, could afford to pose as standing above them. A leader who has called an election out of cycle unnecessarily and is being seen as lacking any serious offer risks seeming weak and taking the electorate for granted. Add to that the generally low expectations of Jeremy Corbyn and the potential for sympathy for a "plucky underdog" to take hold becomes real. The benefit of a wealth of genuinely radical policy propositions enabled him to take the initiative in TV interviews and debates, shift the momentum further and to become the story of the election.

One benefit of this momentum shift was organizational. Labour's half a million members provided a body of local activists way beyond that of any party in any recent election, many of them young and enthused by Jeremy and the manifesto. In terms of the campaign, the pictures on TV showed Corbyn addressing crowds of thousands at open air rallies, his bus being swamped by supporters on the streets. All of this was a breath of fresh air to all those who yearned for a style of politics which was not hamstrung by stage-managed set piece visits and interviews. This election saw the role of digital media, Facebook advertising and online fundraising making a difference as never before in promoting a message and building a political bandwagon.

One other advantage which assisted this process was that, from a position of 25% in the polls at the start of the campaign, literally the only way was up. While the normal mid-term cycles of party popularity were being reversed as the government extended its lead over the opposition, the calling of the election unexpectedly meant that there was structural adjustment to be played out in the partisan balance. Some of those previous Labour supporters who had been undecided were actually unlikely ever to vote for another party, and Labour's true starting point was probably nearer 30%. From mid-May however some polls began to show Labour's share increasing from its 2015 baseline.

The 2017 election may be remembered, like its predecessor, as one where the polls were wrong. In fact in both the truth is rather more nuanced. It was the polls that shifted the perception of the election. The near-unanimity of most candidates, journalists and indeed the electorate as to the outcome of the election was only cracked because the polls appeared to be moving. A YouGov poll published in the *Sunday Times* on 21 May showed Labour on 35%, its highest of the campaign, and the Tory lead down to just nine percentage points. It was accompanied by an article by YouGov's Chris Curtis which carefully explained the source of Labour's new support particularly among previous Greens and non-voters and its reliance on those with a patchy record of actually voting. It rightly drew attention to the uncertainty as to whether these people would materialise in the polling booths. Most pollsters seemed to be finding similar trends but some were more robust in sticking to the well-founded belief that actually the Tories' real lead would be enhanced by turnout differentials. Most of the predictive polls in the week of the election significantly under-estimated the Labour share but they had, over the period of the campaign, identified the trend.

The anecdotal reports from candidates of all parties, amplified by some in their anonymous briefings to journalists, suggested that Labour was likely to lose seats. The only issue was how many. The idea that any might be gained was regarded as fanciful. The shift in the polls did little to modify that received wisdom and it is fair to say that dozens of Labour candidates went to their counts convinced of the prospect of defeat and emerged from them with increased majorities. Not many anticipated a swing to Labour, almost none that the Tories' lead would be just two points.

Nevertheless, it is clear that the reports of large numbers of lifelong Labour voters claiming they were switching to the Tories were well founded. There is plenty of evidence that this was a real phenomenon, and Labour did indeed lose six seats to the Tories, most of which had remained Labour even in previous low points such as 1983. But the picture they painted was partial. The polls showed that the proportion of 2015 Labour voters switching to the Tories was never much above 10% through the campaign, and that is probably what it remained, itself a large number given that the 2015 support was largely a core vote. They were though outweighed across the country and in most constituencies by new supporters from many different sources. These including perhaps one in five 2015 UKIP voters, diminishing the Tories' advantage from their collapse, and most importantly many who had not voted in 2015 as turnout increased by four percentage points. The question is why none of this seems to have been detected.

One answer is that the angry voter who is withdrawing support is always more memorable and disturbing than the floating voter who is moving the other way, and voters with a grievance are also more likely to want to express it. If you are speaking to a Tory representative and want a reason to complain you are likely to raise some nationally contentious issue, like the dementia tax, even if your discontent is rather more generic and ill-defined. If these grievances fit into the narrative which appeared to have been established by the polls over at least a year beforehand, the news agenda or indeed your personal views, it is perfectly understandable that these tales from the doorstep are assumed to amount to the story of the election.

What the 2017 election exposed is the limitation of the vox pop. Even the most assiduous candidate can only speak to a tiny fraction of his or her constituents over the course of a campaign, themselves probably carefully selected. They are one aspect of the story, but they are not as they are sometimes assumed to be, the voice of authenticity, cutting through the anonymity of opinion polls.

It is probably true that these potential distortions were exaggerated in this election by the nature and source of the swing to Labour. It is arguable what precisely was the scale of the increase in turnout among young people and the contribution it made to Labour's increased vote, but it is not arguable that it was significant. The patterns of turnout increase and the swings which it produced make that obvious. It goes without saying that the makeup of Labour's new voters was much more complex and diverse than is explained simply by generational differentials, but they were real. Political parties' communications, of necessity as much as by choice, tend to be with those in older generations. They are more likely to answer a door, to have a landline and to answer it and to live in the same place for a long period of time. This means that they are much more likely to provide those vox pops and the trends in canvass returns which influence local organization and which head offices analyse.

Of course the sophistication of parties' databases and their efforts to identify key voters plays a part in those choices as well. Again, if you have never previously or recently voted, it is not unreasonable that parties regard you as a low priority for their communications and campaigning. That is not to say that those harder-to-reach voters were ignored. There has never been a time when motivating and communicating with young voters has not been a priority for the Labour Party which almost always has much more to gain from an increase in their turnout. It is simply that neither is easy to achieve. In 2017, and perhaps in the two major referendums on Scottish independence and the EU, the new digital technologies made a difference as never before, but it is worth remembering that turnout among under-30s remained resolutely below 60% according to the pollsters' estimates.

One particular aspect of the swing to Labour seems to have been turnout in areas with large numbers of BAME voters, which appears to have increased by more than the national aggregate. The Labour advantage among Muslims of Pakistani origin in particular exceeded its already high 2015 level, and indeed was responsible for a number of seat holds and gains. One can only speculate as to the possibility that this was partly affected by the issues arising from the terrorist outrages which took place during the campaign, but it does seem clear that the security issue was of minimal benefit to the Tories.

All of this meant that that the electoral landscape revealed by the result at least in England and Wales bore little resemblance to that at the start as confirmed by the local elections, apparently making a mockery of both main parties' key seats strategy. Labour held several seats which most had assumed would be lost and made gains, totemically winning the Canterbury constituency for the first time and achieving huge swings in most of London. The Tories failed to win or even to achieve positive swings in several seats which they had hoped to gain. Some claimed that the Labour strategy had been too conservative and that with more ambition and support for seats which were almost won the result might have been better. If you accept the premise that net organizational advantage contributes in any way towards differential swings then that is a truism. But to have offered more support to most Tory-held seats at the start of the campaign would have been whistling in the wind. It would have been legitimate, if bold, to concentrate organizational effort and resources exclusively in seats which needed to be gained in order to have a Labour government, but would obviously have risked being tokenistic and taking support away from Labour-held seats which were genuinely competitive thereby increasing Labour's losses. There was no evidence whatsoever that Labour might gain seats until the latter part of May, and even then it was tenuous. The swing towards Labour was clearly generated chiefly by the circumstances of the campaign and independently of the key seat strategy. In any case Labour lost seats, and would almost certainly have lost several more had they not been supported organizationally so the net benefits of a more ambitious strategy are unclear.

The shift in the polls did mean that some short-term prioritization, particularly for Get Out The Vote activity, was adjusted to assist seats where analysis of the pro-Labour trend meant that gains might be possible. In this respect YouGov's seat-by-seat analysis, which attempted to translate their polls into constituency-level results, was an interesting development in the campaign. However the model of a dynamic key seat strategy, moving money, message, people and materials between seats as the polls shift owes more to the rise of big data and micro-analysis than to actual campaigning practicality. In the 2017 campaign it would have meant constant adjustment not only of the list of priority seats but of the priority voters within them, always behind the game and with hundreds of constituencies supposedly shifting in and out of competitiveness. That is the opposite of a strategy and with all parties doing the same thing would do no more than cancel itself out.

As it turned out, many of the trends in the results reflected and magnified those which had underlain the 2015 election. In 131 seats in England and Wales there was a swing to the Tories counter to the national swing and the patterns that emerged were obvious. This was the election where Labour gained Kensington and lost Mansfield. There was also a superficial parallel between the polarization of the EU Referendum and that of the election in which Labour and Tory shared 85% of votes cast almost evenly. Self-evidently though the polarization was not identical and it is too simplistic to regard the election as a referendum on the Referendum. Perhaps one in four Remain voters voted Tory, roughly the same proportion of Leave voters voted Labour. There was though a clear relationship of sorts between patterns of voting. Most obviously London's 60% vote for Remain must be associated with the Tories' dismal performance in the capital in the election, especially in some of the wealthiest areas where their vote actually fell and the Lib Dems' rose. Here, and in some of the most affluent seats in the South East and elsewhere, there may have been a direct Brexit effect. Equally the apparent collapse of a large UKIP vote mainly to the Tories in some white working class areas was the latest evidence of long-term trends in some of Labour's historic heartlands especially in the former coalfields.

Perhaps May's biggest strategic blunder was in believing she could use an essentially divisive issue as a basis for widening her mandate. The purpose of this election in her own words was not, as it might have been, to bring together a divided nation but to provide her with a strong majority to negotiate Brexit. While most electors regardless of their referendum vote would obviously want the Prime Minister to be strong in those negotiations, she was effectively harnessing herself to one half of the country. Worse, that stated purpose was recognised by most not as a real choice between parties and leaders offering different approaches but as a ruse to take advantage of her popularity, and while they were prepared to tolerate that it left her vulnerable when her campaign ran out of steam. One consequence of May's campaign focus on the Brexit process was that, by failing to concentrate on their message of economic competence (the raison d'etre of the Tory Party) which had won them the 2015 election, and indeed not emphasizing the uncertainties of Brexit as an additional reason for fiscal credibility, she allowed "Austerity" to be portrayed not as responsibility but as no more than intentional callousness.

The 2017 election result is now cemented into British electoral history and it has transformed many previous assumptions about how the electorate behaves. It guarantees that the next election is likely to be the most exciting and uncertain ever. No one will now believe that it will have been decided by "fundamentals" in the years and months beforehand and that the short campaign will not matter. The pollsters will have to interpret their data knowing that previous patterns of turnout are not necessarily to be relied upon.

Mrs. May's breaking of the electoral cycle has demonstrated the capacity of the British electorate to produce the unexpected and brought a new shape to campaigning having proved that digital media has a serious and important role to play. What we cannot yet know is the extent to which the unique dynamics of the campaign and the records broken by the result were a product of the unique circumstances of the election, including the length of that campaign and the almost universal expectation of a Tory landslide. We have evidence going back many years that, when the electorate perceives that an election does not matter very much and/or the result is a foregone conclusion, many will use the opportunity to experiment with their vote and bandwagons develop. The nature of bandwagons of course is that they are jumped on by almost everyone that does not stand in their path. Whether this one has created a new settlement or will prove an aberration remains to be seen.

The Liberal Democrat Campaign

James Gurling

THE LEAST LIKELY OF MANY UNLIKELY THINGS THAT MIGHT HAPPEN

The first inkling I had that that something significant was happening on the morning the election was called was when the podium came out without the Downing Street logo on it. At that moment I popped a message to Tim Farron's chief of staff, Ben Williams. What's this all about? There was a quick exchange—anything from something to do with a Brexit border issue with Northern Ireland to a member of the Cabinet going. It was *possible* that it was a general election, but it just seemed such an unlikely thing to be doing in the middle of an existing campaign for the local elections. So it was the least likely of the many unlikely things that might happen.

After that a cold realization set in, as I started to think through exactly what was about to unfold. By lunchtime I was at HQ for the first of a series of preparatory meetings. A combination of fear and optimism best describes how I felt as we started to organize things in what was, compared with 2015 and 2010, a much more slimmed down headquarters resource.

J. Gurling (✉)
Liberal Democrats, London, UK
e-mail: jgurling@btinternet.com

© The Author(s) 2019
D. Wring et al. (eds.), *Political Communication in Britain*,
https://doi.org/10.1007/978-3-030-00822-2_11

161

FRAMING OUR AMBITIONS

The assumption was that, with the growing disenchantment with the outcome of the Brexit referendum, there was a bigger contingent of target voters to aim at than there had been in 2015. Party membership had grown considerably. Labour were recognized as divided, and poorly led by their Leader. So it seemed to lots of people that there was a fantastic opportunity there for the Lib Dems. However, as I explained it to HQ staff on that first day, we shouldn't get carried away by external optimism because the level of resources available to us was considerably smaller than we ever recently had. Similarly the likelihood that 48% of the voting population was going to vote for us en masse was slight to say the least.

It became clear, as those early days moved on, that the impact on our prospects of calling the election was significant for two reasons. One is that it cut across our local campaigns. We had put considerable resources into the County elections. And there were early indications that voters, who were in the process of returning to us because we were the local campaigners standing up for their issues, were now being diverted back to national politics and into a referendum type way of thinking. The second issue arising from the calling of the snap election was that we had been on a permanent cycle of Parliamentary by-elections, our national campaign staff were, if not shattered, well on the way to being shattered.

Maybe I had rose tinted spectacles, but it also felt that things had been moving quite considerably on the issue of Europe. We had experienced substantial movements in previous Parliamentary by-elections, and had invested heavily in the Manchester Gorton by-election. Two days before May had called the election I had received analysis on Gorton from the Party's campaigns Director (Shaun Roberts) and Deputy Director (Dave McCobb)—both of whom I have worked with for many years and whose judgement I have a great deal of faith in. Their message was that our vote in Gorton had built from single digits to something greater, possibly around the 30% mark. That is quite some progression. The key determinant of this success was communicating to Labour voters their Party's support for the Conservatives triggering Article 50. It added to a notion that reports of a soft Labour vote in Remain areas might be systemic rather than abstract—and explained early perceived vulnerabilities in parts of London and Vauxhall in particular.

But it was not to be. The calling of the General Election ended the need for the by-election and it was cancelled. Had it gone ahead a seismic result could have been achieved for the Liberal Democrats— sufficient to reveal beyond doubt the vulnerability that Labour's Leader had exposed them to on Europe, and sufficient to signal clearly to voters where their best interests sat if they wished to cast their vote effectively on the issue of Brexit and the process of Article 50.

THE PARTY MACHINE

The Party had a limited campaign staff covering quite a large number of seats. The number of seats that were nominally 'in play', by virtue of their standing, their poll rating and their own campaign capacity, far exceeded the numbers of seats that we could provide campaign direction to from the centre. In sum we were stretched.

For a brief time there was also a question of which way we needed to be facing. All the early evidence pointed to the opportunity being in certain Labour areas where their vote was not quite as secure then as it later became. But in many of these same areas we lacked the members and funding required. So we set out to fight the Tories, where our active membership was largely concentrated and where there was greatest motivation over Brexit.

We expanded into the seats that were available by bringing in volunteer staff, including from my campaign and communications committee. They went out into the field to help clusters of seats. And the HQ media and press campaign team, directed by Phil Reilly, expanded and supplemented by former staff and even the occasional peer.

In terms of organisation, we had learned lessons from the 2015 campaign when there had been a bit of a last minute dash for candidates. From the previous summer we had prepared and in 2017, barring one two last minute 'blips' we were ready to go with candidates in place and a Manifesto largely written.

Alongside the manifesto, all the things that were within the party's organisational structure were ready and ready to go. We had conducted some polling, and had seen some initial messaging work. But it wasn't a complete job as staff resources had been dedicated to the diet of unplanned elections. Had we been able to complete that process with the rigor we intended I think I would have been feeling a lot more confident that everything had been done that could have been done in advance of a snap election.

Developing the Messages

We wanted to be clear about the Tory proposition: these were Brexit-focused Conservatives less interested in other domestic politics than they were in leaving the EU at any cost. Despite everyone's expectations, we didn't believe that Europe was going to be *the* defining factor. So, very early on in the campaign, we were promoting ideas that were in the prepared manifesto: we were talking about the NHS and how we were going to fund it; Education; Environment; Security. We had, in many respects, a traditional set of policies.

There was a clear duality in the campaign. If the Tories were heartless and very focused on Brexit, the Labour party had gone along with them on this major issue. Our headline position became to trust the people to have a final say, and to offer them a "the referendum on the deal".

There was considerable body of opinion that said it should have been a straight "we are going to be the party of Remain", come what may. But the position of the party through conferences and the suggested text in the manifesto was quite clear that this is about *the deal*, not the referendum.

And there was a concern that, as we had seen in county campaigns, we were being positioned as against the referendum and in some way anti-democratic. And it was surprising at times how much this rebuttal of our offer took root.

Having a say on the deal was an optimistic and honest message: Tories insisting on hard Brexit, supported by the Labour Party. But it didn't have to be that way. By giving voters a say on the deal they could Change Britain's Future.

We were also challenged by the new broadcasting rules. Based on our Parliamentary representation and our standing in the opinion polls (and now without the boost of good local election results) we were a less commanding prospect in terms of broadcast requirements. Rather than seek political balance programme producers were allowed to make editorial judgements on the news value of the stories available. It was also the first General Election in which the BBC were regulated by Ofcom, rather than by themselves.

Our initial media approach had been very much like in previous elections: we had topic of the day (sourced from the manifesto), we went for it. More often or not, the impact of the new rules meant that if that story was not what the editor of the 6 or 10 o'clock news wanted to cover, if it didn't make sense in the context of the story they had opted for, we simply weren't covered. It was incredibly frustrating for a highly experienced and innovative press team.

There used to be a 'truism' that Lib Dem support went up during election campaigns—which was in no small part attributed to the fact that this was a rare instance where the electorate were actually presented with our view. This was almost entirely absent in the 2017 campaign. There were numerous evening news bulletins with not even a mention of the Party let alone our position. It had a huge impact on our standing in the polls—which in turn served only to re-inforce the broadcasters views as to the value of covering us. The overall outcome of these editorial decisions posed more substantial challenges to the BBC who during the process of the campaign seemed largely to neglect their wider Reithian public service remit to inform and educate.

THE LEADER

Tim Farron had already taken the brave decision on Europe—to stay loyal to our Remain position on EU membership and not to be brow-beaten into a view that the slim majority for Leave meant that everything else had been defined by the Brexiteers. Having been Party President he was also remarkably in tune with our activist base and had been able to motivate and mobilise a Party following the depths of the 2015 election rout. Humorous, engaging, not an identikit politician, Tim offered the prospect of being able to continue the Party's revival.

The challenge we knew he faced was one of profile. No leader—including Ashdown and Kennedy—is really comfortable until they have done 18 months in the public eye. Ideally you need to get your first general election under your belt before you are understood or familiar to the electorate. Cleggmania was in large part a product of the TV coverage revealing to thousands of people for the first time an engaging and intelligent person in post.

Tim's start to the campaign unexpectedly saw him challenged on aspects of his personal faith that weren't easily associated with the values of a modern progressive liberal party. As an introduction to him as Leader, or of the Party to the wider public, it was very far from what was needed. From that point onwards the Party's wider offer was effectively obscured. Tim was placed under a great deal of personal pressure which impacted his performance.

The original plan to introduce Tim recognised that the media campaign was "back ended". The TV debates were at the end of the campaign. The biggest set piece interviews were at the end of the campaign. We were therefore first out of the blocks with the Leader's campaign bus tour. Introducing Tim was one of the reasons the manifesto launch was done in the way that it was.

But these plans to introduce Tim and define his offer were effectively overwhelmed by the pre-introduction publicity over his personal faith, and the need to manage the particular impression this produced. Attempts to draw a line under the issue could be achieved by only one person, and it was for many candidates and activists a demotivating and frustrating start to the campaign.

TARGETING SEATS

Over and above the usual data sources we had an additional index of how people had voted in the 2016 referendum. That went into the mix taken into consideration in thinking about how many votes we might have been capable of bringing across. It was never expected that the 48% would simply transfer across. Looking at all the factors available, not least of which was performance at the May locals it did seem that at the start we could have been looking at a pool of about 20%.

Taking the ferocity of the campaign our former coalition partners had unleashed upon us to such devasting effect in 2015 as a starting point, we had estimated the level of resource needed to defend against a similar campaign in 2020. So from a pool of approximately 50 seats we knew in 2017 we reliably had resource to properly fight in only 30 seats. As the campaign progressed that assessment decreased.

The other thing that we found was that the electorate was very much more volatile than had previously been the case. It wasn't simply the switch between 2015 and 2017. During the period of the election itself people moved with quite some speed between Party options. With our Leader in early difficulties, and over a longer than usual campaign, things seemed to polarise quite quickly culminating in what later became to be known as the Corbyn effect.

THE ONLINE CAMPAIGN

Social media is another area where it's a matter of resources. We certainly put more effort into it than we had in previous elections—but nothing like that available to the other main parties. We were very fortunate to have had some help from people who had campaigned for the Canadian Liberals—who use the same canvassing management tool—who helped optimise some of our online presence. We fought a better campaign within the resources available a result. We were more targeted and more aware of the range of options available to us. Indeed in the first TV debate where Tim took part, the war on Twitter went in his favour.

Volume was an issue to get going on social media, just as it was (for different reasons) on TV. We did little that the other parties hadn't done before. But scale and capability was certainly more integrated this time than it had been last time.

CAMPAIGN SUSPENDED

Not only was this a 'snap' general election, but one which was twice suspended as a result of the terrorist atrocities. During the suspension it is (rightly) the Government that is in the driving seat, but it was interesting to see how quickly media returned to normal procedures—at one stage I heard the Lib Dem position on campaign suspension announced on the radio even before we had informed our campaigners or made a formal announcement. When we asked why this had happened it seemed the media had been informed by 'Government' this was the case and assumed a cross-party discussion had taken place behind the scenes. Each time the campaign resumed there was in effect a natural reset. One suspension came at precisely the same time that Parties were communicating with registered postal voters and suspension also impacted the depth of discussion on the 'Dementia Tax'.

PARTY POLITICAL BROADCASTS

We learnt on April 4 that we were to have four PEB slots. The first of these was due to air in the week commencing May 8. With submission and approval requirements this presented a very challenging turnaround time. Acceptable if you have the resources to be able to throw at it, but a real challenge otherwise. The Liberal Democrat PEBs of the 2017 election therefore tell a story of innovation under financial constraint. The only 'traditional' broadcast we did was the final one—and even that was accompanied by an 'advert' format.

The exception to all this was the PEB following the Manchester attack. Coming right at the end of the period of campaign suspension, it was clear that a traditional party political advert would be inappropriate. The problem was that, with the campaign drawing to an end, there were no further alternative slots for us to use. The BBC very kindly agreed to permit a last minute submission. We chose to do it as a personal statement from the Leader in the wake of the atrocity. Sincere, approachable and reflective of the common mood, it was Tim at his best. It was no mean feat to gather his thoughts into the required length of time and then to do it in one take.

THE CAMPAIGN ON THE GROUND

There were some very bleak days in the middle of the campaign where we had to contemplate some really stark possibilities. At one point nothing was showing terribly well in our data, and the only seat that you could only really hang your hat on was Orkney and Shetland. And it was in Scotland that the first glimmer of success became a reality. Under the leadership of Willie Rennie and with the different dynamic of separatist politics in the mix, the Scottish campaign brought in 3 gains and was only 2 votes away from a fourth.

It is deeply disappointing that the national vote share came down by a further half a percent on the 2015 result. But increasing the Parliamentary Party by 50% is all the more remarkable—a consequence of the ruthless targeting of those seats set against where we had less prospects. It also involved some very difficult decisions and some very awkward conversations with candidates who had worked for the campaign for a long time—the very last thing we expected to have to do was to tell them that, from this point onwards, their activists were encouraged to campaign for different seat.

Clarity on our position that we wouldn't go into coalition allowed our local campaigns to focus once again on the track records and capabilities of our candidates. Combined with a strong 'talent bank' of returning MPs like Vince Cable, Ed Davey, Jo Swinson, or Norman Lamb, the campaign at the grass roots probably did more to shore up the national campaign than ever it had had the opportunity to do before.

But the locality of the campaigns also seems to have made it more difficult to move the member resources between seats—that and the fact that the target seats were rather more geographically spread than they had been in 2010.

BEYOND THE LEADER'S CAMPAIGN

The big names were mostly fighting for their seats. Nick Clegg did some really good national stuff and he cut through on a couple of issues that helped the campaign, particularly in response to terrorism issue. But most importantly he galvanized a lot of people on the issue of Europe. Using people like Paddy Ashdown, who still motivates people to get up and get out there, was a large part of keeping the show on the road. And the likes of Dick Newby were a constant as well—encouraging our team in the Lords in getting out there on the doorsteps and talking to groups on a scale that they had not done before.

LOOKING BACK

Having personally conducted reviews of every round of elections since 2010, the Party is certainly not short of comment and analysis on the positives and negatives of campaign management, and there is undoubtedly some good advice in the review of 2017 for the next snap election. But if faced with a snap election again, the first people I would go and talk to would be the broadcasters so that we could be clear from the outset how they intended to cover it. We will be better set up for clear messaging amongst candidates and activists, but internal communications is certainly something we didn't get sorted right at the start—particularly in comparison to set piece elections where there is greater opportunity to set the scene, introduce messaging, talk through and brief the manifesto in detail and manage expectations.

The 2017 snap election made clear, beyond doubt, the extent that the Party had been hollowed out up to 2015. But it contained within it cause for optimism. Activists returned with a sense of purpose. New members became active and learnt new skills—and even enjoyed it.

Having kept the show on the road, there is no room for complacency. The coming months and years present a huge challenge, but this election proves that the greatest challenge is one of resource not of ambition. Because of the 2017 snap election, the Liberal Democrats can do better next time and deliver more.

Movement-Led Electoral Campaigning: Momentum in the 2017 General Election

Abi Rhodes

Outside the Westminster and mainstream media bubble, social and political movements were tuned into the trends shaping the extra-parliamentary political landscape. One such movement was the grass-roots campaigning group Momentum, which evolved out of the first 'Jeremy Corbyn for Labour Leader' election campaign in the summer of 2015. Since Momentum was established, the group has been intrinsically linked to the Labour leaders' initial success, and, via a rocky road littered with hostile MPs and news reports, eventually to the unexpected surge in votes for the Labour Party in June 2017 (Peggs 2017). In this chapter, I explore the impact that Momentum's movement-led campaigning approach, alongside their use of digital media tools and traditional campaigning techniques, had on the outcome of the 2017 General Election. With particular focus on the personalized political communication strategies the group employed, I examine the role of the activist in the mobilization of Labour supporters and voters.

As an established Officer in Nottingham Momentum, I had the opportunity to speak with other activists, both new and long standing,

A. Rhodes (✉)
University of Nottingham, Nottingham, UK
e-mail: Abi.Rhodes@nottingham.ac.uk

© The Author(s) 2019
D. Wring et al. (eds.), *Political Communication in Britain*,
https://doi.org/10.1007/978-3-030-00822-2_12

in my local area about the political communication strategies devised by Momentum's head office. As the analysis below explores, the message received by the activists I spoke to, and from personal experience, was that YOU and your political knowledge was all that was needed to engage voters on the doorstep. What the Bernie Sanders-inspired training events provided was an extra layer of electoral experience that could facilitate voter engagement, but ultimately the choice to use this communication tactic was left to the individual activist. Similarly, group canvassing and car pools to marginal constituencies offered activists a sense of belonging to a broader movement, one that was supportive but not closely scripted.

The view of these activists was that they were encouraged to personalize their political knowledge and engage with voters on that basis. The result of this was that activist participation was organizationally enabled by Momentum in the 2017 general election campaign as opposed to organizationally brokered. In other words, Momentum invited activists to personalize their engagement with the voter in an individual way, rather than being urged to engage in a way that was pre-defined by either the Labour Party or Momentum.

PEOPLE-POWERED POLITICAL COMMUNICATION

Political consultants and marketing strategies have played an integral part in shaping campaign messages in British politics since the 1980s (Lees-Marshment 2001; Lilleker and Lees-Marshment 2005; Mullen 2015; Savigny 2003; Wring 2001, 2005). Both played a prominent role in the 2015 General Election campaign (Chadwick and Stromer-Galley 2016) with contemporary electioneering engaging in practices of 'personalized political communication' for most of this century (Nielsen 2012). According to the political marketing approach, the parties and candidates are assumed to operate within a political marketplace, each seeking to sell their 'product' to the consumer and each focused solely on the end goal of winning the election (Savigny 2003: 25). Political parties are conceptualized in this model as businesses, competing for votes in a competitive marketplace and in need of consultants who can direct the relationship between political actor and voter (Savigny 2003: 31). The voter (or consumer) is inscribed as the means to that electoral end, and the party or politician is required to structure political communication to meet this 'consumer' demand (Savigny 2003: 25). The personalization of political communication, in such a marketing approach, employs persuasion techniques to reinforce a 'brand' image that constructs a product to meet the desires of the voter-consumer (Harrop 1990: 279; Savigny 2003: 29; Scammell 1995: 20).

During the early part of the twenty-first century, Nielsen contends that there has been a move towards personalization in American campaigning through the pursuit of 'premeditated practices that use *people as media* for political communication' (Nielsen 2012: 14–15, emphasis added). In harmony with long-standing electioneering techniques, the main methods of such communication are the 'ground war' tactics of doorstep canvassing and phone banking, yet the communication is 'personalized' in the sense that people, rather than the mass media or political actor, serve as the primary agents for the message. It can be argued that the activist in this approach is positioned as the carrier of a branded campaign message that targets the voter as consumer, rather than as a person with political knowledge that they wish to share. I argue that Momentum moved away from these approaches toward a movement-led campaign strategy that was aimed initially at the activist and supporter—training and encouraging them to be involved in politics and the political message, rather than as a purveyor of a product. In my own experience, and that of others I have spoken with, Momentum activists did act as agents for the Labour Party's political message on the ground, but not in a premediated way that sought to *use* people as media. Momentum's messaging focused, instead, on encouraging activists to use their personal political knowledge to engage with voters, rather than encouraging them to use a pre-agreed script that would position the activist as nothing more than a messenger. This assessment is based on the movement-led campaigning strategies analyzed below and the digital media content devised by Momentum head office that targeted the activist/campaigner (and thus *indirectly* the voter). The same was true with the traditional ground-war tactics that were employed to target the voter, but which did so *via* the activist.

Momentum's digital media tools were designed to encourage and empower activists to get involved and to then go out to communicate with other voters. This purpose relates to the Bennett and Segerberg (2013) analytic distinction between 'organizationally enabled' participation and 'organizationally brokered' engagement. In their formulation, the former emphasises 'loosely tied coalitions' in which participants are 'invited to personalize their engagement' and the latter emphases 'strong coalitions' in which participants are encouraged to engage in a 'commonly defined' or 'framed' way (Bennett and Segerberg 2013: 11–13). This reflects the differences in how organizations use digital media. In organizationally enabled action, digital media is integral to engagement and individuals are invited to personalize their responses and, in so doing, contribute in important ways to the process and structure of the network (in other words, they have agency over their engagement). In organizationally brokered action, digital media is used primarily as a cost saving tool (both coordination and financial) and does not change the 'logic of participation' because the relations within the network are professionally organized (Bennett and Segerberg 2013: 13). Through this lens, and in conjunction with the analysis below, Momentum activists, myself included, engaged in organizationally enabled participation that encouraged them to use their own political knowledge to respond to concerns raised in conversation with voters. An effect of this, was that the voter was not conceived of as simply a target to be bombarded with official, top-down messaging put out by the national Labour Party or Momentum team, but as a person the campaigner engaged with.

The analysis below of Momentum's use of digital media content and traditional election campaigning techniques to engage both activists and voters, makes the case that this movement-led campaigning contributed, in part, to the unexpected Labour surge, and that it could also represent a shift in how politics is thought to be conducted. In this election, a grassroots movement and its repertoire of extra-parliamentary politics played an important role in the electoral advantage of an established political party and this poses questions about the future of formal parliamentary politics. Moreover, Momentum's organizationally enabled approach was less about choice and may have been borne out of necessity. Unlike in the 1997, 2001 and 2005 general elections, where press coverage of the Party was favourable (Scammell and Harrop 1997, 2005; Wring 1997: 913, 2001), the coverage of Labour under Jeremy Corbyn was hostile during the election and in the years leading up to it (Cammaerts et al. 2016; Schlosberg 2016). Such a political landscape meant that even if there had been a conscious choice[1] to 'market' the Labour 'product' it was highly unlikely to be successful this time around.

---

[1] From his first victory speech in 2015, Jeremy Corbyn made it clear that his relationship with the press would be very different to previous Labour leaders', which suggests that there would have been a conscious choice *not* to court the press even if the landscape had been favourable (Mason 2015).

CONTEXT

The representation of Jeremy Corbyn in the British press had been widely disparaging and overtly aggressive in tone since his election as Labour leader (Cammaerts et al. 2016: 1). A study of British newspapers in late 2015 by LSE's Media and Communications Department concluded that the representation of Jeremy Corbyn 'went well beyond the normal limits of fair debate and disagreement in a democracy' (Cammaerts et al. 2016: 1). It showed that over 50% of all news articles in eight mainstream news outlets from 1 September to 1 November 2015 were antagonistic towards the Labour leader and that he was delegitimized in several ways: through scorn and ridicule over his looks (repeatedly referred to as 'Mr. Corbean' in the tabloid press); through an association of his ideas as 'mad', 'crazy' or 'loony' (also faced by Ed Miliband in 2015; see Gaber 2017) and being portrayed as a terrorist sympathizer; and through a distortion of his voice, a lack of proper context or the complete lack of direct quotations.

In a similar way to this delegitimization of Jeremy Corbyn as a political actor and the undermining of his leadership by the Parliamentary Labour Party (BBC 2016), Momentum has also been confronted with multifaceted establishment derision and a lack of direct representation. Since its inception in October 2015, by former Tony Benn aide Jon Lansman, Momentum has attracted tens of thousands of members keen to campaign en masse to secure a Labour government. With a network, at the time of writing, of 31,000 members, 200,000 supporters and 170 local groups, Momentum has a large number of engaged activists who are ready to participate in Labour Party campaigning.[2] Initially, these members and our enthusiasm for a Corbyn-led Labour government were not received by some within the Party hierarchy. The infighting in the Labour Party between Corbyn supporters and opponents was laid bare in the mainstream news almost from the moment that Corbyn became leader.

A Nexis search of 'Momentum' from 12 September 2015 (the date of the first leadership result) reveals that within weeks of this, media outlets were reporting on the 'deep suspicion' of Momentum held by

[2] See http://www.peoplesmomentum.com/ for latest figures.

some Labour MPs.[3] It was claimed that as a 'pseudo-Marxist militant faction' the campaigning group was set up to 'to act as Jeremy Corbyn's Praetorian Guard' (Hodges 2015) and, in barely more neutral terms, as 'a vehicle to deselect MPs who were critical of the new leadership' (Watt 2015). Descriptions of Momentum as a 'pressure group', as 'controversial' 'rabble-rousers', and a 'clique' or a 'mob' who could destroy the Labour Party circulated in the media throughout 2015/2016. Even as recently as March 2017, the movement was called a 'left-wing faction inside Labour' (Watson 2017) and were issued with the warning that it was 'plotting to "destroy" the party' (BBC 2017a). Yet, during the 2017 General Election the media coverage of Momentum seemed to be less overtly hostile and, on a number of occasions spokespeople for the group made it through to the mainstream media. Days after the dissolution of Parliament on 3 May 2017, the *Guardian* columnist Zoe Williams, highlighted how, in interviews with them, some members of Momentum say that they 'are outraged by the way they're characterized' and she goes on to assert that 'of course they're not Trots; of course they're not hardliners; they just want to do politics differently' (Williams 2017). The movement began to be described in more neutral terms, appearing (again) in the *Guardian* and the *New Statesman* as a 'grassroots organization' (MacAskill and Roberts 2017; Rampen 2017), in the *Independent* as a 'grassroots channel' (Rhodes 2017) and, surprisingly, in *The Times* as a 'network of Jeremy Corbyn supporters' (Fisher 2017).

A few days after the election, Emma Rees, one of the national organizers for Momentum at the time, wrote several articles that appeared in the *Guardian* detailing the numbers of people who had flooded into marginals 'to have millions of conversations with voters' (Rees 2017). By the 12th June, *The Week* published an article on how the movement had 'helped sway the general election' and on the same day the BBC were 'inside Momentum headquarters' finding out how the group had used

---

[3]In order to obtain articles about Momentum as a noun rather than as a verb, the terms 'group', 'movement' and 'Labour' were added to the search and sought within the same paragraph of each article. Over 2000 articles were returned (12 September 2015–4 December 2017) from British newspapers: *telegraph.co.uk* (1290); *Guardian* (London) (669); *Mail Online* (208); *Independent* (United Kingdom) (166); *The Times* (London) (67); *Daily Telegraph* (London) (55); *mirror.co.uk* (52); *Daily Mail* and *Mail on Sunday* (39); *The Observer* (London) (28); *Sunday Times* (London) (23); *Sun* (England) (18); *Sunday Telegraph* (London) (18); *i*—Independent Print Ltd (11); *Express* (10); *Mirror* and The *Sunday Mirror* (8); and *Sunday Express* (6).

social media to encourage people to vote for Labour (*The Week* 2017; BBC 2017b). Towards the end of June, Adam Klug, another national Momentum co-ordinator at the time, appeared in a video posted on the BBC's Politics pages (BBC 2017c). He spoke about the use of 'innovative technology and viral social media content' to mobilize tens of thousands of people to knock on doors across the country. So, despite initial hostility towards members, the voices of Momentum's organizers and the role that creative technology and its activists played in mobilizing the Labour vote made it into the mainstream media reporting. Momentum's use of online campaigning, its imagery and unconventional communication tactics, which led to offline door-knocking, were all designed to cut through the initially frosty but now thawing media reception and negative polling numbers to reach the public.

MOVEMENT-LED CAMPAIGNING

Because Momentum's aim was to secure a Labour government, our digital media messaging was focused on getting people to vote for the party. Complementing the Labour Party's traditional campaigning, the national Momentum team adopted cutting-edge technology in several well-designed approaches aimed at mobilizing its members and supporters to get out there and talk with voters. One of the most useful tools was a website that it created called 'My Nearest Marginal', which I will come back to in detail below, a link to which appeared at the top of almost every Momentum Facebook post and spread across Twitter via #mynearestmarginal. During the campaign the tool sat next to the 'Call your Grandfolks' message, initiated by the *Guardian* columnist and activist Owen Jones, and the #ElectionDayPledge that featured later on in the campaign.

At the start of the campaign, the 'callyourgrandfolks.com/' site was set up by Jeremy for Labour on behalf of Momentum and featured a video of Owen Jones asking us to call our grandparents to convince them to vote for Labour. In the short video, he outlines the negative polling results that Corbyn and the Labour Party were receiving with those over the age of 55 and suggests that this could be combatted with a "phone call to your grandparents" to discuss the policies that the party were putting forward, focusing on the ones that benefitted both the younger and older generations. By the end of the campaign, the website 'electiondaypledge.co.uk/pledge', also developed by Momentum, encouraged people to sign up to take the day off or donate any time that they could on 8th June to help knock on doors and get the Labour vote out. Across social media, there were also frequent links to join the Labour Party and to register to vote. Momentum worked alongside the English grime MC Big Narstie, and the non-partisan RizeUp voter registration campaign to produce, among other things, a song aimed at getting people on the electoral register. It would be the My Nearest Marginal tool, however, that was key to getting people door-knocking for Labour, which is the traditional method of garnering the vote during elections in the UK.

Momentum headquarters believe that more than 100,000 people accessed the 'Mynearestmarginal.com' site, which was four times the number of Momentum members at that time, indicating that the tool had reached way beyond a small bubble of activists (Savage 2017). It allowed the site's visitors to type in their postcodes to find out where their nearest key marginal seat was. Such a specific targeting of marginal seats augmented the official Labour Party site that gave members a list of the campaigning events that were nearest to them. The My Nearest Marginal site also listed these campaign events, but focused on the key marginal constituencies, and provided the mobile number of the local Labour organizer. It also facilitated a car pool service so that people could organize car shares to get to campaigning areas easily and cheaply. Immediately after the website launched in early May 2017, more than 100 Momentum activists turned up in car pools to Derby North, from nearby Leicester, Sheffield, and Burton-on-Trent, to knock on doors for Labour. The appeal to those who used it was not just the coordination element, but also the accessibility that it offered to first-time campaigners and canvassers (as many of those turning up had not canvassed before). For Chris Williamson, re-elected as MP for Derby North in 2017, the site brought in not just a large number of people but also a welcomed boost of energy and a passion for the policies in the manifesto (Shabi 2017).

Growing public enthusiasm for Labour's policies was mutedly reflected in the media by week three (covering 18–31 May inclusively) of the general election campaign. According to analysis of newspapers and television by Loughborough University's Centre for Research in Communication and Culture (CRCC), 'the gap between negative and positive coverage [of Labour was] diminishing', and although it was still broadly critical, there was an increase in media focus on health and healthcare policy (see Chapter A Tale of Two Parties). The latter was good news for Labour as it was one of their key policy areas, however this shift in focus was primarily due to substantial attacks on the Conservative party for its proposed 'dementia tax'. On the ground, I experienced the Labour manifesto proving to be a helpful document for countering media negativity and critics. Some of the voters that I spoke to on the doorstep parroted back to me the consistent ridicule of Jeremy Corbyn's ideas and the unrelenting refrain from many quarters that he is personally unelectable (Finlayson 2016; Rhodes 2016; Seymour 2016: 39–43). But by focusing on the content of the manifesto, my fellow activists and I were able to bring voters around to talking about Labour policy and what the party would do if it got into government. Writing in the *New Statesman*, the Momentum campaign coordinator and Labour party activist Rachel Godfrey Wood, highlighted this when she stated that: '... Labour has only ever advanced when voters are absolutely clear what it stands for. Corbyn has done well in making policy the centerpiece of the campaign, with a manifesto that has both a serious plan and roots in shared values' (Godfrey Wood 2017).

Momentum harnessed this shifting of focus onto policy with the training of new members, which formed part of another key element of Momentum's mobilizing role. The national campaign augmented its focus on digital tools with US-inspired canvassing methods, borrowed directly from the Bernie Sanders 2016 campaign for the Democratic Presidential nomination. Grayson Lookner, Jeremy Parkin, Kim McMurray and Erika Uyterhoeven—all organizers of the Sanders' campaign—were brought into advise on how to extend successful online campaigning activity to the streets with face-to-face conversations. The main message of this canvassing method is that in-person communication is key to changing people's minds and getting them to vote. The motivation behind this approach is that it works well with undecided or disengaged voters and brings the focus on to policy, such as the pledge to save the NHS from further privatization, and away from personality. By having actual conversations with the public at street stalls or on the doorstep, activists could begin to understand *how* people think about politics and to discuss Labour's vision for society in relation to that.

As noted above, Momentum campaigners needed to challenge the pre-constructed, negative image of the Labour Party and Jeremy Corbyn if they were to cut through to voters. In offering the training sessions, the national team fostered a space that encouraged each activist to personalize their engagement with voters on the policies in the manifesto.

By using this method, Momentum's movement-led campaigning further shifts away from marketing and consultant-led campaigning, where image and style is endorsed over policy and substance (Savigny 2003: 29). The linking of policy issues with what matters to people—along with how to have persuasive conversations—formed a fundamental part of the training on offer to both new and experienced activists. Pivotal elements of this training focused on how to find common ground with voters and how to deal with difficult conversations or answer challenging questions. This proved vital in energizing new members who had not been canvassing before (and who therefore did not know what to expect), and helpful to experienced members who wanted a fresher approach. Each of the sessions aimed at being highly participatory and providing attendees with a simple framework for communicating political ideas with others who may have different preconceptions or background knowledge. At my local Nottingham Momentum session, Jeremy Parkin led a discussion about more effective canvassing and engagement with voters that asked door-steppers to focus on finding out what drives someone's voting intention. In the Nottingham context, these new skills were put into action straight away as the training event was then followed by a mass canvassing session in a difficult seat to the North of the city.

Complementing these community-based, face-to-face events, Momentum used a number of mobile phone-based applications. The phone-banking app used during Jeremy Corbyn's second leadership campaign in 2016 was revamped and used to co-ordinate the calling of Labour members during the election. The app allowed you to call the Labour members that Momentum had data for from the comfort of your home and was used by groups electioneering together, anywhere where there was a wi-fi connection. Peer-to-peer texting helped campaigners to text each other about nearby events and canvasses: a tool that was also used by the Sanders campaign. On polling day, Momentum employed a WhatsApp cascade that sent a message to all of its members and supporters reminding them to 'Vote Labour today'. It gave the rallying cry: 'They say we won't turn out to vote. Let's prove them wrong. Let's transform politics and get Jeremy Corbyn elected.' But as well as galvanizing those who were already heavily involved, the main aim of the message was to get people to send a 'WhatsApp broadcast' to as many friends as possible to remind them to go out and vote. The tool asked them to broadcast the message to their contact list, which created a cascade of people texting each other on polling day. A link to the website www.gooutandvote.co.uk/ was contained within the message, which took users to a page urging them to 'make voting go viral'. Alongside this was a link to www.wheredoivote.co.uk/ that asked people to type in their postcode and gave them details of their local polling station. The application and the websites enabled new voters to navigate their way around election protocols by providing them with a map and encouraging them to share the content, which built an inclusive network of other voters. In the post-election interview with the BBC mentioned above, Momentum national organizer Emma Rees estimated that around 400,000 young people received this WhatsApp message on polling day.

The sharing of digital content formed another key component of the movement-led campaigning techniques that were employed so successfully. With a host of volunteer filmmakers and video editors, Momentum HQ made viral social media content that gained huge amounts of traction. The team produced some of the most shared videos of the 2017 General Election, which were estimated to have reached 30% of UK Facebook users (Silvera 2017). A myriad of videos appeared across social media platforms featuring explanations from people about why they were voting Labour, for Jeremy Corbyn and for the policies, many featuring the journalist and economics editor Paul Mason, and plenty explaining how to use the apps and websites. There were videos about tax havens, proposed tax increases, the NHS and the 'garden tax' to name just a few, all with the aim of myth-busting and countering the mainstream media and Conservative Party narratives. Also shared across the platforms were videos from Jeremy Corbyn rallies up and down the country, which delivered, directly to viewers, unmediated content about Labour's political and policy message. One of the most viewed videos of the campaign was called 'Daddy, why do you hate me?' It featured an imaginary conversation about free school meals and university tuition fees between a Theresa May voter and his daughter in 2030 and was viewed more than 7.6 million times across the main social media platforms. All of these were interesting, accessible and provided a knowledge-base for activists when they were speaking to voters in phone banks and on doorsteps.

This networked content-sharing, of signing up to join car pools to help in marginal seats, of phone banking and of door-knocking in groups, offered activists, myself included, a sense of belonging and a belief that all of our contributions were valued equally. Such a notion was reinforced by the horizontality of the campaigning organization, in that there was no requirement to seek authorization about sharing content or making a decision about what activity you felt able to participate in. There was no chain of command telling activists when, where or what to share and no rigid script to stick to when talking face-to-face with the electorate. Of course, there were organized events and technical infrastructure devised by the national Momentum team, but the message that got through online and on the ground was 'here are the tools, now go out and canvass'. Momentum's inclusive messaging and its internal structure that emphasized organizationally enabled participation made it clear that politics was something that *you* can do, which afforded each supporter a sense of agency.

CONCLUSION

In effect, the combination of technology and traditional political techniques helped activist-campaigners to see themselves as political agents who could make a meaningful contribution to an election campaign, rather than simply as a target of it. Momentum's movement-led campaigning gave us a sense of agency over our political engagement, in contrast to the consultant-led campaigning that, as discussed above, conceives of electioneering as an exercise in the marketing and encodes voters as people to whom politics is done (Denver et al. 2012: 153). Momentum's online techniques complemented the traditional ground war political tactics of door-knocking, leafleting and phone banking by engaging with activists and supporters directly and mobilizing them to participate in offline activities. Momentum's use of digital media was integral to engagement by individual activists, supporters and members, who were invited to personalize their responses to the Labour Party's (and Jeremy Corbyn's) political message and to campaign accordingly.

Whether this represents a paradigm shift in how politics is engaged with remains to be seen once more evidence from future elections is available. Here it is contended that the growth of 'party-as-movement mentality' (as championed by Jeremy Corbyn when he took the leadership position), digital activism and movement-led campaigning are adding to citizens' political repertoires and, as argued elsewhere, that 'substantial publics now see election campaigns as another opportunity for personalized and contentious political expression' (Chadwick and Stromer-Galley 2016: 287). Digital media activism and grassroots campaigning are traditionally the preserve of protest politics and social movements, but with the return to its movement-led roots the Labour Party is embracing them. The bringing together of extra-parliamentary politics with electoral politics is something that Momentum did with aplomb during the 2017 General Election and led, in part, to Labour's unexpected share of the vote. A perfect storm of Corbyn's unspun personality, honest approach to politics and non-mainstream message, a sense of establishment skepticism and waning backing for austerity measures in the country (Clery et al. 2016), which was reflected in the Labour Party manifesto, coupled with digital-media activism, an enthusiasm for movement-led politics and a terrible campaign by the Conservative Party also helped Labour. Momentum's organizationally enabled campaigning suited this political landscape and formulated a sense of activist agency with their inclusive messaging and horizontally structured organizing, which empowered individuals to go out and make a (political) difference. In doing so, the movement and its activists played a key role in mobilizing voters and brought the repertoires of extra-parliamentary politics into formal, electoral politics.

REFERENCES

BBC News. (2016, June 28). Labour MPs pass no-confidence motion in Jeremy Corbyn. *BBC News*. http://www.bbc.co.uk/news/uk-politics-36647458. Accessed November 12, 2017.

BBC News. (2017a, March 20). Labour: Tom Watson attacks Momentum-Unite 'secret plan'. *BBC News*. http://www.bbc.co.uk/news/uk-politics-39325559. Accessed November 14, 2017.

BBC News. (2017b, June 12). Jeremy Corbyn: How Momentum HQ perfected social media outreach. *BBC News*. http://www.bbc.co.uk/news/av/election-2017-40255298/jeremy-corbyn-how-momentum-hq-perfected-social-media-outreach. Accessed November 14, 2017.

BBC News. (2017c, June 30). Momentum's Adam Klug says he expects Labour to win election soon. *BBC News*. http://www.bbc.co.uk/news/av/uk-politics-40460842/momentum-s-adam-klug-says-he-expects-labour-to-win-election-soon. Accessed November 14, 2017.

Bennet, W. L., & Segerberg, A. (2013). *The logic of connective action: Digital media and the personalization of contentious politics*. Cambridge: Cambridge University Press.

Cammaerts, B., DeCillia, B., Magalhães, J., & Jimenez-Martínez, C. (2016). *Journalistic representations of Jeremy Corbyn in the British Press: From watchdog to attack dog*. Media@LSE Report. http://www.lse.ac.uk/media@lse/research/pdf/JeremyCorbyn/Cobyn-Report.pdf.

Chadwick, A., & Stromer-Galley, J. (2016). Digital media, power, and democracy in parties and election campaigns: Party decline or party renewal? *The International Journal of Press/Politics, 21*(3), 283–293.

Clery E., Curtice, J., & Harding R. (2016). *British social attitudes: The 34th report.* London: NatCen Social Research. www.bsa.natcen.ac.uk.

Denver, D., Carman, C., & Johns, R. (2012). *Elections and voters in Britain* (3rd ed.). Basingstoke: Palgrave Macmillan.

Finlayson, L. (2016, January 11). Don't elect him, he's unelectable! *Forum for European Philosophy Blog* (Blog).

Fisher, L. (2017, June 2). Momentum runs clever campaign to get out the youth vote for Corbyn. *The Times.* https://www.thetimes.co.uk/article/momentum-runs-clever-campaign-to-get-out-the-youth-vote-for-corbyn-m6gkbjxbx. Accessed November 14, 2017.

Gaber, I. (2017). Othering Ed: Newspaper coverage of Miliband and the election. In D. Wring, R. Mortimore, S. Atkinson (Eds.), *Political communication in Britain polling, campaigning and media in the 2015 general election.* London: Palgrave Macmillan.

Godfrey Wood, R. (2017, June 10). Pavement politics, new media, and a little help from Bernie: How Labour fought its ground game. *New Statesman.* https://www.newstatesman.com/politics/uk/2017/06/pavement-politics-new-edia-and-little-help-bernie-how-labour-fought-its-ground. Accessed November 14, 2017.

Harrop, M. (1990, July). Political marketing. *Parliamentary Affairs, 43*(3), 277–291.

Hodges, D. (2015, October 9). Jeremy Corbyn now has his own Praetorian Guard inside the Labour Party. *Daily Telegraph.* https://www.telegraph.co.uk/news/politics/Jeremy_Corbyn/11922468/Momentum-Jeremy-Corbyns-militant-Praetorian-Guard-inside-the-Labour-Party.html. Accessed November 14, 2017.

Lees-Marshment, J. (2001). *Political marketing and British political parties.* Manchester: Manchester University Press.

Lilleker, D., & Lees-Marshment, J. (Eds.). (2005). *Political marketing: A comparative perspective.* Manchester: Manchester University Press.

MacAskill, E., & Roberts, D. (2017, May 9). Jeremy Corbyn hoping for Bernie Sanders election endorsement. *The Guardian.* https://www.theguardian.com/politics/2017/may/09/jeremy-corbyn-hoping-for-bernie-sanders-election-endorsement. Accessed November 14, 2017.

Mason, R. (2015, September 14). Jeremy Corbyn's victory speech: What he said, what he meant. *The Guardian.* https://www.theguardian.com/politics/ng-interactive/2015/sep/14/jeremy-corbyns-victory-speech-what-he-said-what-he-meant. Accessed November 12, 2017.

Mullen, A. (2015). Political consultants, their strategies and the importation of new political communications techniques during the 2015 general election. In D. Jackson & E. Thorsen (Eds.), *UK election analysis 2015: Media, voters and the campaign*. Bournemouth: CSJCC Publishing.

Nielsen, R. K. (2012). *Ground wars: Personalized communication in political campaigns*. Princeton: Princeton University Press.

Peggs, A. (2017, June 12). How Momentum changed British politics forever. *Huffington Post*. http://www.huffingtonpost.co.uk/adam-peggs/momentum-jeremy-corbyn_b_17054254.html. Accessed April 24, 2018.

Rampen, J. (2017, June 7). "Jeremy Corbyn is the man": Can Momentum help Labour take Croydon central? *New Statesman*. https://www.newstatesman.com/politics/elections/2017/06/jeremy-corbyn-man-can-momentum-help-labour-take-croydon-central. Accessed November 14, 2017.

Rees, E. (2017, June 12). What made the difference for Labour? Ordinary people knocking on doors. *The Guardian*. https://www.theguardian.com/commentisfree/2017/jun/12/labour-knocking-on-doors-jeremy-corbyn-momentum. Accessed November 14, 2017.

Rhodes, A. (2016). The "unelectable" elected man. In T. Unterrainer (Ed.), *Corbyn's campaign*. Nottingham: Spokesman Books.

Rhodes, A. (2017, May 26). Young voters have registered to vote in force—Theresa May made a dire mistake underestimating them. *Independent*. http://www.independent.co.uk/voices/general-election-2017-polls-voter-registration-under25-young-people-a7757976.html. Accessed November 14, 2017.

Savage, M. (2017, June 10). How Jeremy Corbyn turned a youth surge into general election votes. *The Guardian*. https://www.theguardian.com/politics/2017/jun/10/jeremy-corbyn-youth-surge-votes-digital-activists. Accessed November 14, 2017.

Savigny, H. (2003). Political marketing. *Journal of Political Marketing, 3*(1), 21–38.

Scammell, M. (1995). *Designer politics: How elections are won*. London: Macmillan.

Scammell, M., & Harrop, M. (1997). The press. In D. Butler & D. Kavanagh (Eds.), *The British general election of 1997* (pp. 156–185). London: Palgrave Macmillan.

Scammell, M., & Harrop, M. (2005). The press: Still for Labour, despite Blair. In D. Butler & D. Kavanagh (Eds.), *The British general election of 2005* (pp. 119–145). London: Palgrave Macmillan.

Schlosberg, J. (2016). *Should he stay or should he go? Television and online news coverage of the Labour Party in crisis*. Media Reform Coalition report in association with Birkbeck, University of London. http://www.mediareform.org.uk/wp-content/uploads/2016/07/Corbynresearch.pdf.

Seymour, R. (2016). *Corbyn: The strange rebirth of radical politics.* London: Verso.
Shabi, R. (2017, June 1). What use is a group of cultish, Corbynista clicktivists? Quite a lot, actually. *The Guardian.* https://www.theguardian.com/commentisfree/2017/jun/01/corbynista-clictivists-election-jeremy-corbyn-momentum. Accessed November 14, 2017.
Silvera, I. (2017, June 11). Jeremy Corbyn's viral revolution: Momentum's savvy social media strategy hailed. *International Business Times.* http://www.ibtimes.co.uk/jeremy-corbyns-viral-revolution-momentums-savvy-social-media-strategy-hailed-1625760. Accessed November 14, 2017.
The Week. (2017, June 12). How Momentum helped sway the general election. *The Week.* http://www.theweek.co.uk/general-election-2017/85501/how-momentum-helped-sway-the-general-election. Accessed November 14, 2017.
Watson, I. (2017, March 20). Labour: Momentum, Unite and a 'plan' to take over the party. *BBC News.* http://www.bbc.co.uk/news/uk-politics-39333130. Accessed November 14, 2017.
Watt, N. (2015, December 10). Information commissioner launches inquiry into Momentum group. *The Guardian.* https://www.theguardian.com/uk-news/2015/dec/10/information-commissioner-launches-inquiry-into-momentum-group-jeremy-corbyn. Accessed November 14, 2017.
Williams, Z. (2017, May 7). Labour won't be saved by talk at the top. But local action could do it. *The Guardian.* https://www.theguardian.com/commentisfree/2017/may/07/labour-saved-local-action-principles-members-share. Accessed November 14, 2017.
Wring, D. (1997). The media and the election. In A. Geddes & J. Tonge (Eds.), *Labour's landslide: The British general election 1997.* Manchester: Manchester University Press.
Wring, D. (2001). Labouring the point: Operation victory and the battle for a second term. *Journal of Marketing Management, 17,* 913–927.
Wring, D. (2005). *The politics of marketing the Labour Party.* Basingstoke and New York: Palgrave Macmillan.

#GE2017: Digital Media and the Campaigns

Declan McDowell-Naylor

The result of the 2017 UK General Election was remarkable and widely unexpected. Opinion polls had consistently shown that the Conservatives would win comfortably, increasing the party's majority, with many expecting a rout of the Labour Party. Even those sympathetic to the latter such as the Fabian Society, were warning that "when an election comes Labour may end up winning only 140 to 200 big city and ex-industrial constituencies" (Harrop 2017). However, this turned out not to be the case. After six weeks of intense campaigning a resurgent Labour had significantly narrowed the poll gap and in the final vote gained 30 seats and a 40% overall share of the general vote. Shocked commentators have offered several explanations of what happened. Some of these have considered the role and impact of digital media in the election.

Various observers have suggested new forms of campaigning might have played a key factor in the election, with Labour's digital strategy being singled out as a particularly important feature in various commentaries (Booth and Hern 2017; Dommett and Temple 2018; Dutceac Segestem and Bossetta 2017; Walsh 2017). Based around galvanizing

D. McDowell-Naylor (✉)
Royal Holloway, University of London, Egham, UK
e-mail: declan.mcdowell-naylor@rhul.ac.uk

© The Author(s) 2019
D. Wring et al. (eds.), *Political Communication in Britain*,
https://doi.org/10.1007/978-3-030-00822-2_13

187

support for the party, Labour's campaign was notable for the way in which it integrated innovative uses of digital media and an abundance of highly-willing volunteers into "new organizational strategies" which combined "online and offline citizen activism" (Chadwick 2017a). This was in direct contrast with the Conservatives' campaign which, following the election, was described in one *ConservativeHome* piece as a "rusty machine and a hollowed-out operation". It was further claimed that the party's swiftly assembled campaign was left without a clear strategy or leadership, particularly with regards to digital media (Wallace 2017a).

The 2017 result, and the features of the Conservative and Labour party's campaigns, unsettled many assumptions about the state of British party politics and laid bare two remarkable and important shifts in the British political landscape since the 2015 general election. First, this election was defined by the emergence of a strikingly clear, yet multi-dimensional, age divide between Conservative and Labour voters. On an increased turnout among young voters, Labour won every age group up to and including those aged 40–49. This age divide dynamic can be viewed as part of what James Sloam and Rakib Ehsan have referred to as 'youthquake', which they define as "a shock result founded on an unexpected surge in youth turnout" (Sloam and Ehsan 2017: 5; cf. Prosser et al. 2018).[1] Secondly, alongside this dramatic shift in voting behaviour, was the continual evolution of the UK's media landscape and the ways in which citizens consumed news. As Rasmus Kleis Nielsen demonstrated immediately prior to the election, the UK media environment has now become ever more digitally-based, with people increasingly finding their news online and on social media (Nielsen 2017).

---

[1]According to *YouGov* data shown in figure one, there was a strikingly clear set of age gaps between Conservative and Labour voters (Curtis 2017). So dramatic was this divide that age was subsequently touted as the new key predictor of voting behaviour in British politics (ibid.). Interestingly, the firmly centrist Liberal Democrats captured a consistent 7–9% of the vote in every age group, suggesting the age divide was a distinctly two-party voting phenomenon. Broken down the data showed that Labour had a higher vote share in every age group up to and including 40–49. Labour was 47% ahead among voters aged 18–19 year olds, a figure that almost directly mirrors the Conservative Party's 50% lead among voters aged 70 and over. This clearly demonstrated the sharp generational divide in this election. Compared to *YouGov's* 2015 data on British voting behaviour this was the result of a dramatic upsurge in young people voting for the Labour Party, with the percentage nearly doubling among those aged 18–29 (Kellner 2015). Moreover, the fall in young people that voted for the Conservatives was significant, but not as large as the rise in those supporting Labour.

This chapter provides insights into how these shifts in the UK's political landscape were, and continue to be, entwined with the use of online platforms in election campaigns. The 2017 campaign was characterized by remarkable innovations and failures regarding the use of digital media and data and these innovations and failures were inextricably linked to changes in relation to the age profile of voters as well as the UK's increasingly digital media environment. A core idea shapes this chapter: the Labour Party may not have won the 2017 election, but neither did the Conservatives given the workings of the first past the post system. There were, of course, numerous factors behind this surprise result (see Heath and Goodwin 2017). Within this there is much to consider in relation to the role of digital media and data and the potentially pronounced effects of their use in relation to younger people in terms of this demographic's political engagement (see Mossberger et al. 2007). 2017 was "perhaps the first social media election, in terms of the likelihood of political activities taking place on social media having an impact upon voter turnout" (Lilleker 2017: 94).

THE DIGITAL EVOLUTION OF THE UK MEDIA SYSTEM

All media systems constantly undergo change. The Reuters Institute's 2017 Digital News Report, in an analysis that spanned 36 countries, sheds light on some of the key recent changes (Newman et al. 2017). The report suggests contemporary media systems are increasingly characterized by distrust in news coverage, with some countries reporting trusts levels as little as 23%. This low level is strongly connected to perceptions of political bias, particularly in countries such as the United States (US). Social media is also undergoing new and important shifts, with WhatsApp beginning to rival Facebook in some countries as a main source of news. In contrast, many critics also view social media as an enabler of 'fake news'. Overall, the Reuters report suggests that the key issues confronting an increasingly digital world are the growing significance of certain platforms such as Facebook (see Carlson 2017; Nielsen and Ganter 2017; Kreiss and Mcgregor 2018; Kreiss et al. 2018; Stier et al. 2018; van Dijck 2013). Another factor relates to the multi-dimensional challenges facing the traditional news industry, from the redistribution of audiences to online environments to the deep flaws in public discourse that have been exposed in recent years, which offers a broad but important contextualization (see Anderson 2013; Bennett and Pfetsch 2018; Dahlgren 2018; Enli and Rosenberg 2018; Schlesinger and Doyle 2014).

The Reuters report states that the UK's media system is characterized by a "strong public broadcaster (the BBC) and a highly competitive national press struggling with digital transition" (Newman et al. 2017: 52). Shortly prior to the general election Nielsen related the report's findings to the subsequent campaign by pointing to three significant factors (Nielsen 2017). The first is that television and, by a small margin, online digital media are far and away the two primary sources of news as the gradual collapse of print continues. The second factor is the remarkable generational divide between how people source their news (see Fig. 1), with 84% of people in the 18–24 age bracket using online as a main source of news compared to just 21% of those older than 55 using online. When it comes to social media in particular, a quarter of 18–24 year olds use it as their main news source. By contrast 54% of the 55 + age group use television as a main source of news. The equivalent figure for 18–24 years olds is just 9%. Thirdly, those on the ideological left have a significantly lower level of trust in mainstream news compared with those whose political orientation is in the centre or on the right: only around 39% of left-wingers trusted the news most of the time, compared with 57% of those on the right. Reviewing this changing news landscape, Nielsen notes:

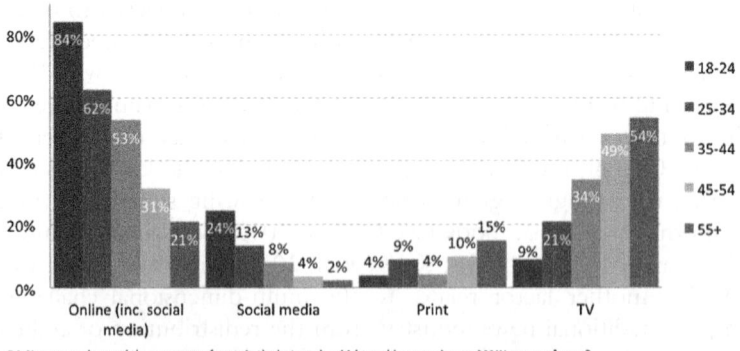

Fig. 1 Main source of news (by age group) 3. https://medium.com/oxford-university/where-do-people-get-their-news-8e850a0dea03

Media developments in the UK are in line with those seen across the world — a move to a more digital media environment, where traditional media like broadcasters and newspapers are still very important producers of news, but where many people increasingly find their news via search engines and social media. (Nielsen 2017)

In the UK, the role of the press in election campaigns has often been regarded as crucial in who wins and who loses—with the oft-repeated truism that *The Sun* always backs the winning party. However, following the 2017 general election, this influence was called into question. Writing for *Buzzfeed's* news division, and for a platform that had only existed since late 2011, political journalist Jim Waterson claimed that, "this was the election where the newspapers lost their monopoly on the political news agenda" (Waterson 2017). The majority of British newspapers are situated firmly to the right of the British partisan spectrum and have overwhelmingly portrayed Corbyn negatively since his assent to the Labour leadership (Cammaerts et al. 2016). This pattern continued throughout the 2017 general election (Waterson 2017). Despite this Labour still managed to win 30 additional seats and more importantly increase its votes share.

At the centre of the UK's changing media system is the digital evolution that Nielsen and others have analyzed. It should, however, also be noted that traditional print titles are seeking to develop and maintain their presence (and with it some potential influence) online, in that: "tabloids are successfully adapting to technologically driven shifts in the consumption of, production, and circulation of news" (Chadwick et al. 2018: 5). These popular media nonetheless face stern competition in this space from "hyperpartisan sites" such as the left-leaning Another Angry Voice, The Canary, and Evolve Politics whose growing success is predicated on the rejection of mainstream news media (Waterson 2017). Moreover, it is not just the right-leaning tabloids that are being challenged as effective campaigning media: evidence drawn from press coverage of the 2016 EU referendum showed both the left-leaning *Guardian* and the centrist *Financial Times* had extremely low audience reaches (Levey et al. 2016: 17). In this environment, emerging media organizations such as *Novara Media* are presenting themselves not just as an alternative to the right-leaning press, but also to what they criticise as a hackneyed liberal commentariat that has been lukewarm in its support for a more radicalized Labour party.

Another key dynamic in the UK is that social media platforms such as Facebook and Twitter have become increasingly important as sources for news and campaign content (Newman et al. 2017: 52; see also Nielsen and Ganter 2017: 1601; Stier et al. 2018: 50). It is now widely recognized that politics operates within what Chadwick has termed a hybrid media system in which newer forms of media, such as social media platforms, are integrated into the established media system (Chadwick 2017b). Both major parties appeared to acknowledge this reality by pouring huge amounts of money into online political advertisements via Facebook and Google during the campaign (Sabbagh 2018). This seemingly paid off, with 16m content shares of articles or videos about Theresa May or Jeremy Corbyn on Facebook between 19 April and 5 June 2017 (Littunen 2017). Media organizations have also embraced these changes, with newsrooms seeking new ways to reach audiences; but this has also resulted in a loss of control over communication channels (Nielsen and Ganter 2017: 1601). Here again, hyperpartisan news sites have therefore looked to take advantage, and now reach larger Facebook audiences than most traditional news brands (Littunen 2017). Some informed observers have argued these trends suggest "social media has opened up a new tactical front for political campaigns" (Dutceac et al. 2017: 91).

In the UK as elsewhere young people's media consumption is orienting away from broadcast and press coverage. This has created a dynamic environment in which new forms of media consumption can emerge and become established. The way in which these shifts interacted with election campaigning are significant for how the Labour Party, and the leadership's grass-roots support group Momentum, produced innovative digital media and data strategies.

"A TALE OF TWO CAMPAIGNS"

BBC News analysis published during the election referred to "a tale of two campaigns", in which the "Labour and Conservative Party appear to be running two entirely unconnected election campaigns" (Cook 2017). The piece focussed on a traditional campaign method, the leader's soapbox, to explore this phenomenon. May, it seemed, was pursuing a straightforward strategy of securing battleground seats, in constituencies the Conservatives expected to win. Corbyn, on the other hand, campaigned in both safe Labour seats and safe Conservative seats, suggesting a more enigmatic strategic approach. The BBC article was also emblematic of two major trends in the coverage of this campaign: the two main parties dominated the news, and the leaders were the focus of this attention (Deacon et al. 2017; see Bale and Webb 2018: 46). In the more submerged battleground of the digital campaign, however, few commentators sensed the entropic nature of the Conservative campaign or the innovations being cultivated by Labour and its sympathisers. As one observer put it, "most pollsters, journalists, and academics were looking for answers in the wrong places" (Walsh 2017).

The growing importance of online platforms in elections has been widely discussed with one recent study concluding "contemporary campaigning has entered a new technology-intensive era where parties and campaigns have invested considerable resources in technology, digital media, data and analytics" (Kreiss 2016: 3; see also Baldwin-Philippi 2017). In this regard, both the Labour and Conservative digital strategies for 2017 should not have come as a surprise given the wider trend of Europe political parties increasingly moving towards a "hypermedia campaign style" (Lilleker et al. 2014; this is akin to that observed in the US by Philip Howard [2006], among others). Further to this Anstead's study of data-driven campaigning during the 2015 UK General Election, based on interviews with numerous practitioners, showed that the Conservatives "seem to have adopted the US model of individual level targeting" (Anstead 2017: 307). The use of these data-driven strategies had received coverage during the 2015 campaign, with attention drawn to the ways in which parties were experimenting with digitally available voter data for door-knocking, Facebook advertising, and big-data acquisitions (Aron 2015; Channel 4 News 2015; Mount 2015; Windsor and Murphy 2014). The Conservatives re-hired Jim Messina,[2] the strategist behind President Obama's 2012 "technology-intensive" (Kreiss 2016) campaign, and he oversaw a spending rise from £1.2 million in 2015 to £2.1 on Facebook this time (Sabbagh 2018). This approach had been eulogized following the 2015 victory, with the directors of the Conservatives' Digital Team writing triumphantly that: "Digital campaigning—through emails, social media, online films and interactive websites—helped win the election for the Conservatives, as we reached over 17 million people a week with targeted online communications during the campaign" (Elder and Edmonds 2015).

[2] Messina's modelling had suggested that the Conservatives would win 371 seats in the 2017 General Election.

The Conservative Party pursued digital campaigning during the 2017 election but obviously it formed part of a less successful strategy this time. An obvious example of this was a prominent Google advertisement the party purchased when the 'Dementia Tax' came under criticism. This advert reflected the nature of a Conservative digital campaign strategy that was different to that of Labour. Fundamentally, the former pursued a rigid, Crosbyite negativity that spent far more on targeting Labour's soft support than on firming up its own. In contrast, Labour benefited from a multi-dynamic multi-platform strategy that was orientated around building support. This differing approach was another important dimension to the 'tale of two campaigns' and raises two interesting propositions that will be further explored. The first is that a previously successful Conservative Party election machine fell apart. The second is that digital media innovations are possibly renewing the Labour Party from the outside inwards. Both statements are presented here with requisite scepticism and are mindful of Kreiss's argument that the analysis of digital campaigning must "move across three levels of conceptualization: changes in underlying social and technological contexts; the strategic actions of campaigns; and the background capacities to act that campaigns have" (2015: 131).

THE CONSERVATIVE ELECTION MACHINE FELL APART

It is widely acknowledged that the Conservatives' 2017 campaign had many problems. There was the robotic and lacklustre slogan: "strong and stable", a reticent leader in Theresa May who sent Amber Rudd to the televised debates in her place and a backfiring social care policy proposal that led to a hasty U-turn. These were basic campaign errors. Following the well-below expectation result recriminations began: Theresa May survived but her key aides Fiona Hill and Nick Timothy were forced out. Lynton Crosby, the strategist behind it all admitted that the campaign had been a failure. Tim Bell, who was central to Margaret Thatcher's successful campaigns, went as far to say that "it was the worst campaign I've ever seen" (Beckett 2017). While there are numerous factors to be discussed in terms of how the Conservatives lost the media war (see Deacon and Smith 2017), the digital campaign can be identified as a key factor. As previously noted, the party had been lauded in 2015 for its digital campaigning. Yet only two years on the Conservatives struggled to successfully maintain this campaign model. This related to systemic problems with the campaign machine (see Bale and Webb

2018; Beckett 2017; Wallace 2017a, b). These might not have proved insurmountable but demographic and media changes combined with Labour's innovative digital approach all contributed to the failure of the Conservative's election gamble.

The systemic failings of the Conservatives' digital campaign were highlighted in a forensic post-mortem published on the *ConservativeHome* website by its Executive Editor Mark Wallace. According to Wallace, the hasty assembling of 2015's key specialists—Lynton Crosby, Jim, Messina, Craig Elder, and Tom Edmonds—left them with very little time to prepare for the election (Wallace 2017a). Moreover, key staff had moved on to new positions within the party, into the private sector, or had simply seen their posts cut. As one senior official told Wallace: "they had let things wither on the vine, starving [Conservative Central Headquarters - CCHQ] of both campaigning platforms and people". Another senior participant said: "The groundwork three months out [from the election] was not ready, but that question wasn't asked" (ibid.). These problems extended right the way throughout the operation. With Conservative party membership and activist resources already limited, between 100 and 120 highly-valuable campaign managers had been let go after the 2015 election, taking with them their campaign experience and established relationships with the local parties (Wallace 2017a; see also Bale and Webb 2018: 48). CCHQ's alleged complacency towards their campaign machine meant "institutional knowledge and expertise had been lost, and other assets had been mothballed or lost entirely" (Wallace 2017a).

Mark Wallace's account also drew attention to the Conservatives' data-driven resources. The party's email address database had grown significantly during the successful 2015 campaign to 1.4 million. But two years on that data had faded. Similarly the canvassing returns that had been ruthlessly exploited in Liberal Democrat seats were also now out of date—not least because those seats were no longer key battlegrounds. Yet data where they needed and wanted it, in Labour seats in the Midlands and the North, was in short supply. Digital campaigning relies on forging effective affinities between the data and the political operative on the doorstep. But as a result of the failures to collect and maintain accurate data, the Conservative activists were left without clear direction or proper resources. According to Beckett:

> Tory activists across Britain were supplied with computer-generated lists of amenable voters by Conservative campaign headquarters in London. But this time, many canvassers got a shock when they knocked on doors. "The

data was only 65 per cent accurate," says a local Tory organiser who has worked in the party's heartlands in southern England for decades. "In the marginals, it was less than 50 per cent." In some cases, canvassers were accidentally sent to the addresses of activists for rival parties. (Beckett 2017)

The problem with this aspect of the campaign apparently stemmed from CCHQ's insistence that a big-data approach—relying on information drawn from swift polling and the mass purchase of consumer data (Wallace 2017a)—should be used to target potential voters, as opposed to locally-led canvassing (Bale and Webb 2018: 48). The effect was disastrous. As Wallace (2017b) accounts, "activists were bemused that they were getting a hostile response from people whom the system told them would have a high chance of voting Conservative". According to one activist Wallace spoke to: "I was knocking up people with data that was, in some places, 15 years old". As in 2015 the Conservatives relied on consultancy services in 2017 to provide the data that would drive the campaign (Aron 2015; Booth and Hern 2017). However, in attempting to repeat the feats of the earlier election, this time around the data-driven approach failed on the doorstep.

The Conservative campaign approached the UK's increasingly digitally based media system, using targeted advertisements on social media as they had done in 2015 as part of a financially well-resourced digital operation with Edmonds and Elder again at the helm (Wallace 2017a). They could also rely upon the traditional support of large sections of the press who, with their own online presence, were "keen to bury Labour's campaign in ordure" (Deacon and Smith 2017). However as Wallace revealed, the effectiveness of this approach was blunted by issues with the campaign machine already explained, and the sheer strength of Labour's digital campaign (Wallace 2017a). The Conservatives' digital campaign was primarily paid-for and had a message that was generated centrally from CCHQ. This online effort came up against not just Labour but also a "red tide" of groups who amplified the latter's campaign message. In the end, as Wallace puts it, "people are more likely to trust a message from a group which is (at least nominally) outside the orbit of a party HQ". Moreover, the messages that the Conservatives put out were consistently at odds with the news agenda (Deacon and Smith 2017).

A combination of factors led to the failure of the Conservative campaign and these were much debated after the result. These included the digital strategy, as Jamie Bartlett wrote:

In fact, the Conservatives almost certainly misunderstood the whole nature of online life. The alt-left media was producing nicely made content and sharing it manically online. Agree or not, it was real stuff shared by real people, some of whom were more active than a Russian bot. The Tories appeared to believe they could match it with lots of sponsored links and micro-targeted adverts. But nothing screams 'not authentic' like links that say 'sponsored by the Conservative Party' underneath. (Bartlett 2017)

While Bartlett suggests the Conservatives lost the digital campaign to Labour, it is, however, too much to claim that CCHQ do not understand how to run an online operation. Despite the loss of key personnel, Conservative strategists were well aware of the underlying social and technological contexts that shape digital campaigning (Anstead 2017). Moreover the renewed presence of Messina, Edmonds and Elder made it clear that the Conservatives were willing to adapt their campaigning to the UK's increasingly digital media system. It is therefore important to caution against creating a myth that the Conservative Party is technologically illiterate. Rather, they simply did not innovate their innovation. The adoption of US-derived data-driven methods has not prevented recent campaigns looking distinctly analogue and mass-media oriented in their reliance on a centralized campaign structure, a single message and an enduring reliance on the tabloid press to articulate the case. There is now evidence of an appetite for change within the party and this was a prominent theme of Sir Eric Pickles' internal general election review (Pickles 2017; see also Ashmore [2017] and Morgan [2017]).

DIGITAL MEDIA INNOVATIONS ARE RENEWING THE LABOUR PARTY

At the outset of the campaign, Labour's joint national elections coordinator, Andrew Gwynne commented: "this is probably the first election where social media will probably have a significant impact" (Stewart 2017). Significantly, Gwynne's operation would outflank the Conservatives in this domain. Many observers concluded Labour "won the social media election", because the party "used Facebook, Twitter and online videos to build and motivate its voter base, rather than to attack the Conservatives" (Booth and Hern 2017). The party did so by clearly recognising the potential of the UK's increasingly digital media system and producing a message that resonated with younger people. Labour's operation "skilfully mobilized an active base of citizen sharers, helping extend the party's reach across Facebook and Twitter" (Dutceac Segesten and Bossetta 2017: 91). The large number of Jeremy Corbyn and Labour social media followers meant that the party had (and continues to have) a large reach when it came to disseminating information online (Walsh 2017). Compared with the Conservatives' highly-professionalized and centralized digital campaign, what emerged was "edgier, savvier and far more share-worthy content and memes [...] produced by Labour, Momentum, and by their supporters on a do-it yourself, 'organic' basis" (Bale and Webb 2018: 50). A prime example of this was Thomas Clark's popular blog Another Angry Voice, which produced 163 articles over the course of the campaign (Waterson 2017). Some believe Clark and others' efforts meant that: "Britain's younger generation and their prolific use of social media had a massive effect on the election outcome" (Polonski 2017).

During the campaign the Corbyn team was clearly willing and able to tap into the potential of viral campaign content. This was well illustrated in the Labour leader's meeting with Grime artist JME—which dovetailed with the popular #grime4corbyn hashtag. Moreover, on Facebook, Labour provided much more content (545 posts) than all of the other parties, with the Conservatives only producing 159 posts (Walsh 2017). Rather than a joined-up strategy, there was an organic synergy between a broad coalition of digital activists who came together to campaign united by Labour's message (Zagoria and Schulkind 2017). Nielsen has previously referred to the phenomenon of a "campaign assemblage" in terms of the conventional ground war but the notion seems applicable here given the enormous scale of the pro-Labour digital effort (Nielsen 2012).

Akin to the Conservatives, Labour made use of data-driven campaigning it had in 2015. By 2017 things had moved on due to technological innovations pioneered by both the party and the Corbyn-supporting activist group Momentum. Labour created Promote which, coupled with its voter database, enabled large number of members to send personalized policy messages on an individual scale (Stewart 2017). Under the guidance of Tom Watson, existing members also gained access to a phone app and web browser that enabled them to read the latest briefings, find the nearest meet up, and get the inside track on campaigning. These tools complemented others developed by Momentum such as CallForLabour and My Nearest Marginal. My Nearest Marginal was a significant innovation, which enabled any willing supporter of the campaign to easily locate their nearest battleground seat on a map and join more than (allegedly)

100,000 other people on the doorstep (Rees 2017). Technological inno-vations infused Labour's campaign, aligning with "significant sections of the public who have started to channel their social media-enabled activism into party politics" that in turn became integrated "with face-to-face door-step campaigning under the guidance of the new Labour party leadership and Corbyn's ancillary movement Momentum" (Chadwick 2017a).

At the time of the election, Labour had over half a million members and Momentum between 20,000 and 25,000 members. Both have since grown. This makes the Labour party membership nearly four times the size of the Conservatives. Although this is nowhere near the mid-20th century peak, shifts in the way in which Labour is organizing and being organized by its members could be important. Chadwick describes what is happen-ing: "Digital media foster cultures of organizational experimentation and a party-as-movement mentality that enable many individuals to reject norms of hierarchical discipline and habitual partisan loyalty" (2017a). This has the potential to recompose Labour's overall approach to political engage-ment both internally and in terms of campaigning. Much, though not all, of this has been created from the bottom up, with Momentum looking to develop more online tools to help establish a long-term digital strategy, including more sophisticated analytics, and its own online payment system (Zagoria and Schulkind 2017). This contrasts sharply with the consultan-cy-based model that the Conservatives have relied on.

Momentum has been criticized from both within and beyond the party. Yet Labour's 2017 result appears to have eased some of the ten-sions within the party, potentially clearing the ground for further renewal led by digital media and data that is orientated around maximising large numbers of more technologically literate younger members and activists. Given time to develop, this has the potential to not just help elect Labour but also change and renew the very nature of British political campaign-ing. This is not to say that, like the Conservatives, the party does not face potential problems with its digital strategy. For example, many of the types of popular content produced during for the election such as memes, have an instinctive, pervasive but time limited presence online. This type of content must remain deterritorialized and 'unofficial' to be effective and, by that virtue, is difficult to plan strategically. It would likely be counter-productive to centralize the production of messages or to try and engineer a broader reflexive effort to create pro-Corbyn memes. Given that the next General Election could be as far away as 2022 the social and technological contexts for digital campaigning will have changed.

CONCLUSION

Changes in the UK's political landscape relating to age are intertwined with an increasingly digital media environment. The 2017 election reflected this and was characterised by significant innovations within Labour's operation and dramatic failures on the part of the Conservative campaign. Strategists appear keen to learn and emulate the effective use of social media by grassroots groups like Momentum. Looking ahead this marks a particular challenge for the Conservatives, who currently suffer from a deficit in support among young people (Davidson 2018). Moreover Momentum and groups like it were not created and directed by Labour, so any parallel attempt by a Conservative equivalent would need to challenge a highly centralized model of campaign organization.

While Labour's renewal under Corbyn has taken on a centripetal nature with the dynamics working themselves from the outside in, the Conservatives appear to be attempting to renew from the centre. Both parties have been clearly attempting to develop the same methods of political engagement that integrate digital media. Going forward this hints at a wider shift orientated around targeting younger voters who until this election had been deemed largely inconsequential. With greater preparedness it is possible that the Conservatives will be able to emulate their past successes. However, given young people are both more likely vote Labour as well as be online, this suggests that the digital battleground in the UK strongly favours Labour.

The 2017 election saw the return of two-party politics. Labour and the Conservatives had the necessary resources to launch the kind of large data-driven, digital strategies which have become increasingly important in reaching and persuading voters. Even so, Britain's political parties are still getting to grips with online campaigning, despite triumphant proclamations of success in the past (see Elder and Edmonds 2015). There are still various issues to be overcome and further research is needed on data-driven campaigning more generally (Baldwin-Philippi 2017). Trends observed in the 2015 and 2017 elections highlight a need to further explore the adoption and adaption of methods used in US campaigns.[3]

---

[3] As Anstead argues, "while it [data-driven campaigning] might play a role in reshaping political parties, campaigning practices, election outcomes, and how voters relate to politics, it will also be grounded in pre-existing political practices in specific contexts" (Anstead 2017: 309; see Sloam and Ehsan [2017: 20]).

REFERENCES

Anderson, C. W. (2013). *Rebuilding the news: Metropolitan journalism in the digital age*. Philadelphia, PA: Temple University Press.

Anstead, N. (2017). Data-driven campaigning in the 2015 United Kingdom general election. *The International Journal of Press/Politics, 22*(3), 294–313.

Aron, J. (2015, April 29). Could smart search for votes swing the UK general election? *New Scientist*. https://www.newscientist.com/article/mg22630195-000-could-smart-search-for-votes-swing-the-uk-general-election/. Accessed May 30, 2018.

Ashmore, J. (2017, July 2). Tories plan beefed up social media operation to take on Labour. *PoliticsHome*. https://www.politicshome.com/news/uk/political-parties/conservative-party/news/87176/tories-plan-beefed-social-media-operation. Accessed May 30, 2018.

Baldwin-Philippi, J. (2017). The myths of data-driven campaigning. *Political Communication, 34*(4), 627–633.

Bale, T., & Webb, P. (2018). 'We didn't see it coming': The Conservatives. *Parliamentary Affairs, 71*(1), 46–58.

Bartlett, J. (2017, June 21). Emotional and authentic: How Labour won the internet. *Wired*. http://www.wired.co.uk/article/how-jeremy-corbyn-won-the-internet. Accessed May 11, 2018.

Beckett, A. (2017, June 26). How the Tory election machine fell apart. *The Guardian*. https://www.theguardian.com/politics/2017/jun/26/tory-election-machine-fell-apart-negative-tactics. Accessed May 18, 2018.

Bennett, L. W., & Pfetsch, B. (2018). Rethinking political communication in a time of disrupted public spheres. *Journal of Communication, 68*(2), 243–253.

Booth, R., & Hern, H. (2017, June 9). Labour won social media election, digital strategists say. *The Guardian*. https://www.theguardian.com/politics/2017/jun/09/digital-strategists-give-victory-to-labour-in-social-media-election-facebook-twitter. Accessed May 25, 2018.

Cammaerts, B., DeCillia, B., Magalhaes, J., & Jimenez-Martinez, C. (2016). *Journalistic representations of Jeremy Corbyn in the British press: From watchdog to attackdog*. http://eprints.lse.ac.uk/67211/1/CAmmaerts_Journalistic%20representations%20of%20Jeremy%20Corbyn_Author_2016.pdf. Accessed May 19, 2018.

Carlson, M. (2017). Facebook in the news. *Digital Journalism, 6*(1), 4–20.

Chadwick, A. (2017a, June 9). Corbyn, labour, digital media, and the 2017 UK election. *Medium*. https://medium.com/@andrew.chadwick/corbyn-labour-digital-media-and-the-2017-uk-election-ac0af06ea235. Accessed May 10, 2018.

Chadwick, A. (2017b). *The hybrid media system* (2nd ed.). Oxford: Oxford University Press.

Chadwick, A., Vaccari, C., & O'Loughlin, B. (2018). Do tabloids poison the well of social media? Explaining democratically dysfunctional news sharing. *New Media & Society*, online first.

Channel 4 News. (2015, May 23). The ruthless reality of the Election 2015 digital campaign. *Channel 4 News*. https://www.channel4.com/news/conservative-snp-election-victory-social-media-behind-scenes. Accessed May 30, 2018.

Cook, C. (2017, May 15). General election 2017: A tale of two campaigns. *BBC News*. http://www.bbc.co.uk/news/uk-politics-39927866. Accessed May 9, 2018.

Curtis, C. (2017, June 13). How Britain voted at the 2017 general election. *YouGov*. https://yougov.co.uk/news/2017/06/13/how-britain-voted-2017-general-election/. Accessed May 11, 2018.

Dahlgren, P. (2018). Media, knowledge and trust: The deepening epistemic crisis of democracy. *Javnost—The Public, 25*(1–2), 20–27.

Davidson, R. (2018, May 18). My fellow Tories, i'm afraid the crash generation just doesn't trust us. *The Guardian*. https://www.theguardian.com/commentisfree/2018/may/18/tories-crash-generation-young-people-conservative-ruth-davidson. Accessed May 30, 2018.

Deacon, D., & Smith, D. (2017, June 14). How the Conservative's media strategy collapsed during the election campaign. *The Conversation*. https://theconversation.com/how-the-conservatives-media-strategy-collapsed-during-the-election-campaign-79291. Accessed May 18, 2018.

Deacon, D., Downey, J., Smith, D., Stanyer, J., & Wring, D. (2017). *National news media coverage of the 2017 general election: Report 4: 5 May–7 June 2017*. http://blog.lboro.ac.uk/crcc/wp-content/uploads/sites/23/2017/06/media-coverage-of-the-2017-general-election-campaign-report-4.pdf. Accessed May 19, 2018.

Dommett, K., & Temple, L. (2018). Digital campaigning: The rise of Facebook and satellite campaigns. *Parliamentary Affairs, 48*(1), 189–202.

Dutceac Segesten, A., & Bossetta, M. (2017). Sharing is caring: Labour supporters use of social media #GE2017. In E. Thorsen, D. Jackson, & D. Lilleker (Eds.). *UK election analysis 2017: Media, voters and the campaign*. http://eprints.bournemouth.ac.uk/29374/10/UKElectionAnalysis2017_Thorsen-Jackson-and-Lilleker_v1.pdf. Accessed May 18, 2018.

Elder, C., & Edmonds, T. (2015, July 23). 2015 really was the first digital general election: Here are 7 lessons you should know. *The Telegraph*. https://www.telegraph.co.uk/news/general-election-2015/11757682/2015-really-was-the-first-digital-general-election-here-are-7-lessons-you-should-know.html. Accessed May 21, 2018.

Enli, G., & Rosenberg, L. T. (2018). Trust in the age of social media: Populist politicians seem more authentic. *Social Media + Society, 4*(10), 1–11.

Harrop, A. (2017). *Stuck: How Labour is too weak to win, and too strong to die.* https://www.fabians.org.uk/wp-content/uploads/2016/12/Stuck-Fabian-Society-analysis-paper.pdf. Accessed May 25, 2018.

Heath, O., & Goodwin, M. (2017). The 2017 general election, Brexit and the return of two party politics: An aggregate-level analysis of the result. *The Political Quarterly, 88*(3), 345–358.

Howard, P. (2006). *New media campaigns and the managed citizen.* Cambridge: Cambridge University Press.

Kellner, P. (2015, June 8). General election 2015: How Britain really voted. *YouGov.* https://yougov.co.uk/news/2015/06/08/general-election-2015-how-britain-really-voted/. Accessed May 11, 2018.

Kreiss, D. (2015). Digital campaigning. In S. Coleman & D. Freelon (Eds.), *The handbook of digital politics.* Cheltenham: Edward Elgar Publishing.

Kreiss, D. (2016). *Prototype politics: Technology-intensive campaigning and the data of democracy.* Oxford: Oxford University Press.

Kreiss, D., & Mcgregor, S. C. (2018). In their own words: Political practitioner accounts of candidates, audiences, affordances, genres and timing in strategic social media use. *Political Communication, 35*(2), 155–177.

Kreiss, D., Lawrence, R. G., & Mcgregor, S. C. (2018). Technology firms shape political communication: The work of Microsoft, Facebook, Twitter, and Google with campaigns during the 2016 U.S. presidential cycle. *Political Communication, 35*(1), 8–31.

Levy, D. A. L., Aslan, B., & Bironzo, D. (2016). *UK press coverage of the EU referendum.* https://reutersinstitute.politics.ox.ac.uk/sites/default/files/2017-06/UK%20Press%20Coverage%20of%20the%20EU%20Referendum_0.pdf. Accessed May 18, 2018.

Lilleker, D. G. (2017). Like me, share me: The people's social media campaign. In E. Thorsen, D. Jackson, & D. Lilleker (Eds.), *UK election analysis 2017: Media, voters and the campaign.* http://eprints.bournemouth.ac.uk/29374/10/UKElectionAnalysis2017_Thorsen-Jackson-and-Lilleker_v1.pdf. Accessed May 18, 2018.

Lilleker, D. G., Tenscher, J., & Steka, V. (2014). Towards hypermedia campaigning? Perceptions of new media's importance for campaigning by party strategists in comparative perspective. *Information, Communication and Society, 18*(7), 747–765.

Littunen, M. (2017, June 7). An analysis of news and advertising in the UK general election. *OpenDemocracyUK.* https://www.opendemocracy.net/uk/analysis-of-news-and-advertising-in-uk-general-election. Accessed May 12, 2018.

Morgan, R. (2017). Richard Morgan: CCHQ must rebuild its digital strategy from the ground up. *ConservativeHome.* http://www.conservativehome.com/platform/2017/07/richard-morgan-cchq-must-rebuild-its-digital-strategy-from-the-ground-up.html. Accessed May 30, 2018.

Mossberger, K., Tolbert, C. J., & Mcneal, R. S. (2007). *Digital citizenship: The internet, society and participation.* Cambridge: MIT Press.

Mount, H. (2015, April 1). Digital democracy: Will 2015 be the year social media wins the general election? *Evening Standard*. https://www.standard. co.uk/lifestyle/london-life/digital-democracy-will-social-media-win-the-general-election-2015-10147384.html. Accessed May 20, 2018.

Newman, N., Fletcher, R., Kalogeropoulos, A., Levy, D. A. L., & Kleis Nielsen, R. (2017). *Reuters Institute digital news report 2017*. https://reutersinstitute. politics.ox.ac.uk/sites/default/files/Digital%20News%20Report%202017%20 web_0.pdf. Accessed May 10, 2018.

Nielsen, R. K. (2012). *Ground wars*. Princeton, NJ: Princeton University Press.

Nielsen, R. K. (2017, May 30). Where do people get their news? *Medium*. https://medium.com/oxford-university/where-do-people-get-their-news-8e850a0dea03. Accessed May 25, 2018.

Nielsen, R. K., & Ganter, S. A. (2017). Dealing with digital intermediaries: A case study of the relations between publishers and platforms. *New Media & Society, 20*(4), 1600–1617.

Pickles, E. (2017). *Eric Pickles' general election review 2017*. https://www.conservatives.com/gereview. Accessed May 29, 2018.

Polonski, V. (2017). From voices to votes: How young people used social media to influence the general election. In E. Thorsen, D. Jackson, D. Lilleker (Eds.), *UK election analysis 2017: Media, voters and the campaign*. http:// eprints.bournemouth.ac.uk/29374/10/UKElectionAnalysis2017_Thorsen-Jackson-and-Lilleker_v1.pdf. Accessed May 18, 2018.

Prosser, C., Fieldhouse, E., Green, J., Mellon, J., & Evans, G. (2018). Tremors but no youthquake: Measuring changes in the age and turnout gradients at the 2015 and 2017 British general elections. https://papers.ssrn.com/sol3/ papers.cfm?abstract_id=3111839. Accessed May 19, 2018.

Rees, E. (2017, June 12). What made the difference for Labour? Ordinary people knocking on doors. *The Guardian*. https://www.theguardian.com/ commentisfree/2017/jun/12/labour-knocking-on-doors-jeremy-corbyn-momentum. Accessed May 30, 2018.

Sabbagh, D. (2018, March 18). Rise of digital politics: Why UK parties spend big on Facebook. *The Guardian*. https://www.theguardian.com/technology/2018/mar/23/facebook-digital-politics-tories-labour-online-advertising-marketing. Accessed May 21, 2018.

Schlesinger, P., & Doyle, G. (2014). From organizational crisis to multi-platform salvation? Creative destruction and the recomposition of news media. *Journalism, 16*(3), 205–323.

Sloam, J., & Ehsan, R. (2017). *Youth quake: Young people and the 2017 general election*. http://www.if.org.uk/wp-content/uploads/2017/11/Youth-Quake_ Final.pdf. Accessed May 18, 2018.

Stewart, H. (2017, April 21). Labour takes to the streets and social media to reach voters. *The Guardian*. https://www.theguardian.com/politics/2017/

apr/21/labour-takes-to-the-streets-and-social-media-to-reach-voters. Accessed May 10, 2018.

Stier, S., Bleier, A., Lietz, H., & Strohmaier, M. (2018). Election campaigning on social media: Politicians, audiences, and the meditation of political communication on Facebook and Twitter. *Political Communication, 35*(1), 50–74.

Van Dijck, J. (2013). *The culture of connectivity: A critical history of social media.* Oxford: Oxford University Press.

Wallace, M. (2017a, September 5). Our CCHQ election audit: The rusty machine, part one. Why the operation that succeeded in 2015 failed in 2017. *ConservativeHome.* https://www.conservativehome.com/majority_conservatism/2017/09/our-cchq-election-audit-the-rusty-machine-part-one-why-the-operation-that-succeeded-in-2015-failed-in-2017.html. Accessed May 18, 2018.

Wallace, M. (2017b, September 6). Our CCHQ election audit: The rusty machine, part two. How and why the ground campaign failed. *ConservativeHome.* https://www.conservativehome.com/majority_conservatism/2017/09/our-cchq-election-audit-the-rusty-machine-part-two-how-and-why-the-ground-campaign-failed.html. Accessed May 18, 2018.

Walsh, M. (2017, November 10). Understanding Labour's ingenious campaign strategy on Facebook. *LSE Blog.* http://blogs.lse.ac.uk/politicsandpolicy/explaining-labours-facebook-success/. Accessed May 18, 2018.

Waterson, J. (2017, June 18). This was the election where the newspapers lost their monopoly on the political news agenda. *Buzzfeed News.* https://www.buzzfeed.com/jimwaterson/how-newspapers-lost-their-monopoly-on-the-political-agenda?utm_term=.ts2e0VE4o4#.ykZQq2z1D1. Accessed May 19, 2018.

Windsor, G., & Murphy, S. (2014, June 20). Big data and the 2015 UK general election: Digital democracy of digitally divisive? *Nesta.* https://www.nesta.org.uk/blog/big-data-and-the-2015-uk-general-election-digital-democracy-or-digitally-divisive/. Accessed May 20, 2018.

Zagoria, T., & Schulkind, R. (2017). *How Labour activists are already building a digital strategy to win the next election.* https://www.newstatesman.com/politics/elections/2017/07/how-labour-activists-are-already-building-digital-strategy-win-next. Accessed May 29, 2018.

PART III

Polling

The Polls in 2017

Will Jennings

The 2017 general election came with the polling miss of May 2015 fresh in many memories. While the official inquiry into the performance of the pre-election polls in 2015 had reported by the time the election was called, citing unrepresentative samples as the major factor in the under-estimation of Conservative support and over-estimation of Labour (Sturgis et al. 2016, 2017), many pollsters were not yet on a war-footing. This meant some planned methodological fixes or innovations had to be introduced hastily or set aside for the future. And while many pundits had declared after 2015 that they would never trust opinion polls again, the polls were once again a central feature of the general election—with a total of 85 polls conducted during the course of the 8-week campaign, compared to 92 in 2015. Some 18 polls were conducted in the final week of the campaign.

In contrast to the previous election, where polls had told a story of relative stability in vote intentions (despite misleading over the likely outcome), in 2017 they revealed an electorate that was in a state of flux. Indeed, they seemingly gave a clear picture of the shifts in support that occurred as the campaign unfolded. The Conservatives began the official campaign with a commanding lead. A ComRes poll fielded just after the

W. Jennings (✉)
University of Southampton, Southampton, UK
e-mail: w.j.jennings@soton.ac.uk

© The Author(s) 2019

D. Wring et al. (eds.), *Political Communication in Britain*,
https://doi.org/10.1007/978-3-030-00822-2_14

election had been called put the party 25 points ahead of Labour, on 50 to 25%. After an initial rally in the polls where they seemed unbeatable, averaging in the high 40s, the Conservatives saw their support falter—following a damaging U-turn over proposals on social care (dubbed the 'dementia tax' by opponents)—back to the mid- to low-40s.

Contrary to the expectations of most people (including many in the parliamentary party), Labour saw its support rise sharply from the mid-20s to the mid- to high-30s—as the party defied predictions of a wipe-out in the Leave-voting parts of its heartlands. The final polls put Labour at anywhere between 33 and 40%—leaving persisting doubts over the depth of its revival with the electorate.

At the same time, the Lib Dems, UKIP and Greens all saw their support squeezed by the main parties during the campaign. UKIP in particular suffered a collapse—from polling above 10% before the election was announced to less than half that by Election Day (and even then the polls substantially overstated their support).

Figure 1 plots all polls fielded in the period between the announcement of the election by Theresa May on 18 April and Election Day on 8 June

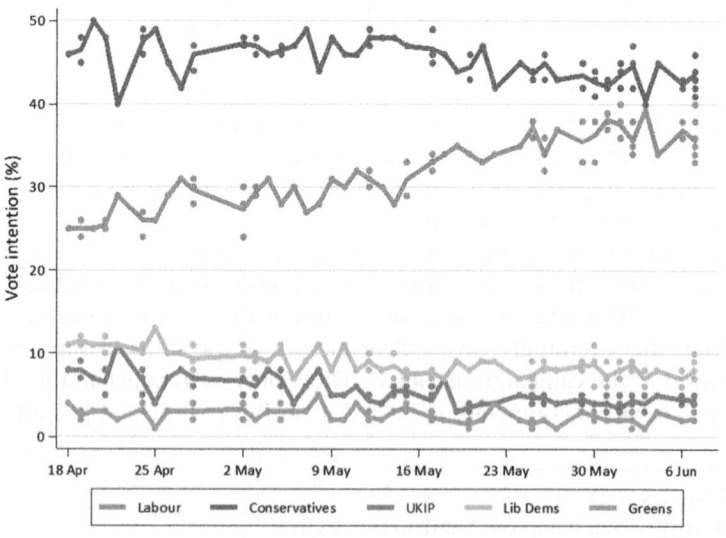

Fig. 1   Vote intention polls during the 2017 general election (Great Britain)

(polls are dated according to the end of the fieldwork period), alongside the daily poll average over this period. What is striking from the graph is that change in voting intentions for each of the parties—whether they gained or lost ground over the campaign—was relatively gradual (aside, of course, from those fluctuations due to sampling error and changes in the mix of polling companies in the field at a given point in time, see Pickup et al. 2011; Ford et al. 2016), rather than being associated with a specific event.

The underlying dynamics of the campaign mirrored the trend in the public's ratings of the two party leaders. Theresa May had started the year with huge leads over Jeremy Corbyn in terms both of net satisfaction with leader performance (as surveyed by Ipsos MORI) and as party leader considered to be the best prime minister (as tracked by YouGov), but saw these slump during the course of May and June. By the time of the election this advantage had largely vanished. These leader polls are displayed in Fig. 2. The general election of 2017 thus was not an exception to the importance of perceptions of competence to elections (see Green and Jennings 2017), but rather confirmed it.

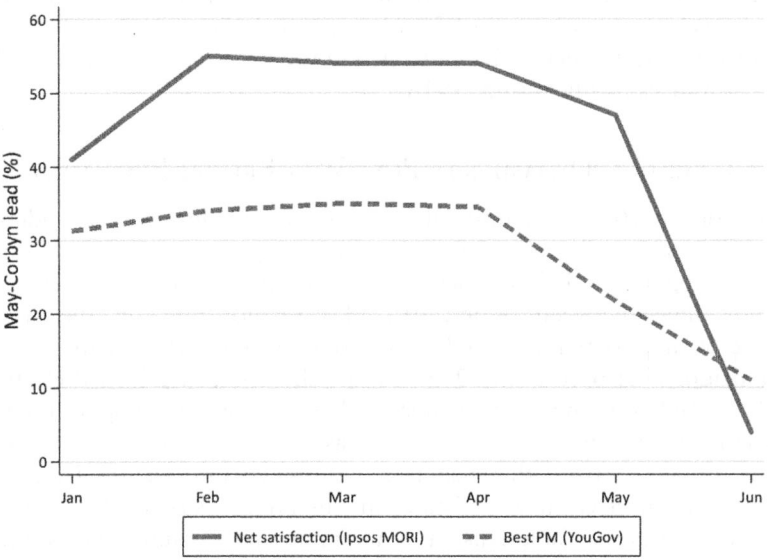

Fig. 2 Theresa May lead over Jeremy Corbyn, net leader satisfaction and best prime minister, 2017

The election also saw a polling innovation new to British general elections: the MRP ('multilevel regression post-stratification') model developed by Ben Lauderdale, Doug Rivers and Jack Blumenau for YouGov (see Lauderdale and Rivers 2017). This used a large sample first to model the likelihood of an individual with specified characteristics voting for a given party—and then used information on the demographic composition of constituencies to estimate the party vote shares. When the model was launched on 30 May, there was much consternation in response to its prediction of a hung parliament, with the Conservatives on 310 seats (Coates 2017), contrary to all expectations. Just a month earlier one pundit had forecast that Labour could lose up to 80 seats (Hawkes 2017). This perhaps should not have come as a complete surprise, however, as some polls around this time were showing the lead at just 5–6 points (although others suggested a much larger gap). It would be an under-statement to say the MRP model was not without its sceptics. Jim Messina—the former Obama advisor and consultant to the Conservative campaign—infamously tweeted "Spent the day laughing at yet another stupid poll from YouGov" in response. YouGov had the final laugh as their model proved extremely accurate on election night, correctly picking the winner in 93% of seats—including some of the most surprising results, such as Labour's win in Canterbury, a constituency the Conservatives had held since 1918.

CAMPAIGN DYNAMICS IN POST-WAR BRITISH ELECTIONS

The polls in 2017 were unusual in seemingly revealing a deep underlying shift in voters' preferences: whereby during the course of the campaign support for Labour increased by around 15 points and its poll rating ranged between 24 and 40%. This was not, however, the largest range of support that a party had previously received during an election campaign. That occurred in 2010, where the first ever televised election debate, and resulting 'Cleggmania', led to a bubble in support for the Liberal Democrats—reaching as high as 34% in the polls (contrasted with a low of 16%)—that had largely subsided by Election Day. The 2017 general election was distinct in observing a sustained change in voters' intentions. Table 1 lists the minimum and maximum poll ratings for each party in all post-war elections, along with the calculated range. Other elections in which parties were subject to a similarly wide range of polling included Labour in 1983—where the party faced the electoral

Table 1   Range of the polls by general election, Britain 1945–2017 (in percentages)

Election	Con			Lab			Lib		
	Max	Min	Range	Max	Min	Range	Max	Min	Range
1945	33	32	1	45	45	0	15	15	0
1950	44	44	0	41.5	41.5	0	12.5	12.5	0
1951	52	52	0	41	41	0	6.5	6.5	0
1955	51	48	3	47.5	44	3.5	7	1.5	5.5
1959	51.2	45	6.2	47.5	42.9	4.6	9.1	4.7	4.4
1964	47.1	44.5	2.6	47	44.1	2.9	9.8	7.1	2.7
1966	42.5	39.2	3.3	53.8	50	3.8	8	6.5	1.5
1970	45.5	39.2	6.3	51.6	48	3.6	7.9	4.5	3.4
1974 (F)	44.5	36	8.5	43	35.2	7.8	23	11	12
1974 (O)	39	31	8	45.5	39.5	6	21	15	6
1979	54.5	42.1	12.4	43.1	33.5	9.6	15	5	10
1983	52	41	11	37	23	14	29	14	15
1987	46	39	7	37	28	9	30	18	12
1992	43	35	8	43	37.5	5.5	23	12	11
1997	37	27	10	56.5	42	14.5	19	9	10
2001	34	26	8	55	43	12	20	11	9
2005	37	26	11	41	35	6	25	18	7
2010	41	31	10	33	23	10	34	16	18
2015	39	30	9	37	29	8	12	5	7
2017	50	40	10	40	24	16	13	6	7

challenge of the SDP—and the Conservatives in 1979 and Labour in 1997 and 2001—all instances where a party that went on to win a comfortable majority was over-estimated in the polls at one point or another (before later falling back). In this regard the historical polling record should have perhaps have forewarned of some 'regression to the mean' in the fluctuation of party support.

Another way to illustrate change in voters' intentions over the campaign is to consider how these poll estimates line up with the election result at different points in time (see Wlezien et al. 2017). In Fig. 3 we plot the difference between the poll share and the vote share for a given party—using poll data for the period between 1945 and 2017 (from Wlezien et al. 2013; Jennings and Wlezien 2016, 2018). A value of greater than zero indicates that the polls over-estimate support for a party relative to the election result, while a value of less than zero indicate that support is under-estimated in the polls. In most instances this

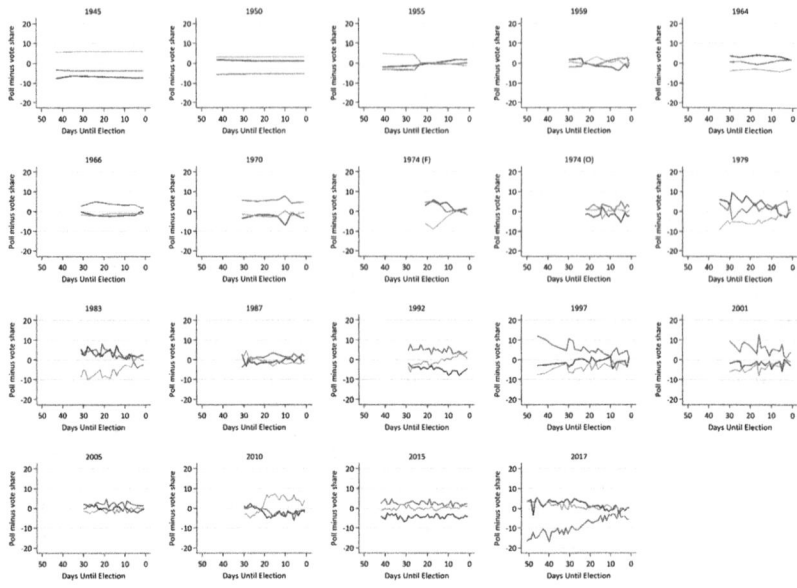

Fig. 3   Poll minus vote share, general elections 1945–2017

net 'error' declines as Election Day approaches as the polls converge on the result. Even at the end of the election cycle, however, polls are not perfect predictors of the election outcome. Visualizing the polls in this way helps reveal changes in voters' preferences over time and also reveals bias in the final poll estimates, such as the tendency—in most elections since 1979—for Labour's support to be overstated. The figure again highlights the unusual scale of the change in Labour's poll share—and that the party gained ground during the campaign (also a rare occurrence).

Performance of the Polls in 2017

How well did the polls perform in predicting the election outcome? Table 2 presents the final poll of the campaign for each pollster contrasted against the result. It considers two measures of polling accuracy—the net error (described above) and the absolute error (simply the absolute value of the net error, which captures how far, on average, poll

Table 2   Final polls for the 2017 general election (in percentages)

Pollster	Fieldwork	Sample	Con	Lab	UKIP	Lib Dem	Green	Con lead over Lab
Ipsos MORI	6–7 June	1291	44	36	4	7	2	8
BMG	6–7 June	1199	46	33	5	8	3	13
Survation	6–7 June	2798	41	40	2	8	2	1
ICM	6–7 June	1532	46	34	5	7	2	12
YouGov	5–7 June	2130	42	35	5	10	2	7
ComRes	5–7 June	2051	44	34	5	9	2	10
Panelbase	2–7 June	3018	44	36	5	7	2	8
Kantar Public	1–7 June	2159	43	38	4	7	2	5
SurveyMonkey	4–6 June	11,000	42	38	4	6	2	4
Opinium	4–6 June	3002	43	36	5	8	2	7
Poll average			43.5	36	4.4	7.7	2.1	7.5
Result (GB)			43.5	41	1.9	7.6	1.7	2.5
Mean absolute error			1.3	5	2.5	0.9	0.4	
Mean net error			0	−5	+2.5	+0.1	+0.4	

estimates for a given party are from the election result—without regard for direction of the error)[1]—taking the mean across all pollsters.

Here we see that in 2017 the polling industry collectively performed well in accurately predicting the Conservative vote, with a mean net error of zero (this represented a substantial improvement on a net error of −4.1 points in 2015, cf. Sturgis et al. 2016). While some pollsters over-estimated their support, and some under-estimated it (reflected in a MAE of 1.3 points across all the pollsters), these errors cancelled out. In contrast, the polling industry systematically under-estimated the Labour vote by 5 points. The MAE is here the same value as the mean net error (apart from the sign of course), because all pollsters' estimates were under the final Labour vote. If the MAE on 'the margin' is taken as our measure instead, i.e. the error on the Conservative-Labour lead, this is equal to 5.3 points. Based on this benchmark the 2017 election polls

---

[1] The mean absolute error (MAE) can be expressed as the mean of absolute error $|x_i - y_i|$ across n observations where x_i is the poll estimate and y_i is the election outcome:

$$MAE = \frac{1}{n} \sum_{i=1}^{n} |x_i - y_i|.$$

were misleading, given consequences of that error when translated into parliamentary seats (as quickly became apparent on election night with the shock when the exit poll predicted a hung parliament). This represented a reversal from the 2015 election where the Conservative lead was under-estimated by 6.5 points. In terms of polling accuracy, 2017 differed markedly from 2015.

Another notable feature of the 2017 election, which has been widely ignored, was the 2.5 point error for the UKIP vote. This might appear small but is large if one considers that the margin of error is a function of the vote proportion[2] (i.e. for a sample of 1000 people the margin of error is equal to 3.0 points for a party receiving 41% of the vote and equal to 0.8 points for a party receiving 1.9% of the vote). Little explanation has been put forward for this since the election, and it could yet be a sign of something awry with pollsters' samples or adjustments—that could matter in future.

THE HISTORICAL PERFORMANCE OF POLLING IN BRITAIN, 1945–2017

It is also helpful to further consider how polls for 2017 general election compare to the historical track record of the polls in Britain. Table 3 reports the vote and poll shares for the Conservative and Labour parties, along with the mean net error and MAE, for all elections between 1945 and 2017. From this, it is evident that 2017 was pollsters' best performance on the Conservative vote share in many years, according to both the mean absolute and net error. However, it was also the largest miss on the Labour vote share in all elections since 1945, and was unusual in under-estimating Labour support. The mean absolute error on the Conservative-Labour margin (5.3 points) was large in historical terms, but not exceptional; the error on the margin was higher in 1951, 1970, October 1974, 1992, 1997 and 2015. It was not much lower in 1983 and 2001.

The Impact of Turnout Adjustments on Polling Accuracy

The final report of the British Polling Council/Market Research Society inquiry into the pre-election polls for the 2015 general election concluded

---

[2]For a proportion p and sample size n, the margin of error is equal to: $\pm 1.96 \times \sqrt{\frac{p(1-p)}{n}}$.

Table 3 Mean absolute error by general election, Britain 1945–2017 (in percentages)

Election	Vote share		Final polls		Net error		Mean absolute error			
	Con	Lab	Con	Lab	Con	Lab	Avg.	Con	Lab	Con-Lab margin
1945	39.3	48.8	41.0	47.0	1.7	−1.8	1.8	1.7	1.8	3.5
1950	42.9	46.8	44.5	43.8	1.6	−3.0	2.3	1.6	3.0	4.6
1951	47.8	49.4	49.8	45.3	2.0	−4.1	3.1	2.0	4.1	6.1
1955	49.2	47.4	50.6	47.4	1.4	−0.1	0.8	1.4	0.2	1.5
1959	48.8	44.6	48.6	45.5	−0.2	0.9	0.8	0.4	1.2	1.1
1964	42.9	44.8	44.3	45.8	1.4	1.0	1.5	1.4	1.5	1.4
1966	41.4	48.7	40.1	51.3	−1.3	2.6	2.1	1.5	2.6	3.9
1970	46.2	43.8	44.0	48.2	−2.2	4.4	3.3	2.3	4.4	6.5
1974 (F)	38.6	38.0	38.6	36.0	0.0	−2.0	1.7	1.3	2.0	2.6
1974 (O)	36.6	40.2	34.1	43.3	−2.5	3.1	2.8	2.5	3.1	5.6
1979	44.9	37.7	44.7	38.8	−0.2	1.1	1.0	0.7	1.3	1.6
1983	43.5	28.3	45.9	25.6	2.4	−2.7	2.6	2.4	2.7	5.1
1987	43.2	31.5	42.4	34.3	−0.8	2.8	1.9	1.0	2.8	3.6
1992	42.8	35.2	37.6	39.1	−5.2	3.9	4.6	5.2	3.9	9.2
1997	31.5	44.3	30.2	47.7	−1.3	3.4	3.1	2.3	3.8	5.6
2001	32.7	42.0	30.9	45.1	−1.8	3.1	2.5	1.9	3.1	5.0
2005	33.2	36.1	31.8	38.0	−1.4	1.9	1.7	1.4	1.9	3.3
2010	36.9	29.7	35.4	27.5	−1.5	−2.2	1.9	1.5	2.2	1.3
2015	37.8	31.2	33.6	33.5	−4.2	2.3	3.3	4.2	2.4	6.5
2017	43.5	41.0	43.5	36.0	0.0	−5.0	3.2	1.3	5.0	5.3

that the polling error was largely due to unrepresentative samples (Sturgis et al. 2016), though it noted a number of potential weaknesses of methodologies that might impact on polling accuracy in future elections. In the 2017 election, pollsters' choice of turnout adjustment appears to have been a critical factor in the size of error on the Conservative and Labour vote share. In an article written prior to the election, 'Will turnout weighting prove to be the pollsters' Achilles heel in #GE2017?', Patrick Sturgis and I noted the substantial effects of turnout adjustments on the Conservative-Labour lead, which on average increased it by 5 points, and in some cases as much as 8 or 9 points. It was understandable that pollsters were concerned with turnout in 2017, given that Labour's support seemed to be being driven substantially by younger voters but it was widely recognized that older respondents have a greater propensity to vote.

Replicating that analysis for the final polls (see Table 4) reveals that the effect of turnout adjustments on the Conservative lead, consistent with our earlier findings, was an increase of 5 points. Without the turnout weights, the poll estimates predicted a lead of 2.6 points, just 0.1 points off the actual result. These methodological adjustments varied by pollster, with some firms using self-reported likelihood to vote to weight respondents and others using turnout probability models (based on the demographic characteristics of respondents). The average error on the lead was around 9 points for those pollsters using turnout probability models, whereas it was just over 3 points for those using self-reported likelihood to vote. Turnout adjustments did reduce the error on the Conservative vote, addressing the bias at previous general elections, but with the side-effect of increasing the error on the Labour vote.

Table 4 Effects of turnout adjustments on poll estimates in the 2017 election (in percentages)

Pollster	Mode	Adjustment	Fieldwork	Poll estimates with turnout weight			Poll estimate without turnout weight		
				Con (%)	Lab (%)	Con lead	Con (%)	Lab (%)	Con lead
Ipsos MORI	Phone	Self-reported	6–7 June	44	36	8	41	41	0
BMG	Online	Turnout probability	6–7 June	46	33	13	41	39	2
Survation	Phone	Self-reported	6–7 June	41	40	1	42	40	2
ICM	Online	Turnout probability	6–7 June	46	34	12	43	38	5
YouGov	Online	Self-reported	5–7 June	42	35	7	41	38	3
ComRes	Online	Turnout probability	5–7 June	44	34	10	40	39	1
Kantar Public	Online	Self-reported	1–7 June	43	38	5	40	39	1
SurveyMonkey	Online	None	4–6 June	42	38	4	42	38	4
Opinium	Online	Self-reported	4–6 June	43	36	7	42	37	5
			Mean	*43.5*	*36.0*	*7.5*	*41.3*	*38.7*	*2.6*
			Actual	43.5	41	2.5			

While it would not be desirable to abandon attempts to better model likelihood to vote, the experience of 2017 highlights the risk of fighting the last methodological war and also that demographic patterns of turnout will not necessarily be fixed from one election to the next.

CONCLUSIONS

The general election of 2017 raised as many questions as it answered in terms of polling. It was far from the British polling industry's finest hour—with a substantial under-estimation of the Labour vote and error on the Conservative-Labour margin—yet there were silver linings. These were found in the unusually good performance on the Conservative vote share and the promise shown by YouGov's MRP model, while the polls accurately told the story of a surprise Labour comeback under Jeremy Corbyn, even if the final estimates fell short. Importantly, the polling 'miss' in 2017 was very different from that in 2015: with the former seemingly associated with turnout adjustments (Sturgis and Jennings 2017) whereas the latter was attributed to unrepresentative samples by the official inquiry (Sturgis et al. 2016). Certainly the experience of 2015 (and the 2016 referendum on Britain's membership of the EU) meant that most in the world of politics and media were rather more prepared for surprises, or at least were less bullish about the accuracy of the polls.

REFERENCES

Coates, S. (2017, May 31). Poll firm predicts shock losses for Theresa May's Tories at general election. *The Times*. https://www.thetimes.co.uk/article/latest-general-election-poll-predicts-conservatives-will-lose-seats-02zfwl8lc.

Ford, R., Jennings, W., Pickup, M., & Wlezien, C. (2016). From polls to votes to seats: Forecasting the 2015 British general election. *Electoral Studies, 41*(1), 244–249.

Green, J., & Jennings, W. (2017). *The politics of competence: Parties, public opinion and voters*. Cambridge: Cambridge University Press.

Hawkes, S. (2017, April 28). End for the reds: Labour heads for its worst election in 86 years as Jeremy Corbyn's leadership and UKIP collapse hands Tories prized seats. *The Sun*. https://www.thesun.co.uk/news/3368305/labour-heads-for-its-worst-election-in-86-years-as-jeremy-corbyns-leadership-and-ukip-collapse-hands-tories-prized-seats/.

Jennings, W., & Wlezien, C. (2016). The timeline of elections: A comparative perspective. *American Journal of Political Science, 60*(1), 219–233.

Jennings, W., & Wlezien, C. (2018). Election polling errors across time and space. *Nature: Human Behaviour,* (2), 276–283.

Lauderdale, B., & Rivers, D. (2017, June 9). UK election: The day after. *YouGov Blog.* https://yougov.co.uk/news/2017/06/09/the-day-after/.

Pickup, M., Matthews, S., Jennings, W., Ford, R., & Fisher, S. (2011). Why did the polls overestimate Liberal Democrat support? Sources of polling error in the 2010 British general election. *Journal of Elections, Public Opinion and Parties, 21*(2), 179–209.

Sturgis, P., & Jennings, W. (2017, June 4). 'Will turnout weighting prove to be the pollsters' Achilles heel in #GE2017? *Sotonpolitics blog.* https://sotonpolitics.org/2017/06/04/will-turnout-weighting-prove-to-be-the-pollsters-achilles-heel-in-ge2017/.

Sturgis, P., Baker, N., Callegaro, M., Fisher, S., Green, J., Jennings, W., et al. (2016). *Report of the inquiry into the 2015 British general election opinion polls.* London: Market Research Society and British Polling Council.

Sturgis, P., Kuha, J., Baker N., Callegaro, M., Fisher S., Green, J., et al. (2017). An assessment of the causes of the errors in the 2015 UK general election opinion polls. *Journal of the Royal Statistical Society: Series A, 181*(3), 757–781.

Wlezien, C., Jennings, W., & Erikson, R. S. (2017). The "timeline" method of studying electoral dynamics. *Electoral Studies, 48,* 45–56.

Wlezien, C., Jennings, W., Fisher, S., Ford, R., & Pickup, M. (2013). Polls and the vote in Britain. *Political Studies, 61*(S1), 129–154.

"Yer Jaiket Is Hanging by a Shooglie Peg!": Fear, Groupthink and Outliers

Damian Lyons Lowe

INTRODUCTION

Survation was founded in 2010 with the ambition of building a general market research firm from scratch. Conducting political polls for media consumption seemed a good way to gain publicity; however, if Survation was to compete with established players, and gain publicity for our work, we would need a reputation for accuracy in collecting public opinion. As a product of this strategy, political work as a proportion of our daily activity is likely the highest in the industry.

As well as making a decent start picking up media clients using online polling, by 2012 we had become a prolific provider of constituency telephone polling, using careful methods with available data to construct representative sample frames of named persons with careful attention to their demographics. Just one of a number of our clients conducted 139 quantitative polls in 73 constituencies between August 2013 and April 2015.

D. Lyons Lowe (✉)
Survation, London, UK
e-mail: damian.lyonslowe@survation.com

© The Author(s) 2019
D. Wring et al. (eds.), *Political Communication in Britain*,
https://doi.org/10.1007/978-3-030-00822-2_15

221

I had hoped that by now, eight years on, I would not be here outlining the methods chosen to produce our accurate General Election polls in 2017 but rather celebrating a second successful General Election prediction.

Sadly, the false comfort of being part of a consensus during the 2015 General Election led us to not question ourselves enough in our online work, and fear of being an outlier led us not to publish our final telephone poll of the 2015 General Election—which turned out to be highly accurate.

However we learned a great deal from these painful experiences, which set us up well for 2017.

At Survation, we successfully resisted the pressures an apparent "outlier" can be subject to in our early years. This benefited the company in many ways, for example correctly capturing the rise of UKIP—being the first company to include the party in the main voting prompt from 2012 (441), despite criticism that this would produce far higher figures than was the reality (sometimes three times the vote share of other methods). But the decision proved sound: in the 2013 elections UKIP won over 140 seats and averaged 25% of the vote in the wards where it was standing (BBC News 2013). Some resisted including UKIP in the main voting intention even for the 2014 European Elections. The reasoned logic was that this would result in an unrealistically high figure for the party, including one company producing detailed research (Kellner 2013) to "prove" that we were wrong. Our "outlier" practice of prompting the purple party in the end became standard practice for the European elections and pollsters including Survation correctly predicted UKIP would win that election, taking more than 27% of the vote in Great Britain.

In the run up to the 2014 Scottish Independence referendum, Survation were among a small group of polling companies (with ICM and Panelbase) forecasting that the vote would be a far closer affair than had been the expectation. Our online methodology in particular was criticized, and in some detail (Curtice 2014).

To add greater certainty to our final figures, and as a secondary check against the possibility something had gone awry with online sampling in Scotland, we initiated our first sample-frame telephone poll design as our final poll for the 2014 Scottish Independence Referendum (the method we chose to use for our final 2015 General Election, 2016 Referendum and 2017 General Election polls). We constructed a pre-stratified sample of named persons we believed to be representative of the Scottish population as a whole, making multiple attempts to contact individual persons via landline and mobile phone appropriate to their age group (so, for example, we would only usually contact a 75+year old via landline and we would only usually contact an 18–24 year old via mobile), taking elements such as time of day into account in order to contact harder-to-reach demographics.

Survation's final poll was the most accurate (by a mere 0.1%)—but effectively sharing "joint honours" with Ipsos MORI.

Survation's 2015 election experience performance was similar to that of the industry—we produced poll after poll (online) for the *Daily Mirror* showing Labour and the Conservatives "neck and neck".

As with the 2014 Scottish Independence Referendum, we had planned for our final poll to be the unique telephone method we had initiated as a guard against potential issues in the case of an unrepresentative sample—calls were made on the eve of polling day with interviews running until 9 p.m. to be published sometime after 10 p.m. We were expecting something along the lines of CON or LAB assuming some sort of small lead, in line with the type of difference we had seen in the 2014 Scottish Independence Referendum.

Our lead statistician at the time came running into our election "war room" in state of high excitement. He was tabulating work for multiple clients that evening, and yet to produce data tables for this final poll, but grabbed a marker pen and wrote the voting intention out:

CON 37.3 LAB 30.6 LD 10.0 UKIP 10.6 GRE 5.2 SNP 3.8

A Conservative lead of 6.7%—completely different to anything we or the industry had in our final online polling. After checking whether there was any obvious reason to suspect the poll was a rogue, we were left scratching our heads. *Had the whole industry including ourselves got the election entirely wrong?*

Our media client in 2015—*Daily Mirror*—had not commissioned this poll but we'd informed them we would be conducting it as a "check" against the online work. I called the *Mirror*'s election desk to relay that we had a poll that was far away from the narrative of all our previous online work. The person who eventually answered the phone explained there was no-one available to publish anything at that time of night.

This left us with one other option in the hour we now had left for the poll to "count" as a final poll—we could self-publish the figures.

We knew what this would mean—we would be either the only polling company that got the 2015 General Election right *or* be the laughing stock of the industry, bottom of any accuracy table and perhaps go out of the political polling business altogether.

After some torturous thought, fear of failure won the day and we decided not to tabulate and publish the data at that time.

The Conservative lead in the 2015 GE was 6.4 versus our 6.7% in this poll—a very harsh lesson to bear about the fear of being an outlier (Belam 2015). We sent the raw data to the BPC the following day, as the data would be relevant to the inevitable polling enquiry that would follow.

WHY DO POLLSTERS FEAR BEING OUTLIERS?

Elections are competitive from the point of view of companies and their political departments "getting it right". Many in the industry only decide to risk conducting election predictions as it brings publicity to their commercial work (nobody gets rich producing only political polls). Getting elections "wrong" brings negative publicity for your company, and some have tactically withdrawn from conducting political polling at all—seeing little upside potential in the risk of staking the company's otherwise good public reputation on a single final political prediction.

The fear of *being* an outlier, and therefore having the potential to be singled out as the "company or pollster that got it wrong", leads to a number of perfectly logical phenomena.

1. If you are not an outlier: you may elect to not change or challenge your methodology. It is producing similar results to others whom you respect based on past performance. You feel you are "getting it right". You may conduct fewer experiments than you might otherwise to test your methods—which may have been the culprit of polling companies including ourselves producing such similar results in 2015.

2. You are becoming an outlier: seeing your data moving away from consensus, you may examine your methodology carefully and be more likely to make what seem like sensible changes that move you closer to the consensus than away from it—consider this paragraph from the official report of the 2015 miss in this context:

The decrease in the variance on the estimate of the Conservative lead in the final week of the campaign is consistent with herding – where pollsters make design and reporting decisions that cause published estimates to vary less than expected, given their sample sizes. Our interpretation of the evidence is that this convergence was unlikely to have been the result of deliberate collusion, or other forms of malpractice by the pollsters. (Sturgis et al. 2016: 5)

3. You are a clear outlier: you or your company may decide that your polling is so far away from the consensus it presents a risk to your reputation and may elect to not publish your poll at all. This happened in the case of Survation's final telephone poll of 2015, and to at least one other company in the 2017 election.

These experiences—both the positive and negative—taught us valuable lessons which I believe set Survation up well for the 2017 General Election. Having a representative sample would be key; other vital steps were:

- Choosing a clear methodology for online or telephone and sticking to it;
- Not making the mistake of even minor adjustments to method based on the figures produced by others;
- Employing sufficient tests to interrogate your assumptions.

If those steps are taken and your assumptions have been sufficiently scrutinized, but you still find yourself as a significant outlier, have the courage to maintain your process and publish, whatever the consequences of failure.

BECOMING THE 2017 OUTLIER

At the beginning of the campaign, our polling showed smaller but comfortable leads for the Conservatives over Labour than the industry. However, as the campaign drew to a close, all other polling companies were still producing voting intention polls showing Conservative leads ranging from "comfortable" to "landslide victory".

Our telephone polling series for ITV's *Good Morning Britain* began reporting successive declines in the Conservative lead through May and

on a memorable Saturday—3 June, with five days until polling day—
I was at home (for a change) for my daughter's tenth birthday party.
A glance at my phone showed data tables arriving for a new online poll
for the following day's *Mail on Sunday*—their final election edition. I
popped upstairs to my home office to check the voting intention table
and felt a sort of sinking feeling—we were to be at that point not only
the outlier pollster with the highest figure for Labour at 39%, but the
figures would indicate that the whole election outcome had flipped for
us from a Conservative majority to hung parliament, something no other
polls were showing.

Needing to call this in to Simon Walters, the *Mail on Sunday*'s
Political Editor, I somewhat nervously requested that the birthday cake
cutting be delayed for a further 10 minutes: "Simon…I think you might
need to hold some space for the front page".

The *Mail on Sunday*'s front page the following day announced:
"Shock poll as Tory lead cut to 1% with just 4 days to go".

We were also conducting UK telephone polling using our carefully constructed methodology on that final weekend—2–3 June—and
a second set of data tables arrived. The voting intention? CON 42%
LAB 40%. Based on this secondary input, which used an entirely different method to the online polling, it was now looking unlikely that the
"shock" poll was a "rogue" poll.

Although the trend of our polling felt in line with the direction of the
campaign and the concomitant improvement of Jeremy Corbyn's ratings
against May's using questions such as "best Prime Minister?", we were
still way out of line with the rest of the industry.

"YER JAIKET IS HANGING BY A SHOOGLIE PEG!"— BROADCASTING HOUSE, 7 JUNE

As the only polling company with results indicating a hung parliament,
we were now in the firing line that an outlier pollster can find himself or
herself in.

I appeared as a guest on the BBC's *Daily Politics* programme on election day eve, my first appearance on the show during the campaign, to
explain why, contrary to consensus, we had confidence in the position
that a *reduced* Conservative majority and hung parliament was the most
likely result.

Despite election fatigue and on-going work ahead, I agreed to appear on the show to highlight a response we had made to the many critics of our methodology via a blog article (Lyons Lowe et al. 2017) published to attempt to explain why—regardless of the consensus of expert and media views to the contrary—we were confident in our numbers, and why we would not change or tweak our methodology despite apparent "flaws" being pointed out as our work was carefully inspected by peers in the industry, media and political academics.

The interview illustrates the direct and indirect psychological pressure of being an "outlier" in elections, as the discussion participants reacted to my prediction of "no overall majority situation with at least the requirement for the support from the DUP" with a mix of derision, mockery and disbelief.

An edited transcript follows with the BBC's Andrew Neil (AN), Ed Vaizey (EV), David Lammy (LAM), Deborah Mattinson (DM) and myself (DLL).

> *AN*: One firm, Survation, said on Monday that it believed the Conservative lead over Labour's down to just one point. Other polling firms think the Tories are as much as 12 points ahead. So we're joined now by Damian Lyons Lowe from Survation and Deborah Mattinson from Britain Thinks, welcome to you both.
>
> *AN*: Now your poll predicts a 1-point lead for the Conservatives, some of us remember in the start of this campaign in some polls over 20 points. One point would mean a hung parliament and the Tories losing a majority, wouldn't it?!
>
> *DLL*: It would mean, using our most recent Scotland figures using our most recent figures from the *Sunday Post* {Scotland data}, plugging those into a Scotland predictor..and plugging in, doing a simple national swing and a few tweaks - nothing too special - it would mean there would be a no overall majority situation with at least requirement for support from the DUP and perhaps not even that.
>
> *AN*: So the answer's yes? [LAM, EV, DM laughter]
>
> *DLL*: That's a yes.
>
> *AN*: That's a yes, a hung parliament? [More laughter]
>
> *DLL*: I was giving you my workings, so yes. Hung parliament.
>
> *AN*: Well we got there in the end! [Laughter] I was losing the will to live. [Laughter]
>
> *DLL*: Andrew, I'm a massive outlier here, I'm gonna to be the most wrong or the most right so I think, showing my working...

AN: As they say in Glasgow, "yer jaiket is hanging by a shooglie peg" on this.[1]

DLL: That's right! OK so....

AN: Translations will follow. [Laughter] Deborah Mattinson... Is this Survation poll an outlier or in the mainstream?

DM: It's an outlier and erm, er, you know in a word no! I don't think, ha ha, no I don't think so...not feeling that! I think what Survation's done is interesting and Damian shows his workings on his website, but I think there is a big presumption about turnout, about young people, I think there is a danger that his sample includes too many voters who are highly engaged in politics, also the fieldwork - am I right is was before Saturday night - things have changed a bit since then?

AN: What turnout among younger people are you assuming?

DLL: In the post which is on Survation.com - we walked through - you can give an 2015 assumption of turnout and the results don't really change... you can use a 2015 assumption of turnout, it makes 2 points difference, you can use a (this is by micro age category) - you can use if you like an EU referendum turnout by age.

AN: I think in 2015 turnout was about 46 per cent among 18-24s.

DLL: It was 43 per cent.

AN: 43 per cent among them - What are you assuming will it be this time?

DLL: I wrote that article, I let people do whatever they want to do {regarding turnout by age}, because it doesn't change our figures. We all have the same numbers on ... all the pollsters have the same numbers, except their turnout weights are jamming up their Tory numbers. I did warn people about this, that this would be a problem.

DM: I'm not really sure I entirely followed that. (Laughter) I did think voter engagement is a bit of an issue with the sample...

DLL: ...there is no issue with voter engagement; we start off with a representative sample...

DM: ...but you've got 1.2 per cent saying that they didn't vote in last year's referendum, er, and a further 10.6 per cent saying that they can't remember, only 12.5 per cent saying that they did not vote in 2015.

DLL: That's because people always...

AN: We're running out of time, we want to have you both back of course, what do you think the results will be?

DM: I think a comfortable win for the Conservatives.

DLL: No overall majority.

---

[1] In Scots, "*yer jaiket/coat's on a shooglie hook/nail/peg*" means "You are in a precarious position, you are likely to lose your job."

Andrew Neil's pertinent questions, were actually rather more challenging to answer than they seemed, but we did consider these concerns about our methodology.

One Point Would Mean a Hung Parliament and the Tories Losing a Majority, Wouldn't It?

The answer to this question could have been "not necessarily, an opinion poll such as this is designed to forecast national vote share not seats".

Internally, given our public data had raised the probability the Conservative party could be unable to form a government—an SNP/LAB/LD/GRE coalition could be in play—further checking work was undertaken.

We ran an in-house model with Chris Hanretty (Royal Holloway, University of London), based on a different sample to our other polling—12,000 online interviews using a multilevel regression and poststratification (MRP) technique to forecast seats specifically. While not published, it independently forecast a 60% probability of a hung parliament. This demographic-based modelling technique was run as an entirely separate private project, to forecast seats to calculate the probability of the Conservatives being able to form a government.

Complicated. So the answer I gave to answer question was on the basis that: If one was to input our published polls into a publicly-available model such as Baxter's Strong Transition model—a modified way to impute the effect of simple national swing onto seats, with the added detail of using our Scotland polling into his six-party Scotland model—you would indeed see a *modelled prediction* of a hung parliament.

What Turnout Among Younger People Are You Assuming?

We were not making "assumptions" about turnout by age. The answer I should have given was that we were using the self-declared turnout—0 meaning would not vote then scaling 1 through 10 to adjust for a respondent's likelihood to vote.

Neil was pursuing that only 43% of 18–24s actually turned out to vote in 2015, but our tables showed a far higher self-declared turnout. This was fair. However, what we illustrated in the pre-election article was that all age groups were exaggerating likelihood to vote (including older groups more Conservative supporting than Labour). Our analysis showed that exaggerated turnout among the young in our data was off-set by exaggerated turnout for older groups. If we applied 2015 or 2016 levels of turnout by age instead, the shape of the voting intention barely changed.

Exaggeration of intention to vote and past vote is a known social desirability phenomenon when conducting polling—the point I had begun to address in response an "overly politically engaged sample"—which others had picked up on.

Another legitimate concern was that even if increased turnout among certain groups favoured Labour it might fall in unhelpful places—their safe seats. Regarding this issue, another internal study was carried out—a telephone poll on a sample of 3000 respondents from a sample frame representative of the adult population in 123 constituencies considered marginal. Results were input into a simple Excel-based constituency-level electoral simulation based on the vote shares for marginal constituencies which assumed and applied a uniform swing across non-marginal constituencies. The results from this separate telephone exercise, in addition to Hanretty's online MRP model, were consistent with our public polling. We maintained the search for empirical evidence that might justify changes to our planned public methods, but found none.

TURNOUT GROUPTHINK?—THE 2015 ELECTION HANGOVER

A key question in terms of understanding our methodology decision-making process going into the election would be: Why did Survation decide to not use a "probabilistic turnout model", given our 2015 online inaccuracy, instead using the self-declared system that failed to correct our unrepresentative online sample in 2015?

The main conclusion of the report of the inquiry into the failure of the 2015 polls was that

> the primary cause of the polling miss in 2015 was *unrepresentative samples*...The statistical adjustment procedures applied to the raw data did not mitigate this basic problem to any notable degree. The other putative causes can have made, at most, only a small contribution to the total error. (Sturgis et al. 2016: 4)

So, given the report's main conclusion—that unrepresentative samples were the cause of the industry's miss, and, importantly, that "other putative causes can have made *at most* only a small contribution to the total error"—improving our sample was the focus for the changes to our online methodology, outlined below.

Within the report's twelve sensible recommendations (which were *not* instructions to be adhered to with a prescriptive priority or weight) relating to turnout and model-based imputation procedures were:

1. review existing methods for determining turnout probabilities.
2. review current allocation methods for respondents who say they don't know, or refuse to disclose which party they intend to vote for.

Our thought process was that if we worked to improve the representativeness of online sample, then an approach some took based on the question "What should our methodology have been to get it right in 2015?" was the wrong question for 2017 *if* issues with sample were addressed. Further, in an election situation where voter groups behaved differently to past election behaviour, "retrofitting" a turnout model referencing 2015 behaviour would bring the danger of making headline figures even less accurate.

SURVATION'S TELEPHONE METHODOLOGY PROVIDED A BENCHMARK

The telephone methodology Survation initiated for final polls was essentially unchanged from 2014 to 2017. Polling, both published and private, using these methods in the EU referendum, the Scottish independence referendum, Holyrood government election, and our fateful telephone poll of 2015, accurately reflected the final results, with applied standard weightings having very little effect on the collected data. We believed strongly that our telephone method *already* addressed the primary cause of the 2015 polling miss—unrepresentative samples.

We construct a pre-stratified sample of persons we believe to be representative of the population as a whole. Multiple attempts to contact individual persons via landline and mobile contact appropriate to age group are made, taking elements such as time of day into account in order to contact harder-to-reach demographics.

We employed a standard prompt: CON, LAB, LD and UKIP in GB, plus SNP in Scotland and PC in Wales; DUP, SDLP, Sinn Fein, and UUP in Northern Ireland; with 'Another Party' concluding all prompts.

Respondents indicating a vote for Green Party or UKIP were asked a secondary question—how they would respond if a candidate for their preferred party was not standing? Their second preference (or not vote) was re-allocated accordingly where their preferred party was indeed not standing.

This final 2017 poll did, as in 2015, include full ballot paper order prompt of candidates, including independents and minor parties standing in each respondent's constituency. It also included a 'squeeze' of undecided voters who were asked "If the General Election was today and you had to choose, for which candidate would you vote or would you not vote?

Regarding turnout, a simple question for the period after postal votes dropped was employed: "How likely do you think you will be to vote in your constituency at the General Election tomorrow, or have you already voted by post?"

We maintained our regular likelihood to vote system—those who self-prescribe their LTV as 10/10 adjusted to a factor of 1.0, 9/10 to a factor of 0.9 and so on. A factor of 1.0 applied to those who told us they had already voted.

Meanwhile, steps to improve our online sampling methods since 2015 included targeting our sample with more granularity by income, education, age and time of day based on the analysis of response rates of different demographic groups. Fieldwork ran at optimal times to allow different groups to participate. We also took similar steps to our telephone method in reallocating the second choices of UKIP and Green voters in constituencies where there no candidate was running. There was no 'undecided squeeze' in our online polling.

CONCLUSIONS

The methodological success we had in the 2017 General Election was based on the lessons learned from prior elections. The challenge of having a representative sample will always be most important but also the most difficult problem to solve.

Our choice not to use a probabilistic turnout model worked particularly well in this election as voting patterns by age and region and party support were very different to those seen in 2015—simply put, when voter attitudes shifted sharply during the campaign, the method we had was responsive enough to reflect those attitude changes in our headline figures.

The media and political science community should welcome "outlier" polls and new innovations with interest—if it becomes more acceptable to be wrong, there will likely be more outlier results in different directions to analyse.

Finally, there are likely to be other small but significant contributory factors that we employ that bring accuracy that are not each easily quantifiable—from the quality and training of our telephone interviewers and online sample team to the political experience of the team as a whole.

REFERENCES

BBC News. (2013, May 3). Local elections: Nigel Farage hails results as a "game changer". *BBC News.* http://www.bbc.co.uk/news/uk-politics-22382098. Accessed March 29, 2018.

Belam, M. (2015, May 9). Did this polling company predict the correct general election result—And then decide not to publish it? *Daily Mirror.* https://www.mirror.co.uk/news/ampp3d/survation-unpublished-poll-conservative-lead-5667287. Accessed March 29, 2018.

Curtice, J. (2014, July 16). Who is right? YouGov or Survation? *What Scotland Thinks* (blog). http://blog.whatscotlandthinks.org/2014/07/who-is-right-yougov-or-survation/. Accessed March 29, 2018.

Kellner, P. (2013, January 15). Measuring UKIP's support, *YouGov.* https://yougov.co.uk/news/2013/01/15/measuring-ukips-support/. Accessed March 29, 2018.

Lyons Lowe, D. (2012). Will "Some other party" decide general election 2015? *Survation* (blog). http://survation.com/will-some-other-party-decide-general-election-2015/. Accessed March 29, 2018.

Lyons Lowe, D., Hopkins, C., & Bristow, T. (2017). Conservative lead over Labour has dropped 16 points in a month—What's going on? *Survation* (blog). http://survation.com/conservative-lead-labour-dropped-16-points-month-whats-going/. Accessed March 29, 2018.

Sturgis, P., Baker, N., Callegaro, M., Fisher, S., Green, J., Jennings, W., et al. (2016). *Report of the inquiry into the 2015 British general election opinion polls.* London: Market Research Society and British Polling Council. http://eprints.ncrm.ac.uk/3789/. Accessed March 29, 2018.

An Ever-Changing Mood: Qualitative Research and the 2017 Election Campaign

Paul Carroll and Suzanne Hall

If there's one thing that the political turmoil of the past few years has taught us it is that, while polling is invaluable for checking the temperature of the nation, other complementary methods—particularly qualitative ones—can get us closer to what people are really thinking and feeling. From the qualitative discussions Ipsos MORI conducted throughout May and June 2017 it was clear that both the issues that mattered to the electorate, and their confidence in the main parties' responses to these, shifted as the campaign unfolded. And qualitative approaches—such as the classic 90-minute focus group—are especially suited to identifying these "late-breaking influences on voting behaviour",[1] augmenting data from snap polls and developing a more nuanced understanding of people's feelings and motivations. In particular,

---

[1] http://the-sra.org.uk/wp-content/uploads/sra-research-matters-march-2017-edition.pdf.

P. Carroll (✉) · S. Hall
Ipsos MORI, London, UK
e-mail: paul.carroll@ipsos.com

S. Hall
e-mail: Suzanne.Hall@ipsos.com

© The Author(s) 2019
D. Wring et al. (eds.), *Political Communication in Britain*,
https://doi.org/10.1007/978-3-030-00822-2_16

through analysis of both what people saying and the ways in which they discussed the issues of importance to them, this qualitative work enabled us to understand why the polls narrowed.

Before looking into this in detail, it is worth recalling the received wisdom of spring 2017; that the Conservatives would be returned to government with an increased majority, with a mandate to press ahead with their vision for Brexit. Talk that the Labour party could be destroyed as a political force was not considered outlandish. These views hinged on what we knew of people's perceptions of the two party leaders at that time; prior to the election, Theresa May was routinely described by focus group participants as a strong leader, someone they looked up to. In contrast, Labour's Jeremy Corbyn was frequently derided, particularly for his policies, which were thought to be both outdated and economically reckless. Our participants, however, changed tack as the weeks progressed to the extent that, by the end of the campaign, it was Corbyn—not May—who was seen as most in touch with voters' concerns. As the mood of the nation shifted, and the polls started to show increasing support for Labour, qualitative work enabled us to track and better understand exactly what was happening. This chapter explores how and why voters' perceptions changed.

Pre-election

Immediately prior to the election being called, Brexit dominated the political discourse; the focus groups we held highlighted the profound societal divisions that still existed over the referendum. Remain voters, while respecting the outcome, nonetheless continued to rue the result and expressed concern about the social and cultural consequences—especially for non-British citizens. Leave voters, in contrast, were keen for the government to move as quickly as possible to secure the country's exit from the EU. They felt progress has been slow, and that "the will of the people" was not being enacted.

> I wish they would get on with Brexit faster, and stop bickering amongst each other.
> Leave voter

> Socially and culturally it's terrifying. It's so sad and I feel very much for people who have lived here for years being made to feel unwelcome.
> Remain voter

But while Brexit was the top-of-mind response when we asked participants about the main issues facing the country, this was underpinned by a broader unease about the state of the nation. To say that people felt that the government faced several significant challenges would be an understatement. Aside from Brexit, participants also frequently mentioned the housing crisis, funding shortages in the NHS, the lack of social care provision, and perceived high rates of immigration putting public services under pressure—all of which were taken as indicators that the country was not working in the way it should.

Compounding all this was a deep sense of distrust with the "establishment", expressed as a concern as to whether their elected representatives would do what was in the interests of the people. Leave voters voiced these concerns most frequently, suspecting that the government was reluctant to push forward with exiting the EU due to—in their view, unfounded—fears about the impact that doing so would have on the economy. In their view, the dire warnings voiced by economists in advance of the Leave vote had been just scaremongering; the country had voted to leave and yet the ravens remained in the tower—thus, to their mind, proving these experts wrong. As a result of this though, they took the government's slow progress on Brexit as a sign that those in power cannot be trusted to do what is right.

> The economists have got it all wrong so far. Britain was going to the dogs as far as they were concerned after the referendum. But they were all proved wrong.
> Leave voter

But while participants were able to talk about the issues facing the country at length, their views on the two party leaders were less well formed; though a political presence for some years, Theresa May had been Prime Minister for barely a year, while Jeremy Corbyn was approaching just his second anniversary as Labour leader. Because both were relatively new in their roles, participants had had limited exposure to them prior to the election. Consequently, when asked for their opinions on the two leaders, they fell back on stereotypes or reached for emotional responses—their gut instincts—rather than being able to contribute anything more evidence-based. So Corbyn, by virtue of being a Labour politician, was assumed to struggle with economic management and his policies were viewed through this lens and typically discredited as a result. He was also personally seen as weak, and unable to unite a divided Labour party.

> I am sure he is very well meaning but does not strike me as a strong politician....he stands up and says nothing.
> Remain voter

In contrast, May was seen as someone who, to her credit, had stepped into a difficult situation created by David Cameron; participants felt sorry for her having to deal with problems that others were thought to have backed away from and thought that this was a demonstration of leadership. Building on this, our participants saw her as effective, reliable, and credible—and someone who was more in touch with the public than her immediate predecessor, David Cameron.

> Theresa May did a fantastic job as Home Secretary I thought, and she is continuing the same ethos.
> Remain voter

Crucially though, these opinions had been formed from relatively low levels of awareness. Precisely as a result of calling the election—which had the immediate and obvious consequence of exposing the two main party leaders to the scrutiny of the electorate—were they able to come to informed views which, as it turned out, were very different to the ones they had previously held. And it was this process which was central to how perceptions—and popularity—shifted in Jeremy Corbyn's favour.

THE ELECTION CAMPAIGN

Over the course of the election campaign, we spoke to a wide range of voters across England about what mattered to them. We spoke to working class Leave voters in Halifax, middle class Remain voters in Bedford, and "just about managing" ("JAMs") voters in Eltham. We also spoke to people in Walsall during the week of the election, and in Enfield one week after the results were in. The group discussions were filmed by BBC News and used in the Today programme and Newsnight.

The findings from these groups throughout the campaign echoed the numbers in the polling. As the campaign got underway, we conducted groups in Halifax and Bedford where participants argued that Theresa May was the leader most in tune with the big issues of the day, especially the need to "get on with" Brexit. Further, she was perceived as much stronger and more effective a leader relative to Jeremy Corbyn—there was a sense, even among those who didn't necessarily like her, that she must be strong to have become leader of the Conservatives and Prime Minister. However, by the time we reached Eltham with a fortnight to go before polling, the conversation had shifted. The Prime Minister's response to the controversy over the Conservative Party manifesto and the so-called "dementia tax" was eating into Theresa May's popularity—the poor initial reception to the policy, followed by a partial U-turn on how social care would be funded, played badly with voters, undermining the Prime Minister's existing reputation for professionalism and effectiveness. And, when we got to Walsall just before election day, then an election that had previously seemed like it would be a "done deal" was being talked about by participants as too close to call.

From these discussions with voters, we identified four main themes that influenced voters' views throughout the election campaign: austerity fatigue, Brexit, dissatisfaction with and remoteness from the "Westminster elite", and how competent (or not) the party leaders were seen to be through their responses to events during the campaign.

AUSTERITY FATIGUE

Evident from the start of the campaign was that living with seven years of austerity measures was clearly taking its toll on people—particularly those claiming state benefits. They spoke about the difficulties they faced in their everyday lives—from finding the money to cover the essentials like their weekly food shop or their utility bills, through to the shame they felt when they couldn't quite manage this and needed to visit food banks for help and support. There was a strong sense that people's standard of living had declined under austerity and that even full-time employment was not necessarily a guaranteed passport out of poverty.

The Leave voters we spoke to in Halifax, however, did not believe that the policy proposals laid out in the Conservative manifesto tackled these issues meaningfully. They felt capping energy bills, for instance, would only make the smallest difference to the amount of money they had in their back pocket. More importantly though, these kinds of policies simply weren't credible coming from the Conservative party. For these voters, the government was very much thought to comprise a 'type'—well off, well educated people with little understanding of the daily struggles most people face. As a result, these participants ignored the Conservatives' proposals designed to help them, as they just weren't convinced that they could offer anything that would be designed with their needs in mind.

> They have all come from privileged backgrounds. None of them were brought up on council estates, none are single parents, none of them have used benefits, or queued for a food bank.
> Leave voter, Halifax

Similarly, the just-about-managing voters in Eltham also expressed frustration that they didn't see anyone speaking to their concerns. The Labour manifesto was seen by these voters as a "wish list" of things that would be nice to have but—due to the party's perceived lack of economic reliability—was thought to be lacking in credibility. Participants, even those who were current supporters or past Labour voters, worried about the party's ability to balance the books; particular scepticism was reserved for the affordability of abolishing student tuition fees. And, as in Halifax, these participants simply did not believe that the Conservative party understood the issues that people like them faced. By way of illustration, this group spontaneously raised the cuts to Free School Meals as laid out in the Conservative manifesto. Participants argued that this undermined the Prime Minister; if she really wanted the government to help people, why would she suggest a policy which would make their already precarious household budgets even trickier to balance?

> How does she want to help us when she wants to take them [free school meals] away?
> Just About Managing voter, Eltham

As the election approached, however, the terror attacks in Manchester and London prompted many people to think about the wider consequences of austerity measures and, in particular, the issue of police budget cuts. Further, Labour's response—essentially, to increase spending on security and police—chimed with participants' broader mood; that the austerity measures had gone too far. Building on this, participants in our groups also started to raise the issues of homelessness, believing this to be both on the rise, and a result of government policies since 2010. These issues led some participants to consider the wider impacts of austerity; it wasn't just their families that were struggling but, rather, the whole country. Consequently, people were primed for Labour's message about ending austerity, and they began to interpret their policies differently; what was once seen as a wish list, was now a desirable blueprint for change. This, in turn, highlighted the Conservative "ownership" of austerity programmes and forced a clear distinction between the two main parties.

> Jeremy Corbyn is thinking of getting more police, while May is talking more about finance – for some things, cost shouldn't be an issue.
> Undecided voter, Walsall

Brexit—And the Decline of the Smaller Parties

Despite the EU referendum remaining a dominant issue in discussions before and during the campaign, our focus group participants did not see the 2017 General Election as a chance to re-fight the Brexit battle; in their eyes, this was not a second referendum. Rather, what voters seemed to want instead was for the government to get on with the job of exiting the EU.

This view, however, had repercussions for two of the smaller parties—and particularly the Liberal Democrats whose campaign focussed on a second referendum. Yet the "ReLeavers"—those who had voted Remain but were now reconciled to leaving the EU—we spoke to in Bedford had no desire to reignite the bitterness that they felt had marked the referendum campaign. Because of this, these voters felt they could safely ignore the party whose campaign promises could end up doing just this.

Reflecting a similar dynamic on the other side of the referendum divide, our Leave voters in Halifax felt UKIP to have little relevance. With the Brexit vote secured, they felt that the party—which they very much saw as a single-issue campaigning organization—had served its purpose. That said, there remained admiration for Nigel Farage; participants felt he might be able to secure a good deal for the UK in Brexit negotiations. However, they did not feel that he, or the party he used to lead, would be able to speak to them about other issues that mattered—for example, housing or the NHS.

> We need someone who is strong, who is going to get the best deal for Britain and not just take the bill they throw at us.
> Leave voter, Halifax

DISTANCE FROM WESTMINSTER

Regardless of where in the country we conducted our focus groups, all the participants felt a long way from Westminster. As previously discussed, the Conservatives were widely seen as the party for the rich—and still, perhaps, in the Prime Minister's famous phrase from more than a decade previously, the "nasty party".[2] The ways in which the campaign played out fed into this. To illustrate, in the week prior to the election itself, undecided voters in Walsall criticized the inclusion of lifting the ban on fox hunting[3] in the Conservative manifesto. For these voters, it seemed a particularly odd thing to focus on when people are struggling, financially, and only emphasized how out of touch the Conservative party was with the lives and concerns of ordinary working people.

These voters also spoke about the sense that the election was unnecessary. They did not see this election as being in either the national or their interest; rather, they simply believed it had been called to strengthen the government's position, and to legitimize the Prime Minister's stance on Brexit—particularly within her own party. This caused some anger among the voters we spoke to; they felt that there were more pressing issues that the government should be dealing with over and above trying to resolve squabbling about Europe among the different factions of MPs in the Conservative party. Again, this was taken as a sign of just how distanced the government was from the people it was elected to serve.

This, in turn, played to Jeremy Corbyn's "new kind of politics."[4] Corbyn himself seemed authentic and his delivery unscripted compared to his political opponents; something that scored him and the Labour party points with an electorate tired of being taken for granted and 'spun' lines about what was in their interests. What's more, Labour's policies struck a chord; the Labour party manifesto—cleverly leaked,

---

[2] https://www.theguardian.com/politics/2002/oct/08/uk.conservatives2002.

[3] The Conservative Party's manifesto pledged to hold a free vote on overturning the ban, rather than it being part of their formal legislative programme https://www.independent.co.uk/news/uk/politics/theresa-may-fox-hunting-bring-back-ban-repeal-conservative-tories-general-election-rural-vote-a7726506.html.

[4] https://www.theguardian.com/politics/2015/sep/11/jeremy-corbyn-aims-to-throw-out-theatrical-abuse-inparliament.

perhaps—managed to move the conversation onto fertile ground for the party and appealed to voters' anti-austerity and anti-establishment instincts—such as building more houses, or tackling student debt. What's more, this appeal was cross-generational; while young voters we spoke to felt these policies would help them directly, older people also welcomed that there were measures being suggested that could help build a decent future for their children.

> We look after our children today, we look after tomorrow.
> Undecided voter, Walsall

THE LEADERS

As we have seen, at the outset of the campaign Theresa May was seen as much the superior party leader. The Conservative campaign itself, however, destroyed this picture. Jeremy Corbyn's response to the terror attacks, austerity fatigue, and apparent passion and conviction gave a more positive sheen to the Labour leader.

In Walsall, Corbyn's promise to increase police numbers in wake of Manchester and London terror attacks was a factor in persuading those who had been on the fence about him that they should vote Labour. The incidents gave the Opposition leader more airtime than before—and by this late stage of the campaign our undecided voters seemed to be more familiar with Labour's "for the many, not the few" slogan than voters in earlier groups had been with "strong and stable". Corbyn was also praised for how he handled himself and responded to attacks on his own performance; his passion and conviction made people pay closer attention and, in turn, they found that he well exceeded the low expectations that they previously had of him.

> He's answered and explained himself even though people have tried to disrupt his campaign.
> Undecided voter, Walsall

Meanwhile, a poor reception to proposals for funding adult social care in the Conservative manifesto—the so-called dementia tax—and May's uncertain response to this contributed to a re-evaluation of her supposed competence. Previously seen as unflappable—"a businesswoman" to quote the pre-election focus group with Remain voters in Bedford—but now starting to sweat.

> I initially though she was quite clever to ask for this election. But as the time has gone she has shot herself in the foot.
> Undecided voter, Walsall

All this conspired to give Corbyn "a second chance to make a first impression" with voters.[5]

So, What Did We Learn?

A final focus group was conducted one week after the election, comprising a mix of Conservative and Labour voters in Enfield Southgate, a gain for Labour from the Conservatives. This gave voters a chance to reflect on what happened, to discuss why they voted the way they did, and ponder the implications of a result few saw coming.

Firstly, it turned out that voters want a bit of light in their politics—something that Corbyn and Labour offered, especially among the young. It felt like Labour voters had someone and something to cast their ballot *for*, rather than *against*. After a number of difficult years, the choice before them offered hope of a change from the existing status quo with two clearly different approaches. The options available felt different to 2015 for these voters, even among those Labour supporters who remained reluctant to praise Corbyn himself.

> Being 18 now just after Brexit a lot of young people now felt cheated out of the future … to vote in this election was important, and it felt like a choice.
> Labour voter, Enfield Southgate

Secondly, if you are going to build an election campaign around competence, you have to deliver on that. Theresa May had a poor campaign personally, which directly contradicted the core slogan of offering "strong and stable" government. Those that voted Conservative talked about doing so *in spite of* May, rather than because of her. On top of

---

[5] https://www.newstatesman.com/politics/uk/2017/06/it-s-now-all-about-jeremy-labour-mps-way-forward.

that, Corbyn outperformed against expectations—albeit this was a low bar. Trying to undermine an opponent by attacking them as incompetent needs that opponent to be truly seen as incompetent for the label to stick. In this case, the Conservative attacks on Corbyn lost traction the more people saw of the Labour leader.

> She called an election because her polling was high...I don't see her as a saviour at all...I think at a time when we need complete stability it's been unnecessary.
> Conservative voter, Enfield Southgate

Despite all this, while Corbyn may now be seen in some quarters as "the Prime Minister in waiting",[6] May remains the Prime Minister in reality. Across the campaign and in its aftermath, it was clear that there is a lingering distrust of the Labour Party's management of the economy.

> We were fed headlines after headlines about the economy and it worried me...it sticks eventually, you hear about how the Labour government spent all the money...it all sticks.
> Conservative voter, Enfield Southgate

Thirdly, Brexit receded in importance as the campaign proceeded. In part, this was because events overtook the campaign, and our discussions with voters turned to terror attacks and cuts to public services. Additionally, Brexit remained relatively distant and abstract to the electorate—for the most part, the voters we spoke to had little appetite to repeat the arguments of 2016 and the referendum campaign. Whether they liked the result or not, they largely believed the issue to be settled and that Parliament should press on with making a success of Britain's departure from the EU.

All told, our focus groups demonstrated that election campaigns do still matter, that what political actors do and say, and how voters react to this, can shift perceptions and voting intentions. Prior to the campaign, the election seemed a foregone conclusion. Yet, put together, the story voters told us in the run-up to polling day was that the election was not going according to the script written beforehand inside the Westminster

---

[6] https://www.economist.com/news/leaders/21729431-labour-track-rule-britain-who-rules-labour-party-jeremy-corbyn-britains-most.

bubble. The Conservative campaign stumbled and Theresa May failed to live up to her "strong and stable" billing. Austerity fatigue rose in prominence and Jeremy Corbyn managed to earn a second hearing, connecting with more voters than his opponents—including those within his own party—expected.

But while the 2017 General Election showed us that political campaigns matter, what's equally clear is how we research these campaigns matters too. Polling is fundamental to our understanding of what the shifts are during a campaign. But going out and talking to people is one of the key ways we can understand *why* the electoral weather is changing.

Seismographs for Youthquakes—How Do We Know How the Public Voted in British General Elections?

Roger Mortimore

INTRODUCTION

In the immediate aftermath of the 2017 general election, journalists and campaigners alike sought to understand an outcome that had taken almost everybody by surprise. The early published estimates of voting behaviour seemed to provide that explanation: the overall rise in turnout came mainly from a substantial rise in participation by younger age groups, and those same age groups had swung to Labour from nonvoting and from the smaller parties, which played a major part in reducing the Conservative lead and delivering a hung parliament. This explanation apparently seemed plausible to campaigners on all sides reflecting on their experiences in the field, but was especially welcomed by those who felt that it vindicated Jeremy Corbyn's unconventional campaign strategy. The term "youthquake" was quickly adopted to describe the shock to the political system delivered by

R. Mortimore (✉)
King's College London, London, UK
e-mail: roger.mortimore@ipsos-mori.com

© The Author(s) 2019
D. Wring et al. (eds.), *Political Communication in Britain*,
https://doi.org/10.1007/978-3-030-00822-2_17

247

previously-unregarded young voters, and was so widely used that it was declared the "word of the year" by Oxford Dictionaries.[1]

There was, therefore, a degree of consternation when, some seven months after the election, the British Election Study (BES) team published new data which, they said, showed that the youthquake was "a myth" (Prosser et al. 2018; BBC News 2018). This conclusion was quickly attacked, both by pollsters (Kellner 2018) and by other academics (Stewart et al. 2018); the BES team, however, defended and reiterated their conclusion (British Election Study Team 2018).

Perhaps none of the available evidence is robust enough to make a definitive pronouncement as to whether there was or was not a youthquake, and this chapter will not make the attempt; but it will outline some of the methods which are used to estimate voting behaviour in Britain and the data sources on which they are based, and will explore their strengths and weaknesses as sources of evidence about youth voting in 2017. In the process, it may also throw light on how far the publication of research on electoral behaviour helps to establish an accurate popular understanding of how the British voter thinks and behaves.

EXIT POLLS

In many countries, notably the USA, the first indications of the main trends in voting behaviour and turnout come from the exit polls. Demographic information is collected from voters who answer questions about their opinions of the candidates and policy issues as well as how they have just voted, and tabulated figures are often available early enough to be discussed on election night results programmes and in the following day's newspapers.

In Britain, this is not the case. There is an exit poll, commissioned jointly by the BBC, ITV News and Sky News. Fieldwork is by Ipsos MORI and GfK, and a team of political scientists led by John Curtice analyses the data to produce a prediction of the election result, which is released simultaneously on all three channels' results programmes at ten o'clock, the moment that the polls close. But their efforts are directed entirely towards predicting the number of seats that each party will win, and the poll's design reflects this. The sample is not nationally

---

[1]As the *Guardian* noted, "youthquake" was already dictionary-listed, having been coined in the 1960s, but 2017 saw a 400% increase in its usage (Cain 2017).

representative: interviews are mostly concentrated in marginal constituencies (and as far as possible are conducted in the same polling districts as at the previous election), since this provides the most useful data for making the prediction. The interview consists solely of asking the participant to complete a duplicate ballot paper and place it in a ballot box, and is over in seconds: there are no demographic questions and none about election issues or personalities. This very short interview length probably helps to maintain the exit poll's high response rate, usually over 80% (a lengthy questionnaire might make it much harder for interviewers to persuade the randomly-selected voters to participate), contributing to its excellent record of accuracy in its predictions.[2] But it offers no evidence on who has voted which way, or why.

In the past, there have occasionally also been analysis exit polls conducted at British elections, but the last was a number of years ago. Exit polls are expensive exercises, and the media presumably feel that they would not make sufficient use of the data to justify the cost; academics, for whom depth of content in the data is more important than the speed with which it can be produced, find the British Election Study a better use of the available research funds. But for reliability in measuring the basics of electoral behaviour, exit polls have important advantages. An exit poll interviews people known to have voted, and does so within minutes of their vote. Other polls have to distinguish those who have voted or will vote from those who have not or will not, and to ask about voting intentions before the vote (when there is still the possibility that the voters might change their minds) or some time afterwards (when voters might misremember, might fail to report their tactical votes, or when answers might be distorted by knowledge of the election result).

Evidence from the Official Results

One obvious way to find evidence about voting behaviour is to look for patterns in the constituency results. In the absence of survey data, this might be the best source that there is, and very valuable it can be,

---

[2] The 2017 exit poll interviewed 26,272 voters at 144 polling stations; its 10 pm headline projection of 314 seats for the Conservatives and 266 for Labour was within four seats of each party's final total. The methodology is explained in detail by Curtice et al. (2017).

especially with the wealth of constituency-level statistical data which is available these days; indeed, the analysis of constituency results and what they imply about the underlying movements of votes has often been central to the statistical appendices to the Nuffield election studies. And after the 2017 election, it was quickly noted that constituencies with the highest proportions of young adults in their populations tended to have significantly higher increases in turnout and higher swings to Labour.

But there is a difficulty in diagnosing age-based differences in voting behaviour from constituency results: constituencies do not, in fact, differ that much in their age profiles and these differences tend to go in tandem with other, more distinctive, constituency characteristics. For example, constituencies with high numbers of young people tend also to be urban and unusually ethnically diverse. Heath and Goodwin (2017: 349) analyse the data in considerable detail, and although they find that the proportion of young people is a statistically significant predictor of increased turnout, the relationship is a weak one once they control for other factors. Prosser et al. (2018: 6) go further, showing that the relationship disappears altogether when a control for population density is added.

Moreover, there is a drawback to all aggregate-level analyses: there is no guarantee that the patterns in the aggregate level data are directly caused by the individual characteristics that are being considered. The standard statistical tests can ensure that the correlation between two variables (such as a constituency's proportion of 18–29 year olds and its turnout increase) is strong enough to rule out total coincidence, but it cannot confirm exactly what the causal relationship might be. This is known as the "ecological fallacy" (Robinson 1950). Turnout might have increased most in youth-heavy constituencies because more young people voted than in 2015. But in theory, at least, it is equally possible that greater activity by Labour campaigners in constituencies with lots of young people had the effect of driving older voters to the polls in increased numbers.

There can be no certainty here. If there is other, clearer, evidence against a youthquake then the constituency voting analysis cannot be taken as proving its existence. Nevertheless, if a youthquake did place we would expect the pattern of constituency results to be very similar to what it was, and had there been no such pattern it would certainly have raised legitimate doubts.

EVIDENCE FROM PRE-ELECTION POLLS

Perhaps the most-cited figures on voting behaviour after the past few elections have been those compiled by MORI (now Ipsos MORI), which have been released within a few days of the vote at every general election since 1979. These estimates are based on data from voting intention polls conducted during the campaign, aggregated over a period of several weeks; in 2017, they were based on a total of 7505 interviews, some by telephone and some online (Skinner and Mortimore 2017). Estimates of the voting and turnout breakdown are calculated from this data with the benefit of hindsight once the exact result of the election is known. Each respondent is identified from his or her pre-election voting intention and likelihood of voting as a Conservative voter, Labour voter, etc., or as a non-voter; the size of each group is then adjusted by weighting to match the known eventual numbers of each group in each region and reassembled into a national data set to calculate the estimates.

However, this method assumes that the only cause of difference between the projected voting of the unweighted sample and the real election result is sampling error. If the voting behaviour of significant numbers of respondents has been wrongly identified—so that many in the end vote differently from the way they intended to vote when they were interviewed, or vote when they were not expected to vote at all—the estimates may be distorted.

Usually, the biggest complication here is turnout: distinguishing between those interviewees who will vote and those who will not is one of the most difficult tasks in interpreting data from pre-election polls. But since what is measured is pre-election voting intentions, a swing of support between the parties is potentially just as much of a problem. If Labour picks up support late in the campaign, then the estimated characteristics of Labour voters will be skewed towards the sort of voters who supported Labour throughout the election and away from those who switched to the party as the campaign progressed; if, for example, the late swingers were disproportionately in the youngest age groups, then the number of young Labour voters would be under-estimated since many youngsters who eventually voted Labour would have been interviewed before they had decided to do so. At most British general elections, the received wisdom is that there is not much movement during the campaign, but in 2017 it seems generally accepted that there was a swing to Labour in the final weeks; for this reason, Ipsos MORI urged particular caution when it published its 2017 figures.

There is a complication in the measurement of turnout which needs to be mentioned, because it has led to some confusion in the interpretation of the published figures, which have been calculated on three different bases. "Official" turnout figures in Britain express the number of votes cast as a percentage of the number of names on the electoral register; on this basis, the overall turnout in 2017 in Great Britain was 69%, since roughly 31.4 million voted and the electorate was about 45.6 million (Electoral Commission 2017). But the number of entries in the register is not quite the same as the number of real people whose names appear on the register—some are listed more than once, some names appear in error or are out of date, and some people have died since the register was compiled without their names having been removed. Even a perfect poll of people listed on the register would not therefore give quite the same turnout as the official figure.

A more substantial complication however is that not everybody who is eligible to be registered does in fact have their name on the list; the Electoral Commission's most recent estimates suggest that only around 85% are included. Certain groups, including the young, are much less likely than others to be registered (Electoral Commission 2016). This means that a demographic breakdown of the official turnout would be in some respects misleading. A lower proportion of registered electors in the youngest age group than of those in other age groups turn out to vote, but young people are also considerably less likely to be registered in the first place, so the registered turnout will understate the degree to which young people are failing to vote.

In any case, most polls—including Ipsos MORI's—attempt to interview a representative sample of all adults, not only of those on the register.[3] For these reasons, Ipsos MORI's turnout estimates in 2017 were calculated as a proportion of the voting age population: the overall turnout for Great Britain calculated on this basis was 63%. But some of the other polls preferred to calibrate their turnout estimates against the official turnout of 69%. The BES took a third approach, reasoning that some people who live in Britain (foreign citizens, for example) are not

---

[3] This is for practical reasons. Polls need to be calibrated against reliable population profiles: these are easily obtained for the whole population (the basis on which most official statistics are compiled), but little is known in detail about who is not on the registers.

entitled to vote at all; turnout as a proportion of the eligible population is a more appropriate measure. On this basis, the national turnout was 68% (Prosser et al. 2018: 10).

Ipsos MORI estimated that 54% of Britain's 18–24 year olds voted (roughly 2.8 million), and that of those that did 62% supported Labour. The corresponding figures in the Ipsos MORI 2015 projections were 38 and 43% respectively.

EVIDENCE FROM POST-ELECTION POLLS

Several other estimates of the voting were released on or soon after polling day based on vote recall questions in post-election interviewing; some were weighted to the known national result, others were not. Post-election vote recall has the advantage that it is a measurement of past fact rather than of future expectation, and so is not vulnerable to distortion by voters changing their minds. Nevertheless, making an accurate measurement still poses difficulties. Samples may of course be unrepresentative and, except in a true exit poll, dealing with turnout is also still a significant challenge, since some non-voters are reluctant to admit that they failed to vote; nor does previous experience suggest that everybody reports how they voted with perfect accuracy.[4]

The first figures available in 2017 were from the music magazine and website *NME*, which were published before midnight on the day of the election and based on what it described as an "exit poll of young voters", although details of methodology were not given; it seems probable from the context that it was a conventional online poll rather than a literal exit poll. This interviewed 1354 18–34 year olds and found a 53% turnout of 18–24 year olds, which was stated to be a 12-point increase on a 41% turnout in 2015 (Britton 2017). Labour's share of the vote among 18–24 year olds was measured at 66% (Price 2017). The survey was conducted for *NME* by The Stream, which does not belong to the British Polling Council, and no details seem to have been made available online beyond the brief write-up in the article cited; however, its figures were published before those of any of the professional pollsters and are in relatively close agreement with them.

---

[4]These same problems have been observed in many countries—see, for example, van Elsas et al. (2014) and Hanmer et al. (2014).

Lord Ashcroft interviewed more than 14,000 adults who said they had already voted[5] between Tuesday and Friday of election week, some by telephone and some online (Ashcroft 2017). Although the data was not weighted to the final result, it came close to matching it (overall shares of 41% Conservative and Labour 39%), and so can be regarded as reasonably comparable to those from other sources. He found that 67% of 18–24 year olds who voted supported Labour. In a similar exercise at the 2015 general election, he put Labour's share of the vote among 18–24 year olds at 41% (Ashcroft 2015). Since Lord Ashcroft interviewed only those who said they had voted, his data provides no direct turnout estimates.

YouGov interviewed 52,615 adults online very shortly after the election (Curtis 2017); unlike the *NME* and Lord Ashcroft polls, the data were weighted to the election result and turnout. With so large a sample they took the opportunity to sub-divide the 18–24 age group, into 18–19 year olds and 20–24 year olds, but for comparability with the other sources we have calculated a weighted average of the two. This gives a turnout estimate for 18–24 year olds of 58%. However, YouGov calculate turnout to match the official figures: this means that their 58% estimate for 18–24 year olds probably implies a turnout slightly lower than Ipsos MORI's 54% calculated on a different basis. Labour's share of the vote among 18–24 year olds was put at 63%.

YouGov did not make any estimates of change since 2015 in their published figures. They did conduct a comparable exercise at that election (Kellner 2015), but the published tables treat all voters aged 18–29 as a single block. However, the House of Commons Library reported (Baker et al. 2017: 9) that the 58% turnout YouGov found among 18–24 year olds compared to 42% in 2015, giving the same 16-point rise as Ipsos MORI (although based on a different metric).

It might be noted that all four survey sources so far discussed are in fairly close agreement on Labour's share of the 18–24 year old vote, ranging in their estimates from 62 to 67%—similar figures from four medium-to-large independent samples using four rather different methodologies—and that the three making a turnout estimate are in even closer agreement, allowing for the YouGov figure having been calculated on a different basis.

---

[5] Those interviewed before election day may have already voted by post, of course.

ACADEMIC-LED PANEL SURVEYS

As well as the opinion polls, academic-run surveys were also exploring the voting and publishing their conclusions. Two of these, the British Election Study Internet Panel (BESIP), run by the BES team, and the Essex Continuous Monitoring Survey (ECMS), run by a team which includes former BES principal investigators, are panel surveys, which interview the same individuals a number of times at different stages in the electoral cycle. They do not use probability sampling, and being panels may also be prone to "panel effects", in which the sample (either through attrition or conditioning) becomes unlike the population as a whole. Both these online panels are conducted by YouGov.

The ECMS post-election wave was conducted on 9–29 June, interviewing 5134 participants in total (Clarke et al. 2017). They initially published their figures only for a wider group of young people, those aged 18–29. They reported that turnout among this group was 61%, up from 42% in 2015, and that 63% of these voters (Whiteley and Clarke 2017), later given as 65% (Clarke et al. 2017), backed Labour; a subsequent blog post also gave their vote share figure for 18–24 year olds—64%, up 23 points (Stewart et al. 2018). (The full ECMS dataset has not been published.)

The current BESIP exercise began in 2014, and the 2017 post-election survey, in which 31,196 people were interviewed, was its thirteenth wave of interviews. The BES team did not make any youthquake estimates from their panel, noting that "This sort of data is invaluable for examining the evolution of attitudes over time [but] one thing it is not as good at is measuring turnout" (British Election Study Team 2018); however, the data was published and perhaps for completeness should be shown for comparison with the other sources of evidence. The BESIP sample is not weighted to the election results or turnout: its reported voting behaviour is close to perfect in measuring overall Labour share of the vote, but very substantially under-represents non-voters. Of the 18–24 year olds, 79% claimed to have voted, and of these 64% said they had voted for Labour (Fieldhouse et al. 2017).

ACADEMIC SURVEYS WITH PROBABILITY SAMPLING

Finally, we come to two academic-led surveys using probability sampling, the BES and the British Social Attitudes survey.

One inevitable drawback of surveys with probability sampling is that they take a long time—to achieve a reasonable response rate requires many repeated attempts to contact some potential respondents and persuade them to take part. This means that there is always a hiatus of several months before the first results are published, so that impatient journalists naturally turn to the other estimates that are more quickly available. It may also be a problem that many of the interviews are conducted months rather than days after the election: if the accuracy of vote recall deteriorates as time passes, the BES and British Social Attitudes may record the voting of their participants less accurately than the immediate post-election polls.

But that is probably offset by probability sampling's stronger guarantee of producing a representative sample. The track record of the pre-election polls in recent British elections, all using some form of quota sampling, has been weak. It could be argued that many of the weaknesses of pre-election polling do not apply to post-election analysis, when the result is known and unrepresentative samples can be corrected by weighting. However, if quota samples are in effect missing a whole group of the public completely, as most analysts believe happened at the 2015 general election when the polls failed to include the politically disengaged (Sturgis et al. 2016; Mortimore et al. 2017), then even weighting will not create a perfectly-representative sample.

The BES post-election face-to-face survey has been conducted after most general elections since 1964. In the past, the BES data was not always weighted to match the election result before publication, which limited its usefulness to journalists and other interested non-specialists,[6] but in recent years this has been done, and the full datasets published—see Fieldhouse et al. (2016, 2018)—so that its findings for sub-groups of the population can be treated as direct estimates of what actually happened, based on what should be the best available sample. (Yet even probability samples can suffer from sampling error, including non-response bias.) It uses a lengthy questionnaire, which includes asking respondents whether or not they have voted, and if so for which party; but it goes further, attempting as far as possible to validate the reported turnout of its respondents by checking their names against the

---

[6]A voluminous and fascinating compendium of findings from all the studies then completed was published in 1991 (Crewe et al. 1991), but no correction was made in the data to allow for the known result, instead retaining any sampling errors from the original surveys. In 1979, for example, it reports that 45.3% of men and 48.5% of women voted Conservative; since in fact only 43.9% of all voters did so, the figures cannot be taken literally.

marked-up electoral register (the official list from each polling station on which voters' names are ticked off on election day when they are issued with a ballot paper, which remains open to public inspection for a period after the election). The BES therefore has higher quality information about the turnout of its respondents than any of the other surveys; it usually finds that there is significant inaccuracy in the reported turnout of those that it questions.

However, vote validation is not without its difficulties. In the first place, postal voting cannot strictly speaking be validated, since the electoral register records only that a postal vote was issued, not whether it was exercised. Nor is it possible in practice to find all the survey respondents on the electoral register: in some cases this may be because the individual is not registered (and therefore did not vote), but in others it will arise from errors or ambiguities in the recorded address or name; the matching rate in 2017 was around 90% (Prosser et al. 2018: 12). Moreover, privacy considerations now force the BES to obtain permission from respondents before linking their survey answers with information from the electoral register, and not all give it. This leaves uncertainties in the data (although, of course, it is still better to have validated turnout for most of the sample than for none of it, as is the case with all the other surveys).

But a bigger weakness in the 2017 BES as a source of evidence on the existence of a youthquake is that its sample of young people is very small for the purpose—only 151 18–24 year olds were interviewed about their turnout, and only 109 of these reports were validated (Prosser et al. 2018: 14). Of course, bigger samples are not necessarily better: if the other samples were unrepresentative then all their extra interviews cannot help make them more accurate. All pollsters know the story of the *Literary Digest* fiasco of 1936: an unscientific poll by that magazine, with a sample size in the millions, predicted that Alf Landon would beat F. D. Roosevelt in the US presidential election, while George Gallup, Archibald Crossley and Elmo Roper polled only a few thousand and each separately predicted Roosevelt's landslide victory correctly (Crossley 1937; Hillygus 2011). *Literary Digest* folded, and Gallup and his rivals laid the foundations of the worldwide polling industry that exists today.

Nevertheless, the smaller a poll's sample size the wider its "margin of error". The conventional standard for reporting sample surveys in the social sciences is to rely on 95% confidence intervals and to regard any difference within these as statistically insignificant. The BES reports the turnout of 18–24 year olds as 43.1%, but the 95% confidence intervals

Table 1   Estimated 2015 and 2017 voting behaviour of 18–24 year old voters in various studies

Source	Fieldwork 2017	Sample size 2017 (18–24)	Weight to result?	Labour share of the vote			Turnout		
				2015 %	2017 %	Change	2015 %	2017 %	Change
Ipsos MORI	22 April–7 June	614	Yes	43	62	+19	38	54	+16
Lord Ashcroft	6–9 June	734	No	41	67	+26	n/a	n/a	n/a
NME "exit poll"	9 June	†	No	n/a	66	n/a	41	53	+12
YouGov	9–13 June	3756	Yes	n/a	63	n/a	42*	58*	+16
BES Internet Panel	9–23 June	1780	No	37	64	+27	85**	79**	–6
Essex CMS	9–29 June		Yes	41	64	+23			
BES face to face									
(i) self-reported voters	26 June–1 October	151	Yes	44	67	+23	47	48	+1
(ii) validated voters	26 June–1 October	109	Yes	40	68	+28	49	43	–6
British Social Attitudes	July–November	162	No	n/a	n/a	n/a	56**	61**	+5

Sources See chapter text
*Percentage of those registered, not percentage of population
**Reported turnout, not weighted to actual turnout/result
† Figure for 18–24 year olds not given: total of 18–34 year olds was 1354

for a simple random sample of 109 and a finding of 43.1% stretch from 33.8 to 52.4%; and the intervals for their 48.7% measurement for 2015 on a validated sample of 157 are not much narrower. Moreover, the BES is not a simple random sample since it is clustered and the data has been weighted, both of which will widen the confidence intervals, probably substantially. In fact, the consequence of this is that there is probably no statistically significant difference between the BES finding and any of the opinion poll estimates shown in Table 1. However, the BES team argue that their conclusion that there was no significant increase in youth turn-out is based not only on the direct comparison between their 2015 and 2017 data for the age group, but on the patterns observed in the data for other age groups (British Election Study Team 2018).

The British Social Attitudes survey is not primarily intended to investigate electoral politics, and its data is not therefore weighted to the actual result or turnout; nor is its turnout validated against the register like the BES. The 2017 survey overstated Labour by three percentage points and understated the Conservatives by a similar margin in its overall vote recall. It found an increase in reported turnout among 18–24 year olds, but a much more modest one than that of the opinion polls, from 56 to 61%, a change which was not statistically significant given its sub-sample of only 162 members of that age group (Curtice and Simpson 2018). The party preferences of the 18–24 year olds were not reported. Once again, the small sample size somewhat limits the power of the evidence this survey can give.

CONCLUSION

Was there was a youthquake in 2017 or not? All sources agree that there was a very substantial swing to Labour among those young people who voted, but they disagree on whether there was also a substantial increase in young people's turnout. The case does not seem convincingly proven in either direction, although two observations might be in order: that the discrepancy is as much a disagreement over how low youth turnout was in 2015 as over how high it was in 2017; and that even the highest estimated increase would have contributed only a small part of the national result.[7]

---

[7] Taking the Ipsos MORI figures for turnout change and vote share, it would be worth about 0.5 million votes. Labour's total vote increased by 3.5 million between 2015 and 2017, and still finished almost 1 million behind the Conservatives.

When an election throws up interesting questions, we cannot expect that the available evidence will always be conclusive. But perhaps we can expect that the evidence will at least be presented clearly so that readers can judge it. Without trying to single out any cases, not all of the post-election analysis in 2017 was published in the clearest or most helpful form. Basic technical information such as sample sizes was not always published with the data. Not all the findings had been translated into a simple best estimate of what actually happened, which a journalist and his or her audience could easily understand. Important caveats or points of interpretation (such as the different, incommensurable ways of measuring turnout) and degrees of uncertainty involved were not always prominently pointed out.

Communication with the public is an important part of the role of both academic researchers and pollsters. We know more about our field than most journalists, and therefore need to do what we can to help journalists report our work correctly so we can accurately inform their audiences. Above all, we must be careful enough to distinguish between statistical certainties which can fairly be headlined as established fact and mere probabilities which need to be treated with more caution. If evidence is inconclusive, we must say so.

References

Ashcroft, Lord. (2015, May 8). Why did people vote as they did? My post-vote poll. *Lord Ashcroft Polls*. https://lordashcroftpolls.com/2015/05/why-did-people-vote-as-they-did-my-post-vote-poll/. Accessed June 4, 2018.

Ashcroft, Lord. (2017, June 9). How did this result happen? My post-vote survey. *Lord Ashcroft Polls*. https://lordashcroftpolls.com/2017/06/result-happen-post-vote-survey/#more-15330. Accessed June 11, 2017.

Baker, C., Audickas, L., Bate, A., Cracknell, R., Apostolova, V., Dempsey, N., et al. (2017). *General election 2017: Results and analysis*, House of Commons Library Research Paper No. CBP 7979, House of Commons Library, London, p. 54.

BBC News. (2018, January 29). The myth of the 2017 'youthquake' election. *BBC News*. http://www.bbc.co.uk/news/uk-politics-42747342. Accessed January 29, 2018.

British Election Study Team. (2018, February 12). Youthquake—A reply to our critics—The British Election Study. *British Election Study*. http://www.britishelectionstudy.com/bes-impact/youthquake-a-reply-to-our-critics/. Accessed April 30, 2018.

Britton, L. M. (2017, June 9). Here's the NME exit poll of how young people voted in 2017 general election. *NME*. http://www.nme.com/news/nme-exit-poll-young-voters-2017-general-election-2086012. Accessed June 4, 2018.

Cain, S. (2017, December 15). 'Youthquake' named 2017 word of the year by Oxford dictionaries. *The Guardian*, London. http://www.theguardian.com/books/2017/dec/15/youthquake-named-2017-word-of-the-year-by-oxford-dictionaries. Accessed May 16, 2018.

Clarke, H., Goodwin, M., & Whiteley, P. (2017, October 6). Underpaid, overworked and drowning in debt: You wonder why young people are voting again. *The Conversation*. http://theconversation.com/underpaid-overworked-and-drowning-in-debt-you-wonder-why-young-people-are-voting-again-85298. Accessed June 13, 2018.

Clarke, H., Goodwin, M., Whiteley, P., & Stewart, M. (2017, September 23). How the internet helped Labour at the general election. *BBC News*. https://www.bbc.co.uk/news/uk-politics-41349409. Accessed June 1, 2018.

Crewe, I., Day, N., & Fox, A. D. (1991). *The British electorate 1963–1987: A compendium of data from the British Election Studies*. Cambridge: Cambridge University Press.

Crossley, A. M. (1937). Straw polls in 1936. *Public Opinion Quarterly, 1*, 24–35.

Curtis, C. (2017, June 13). How Britain voted at the 2017 general election. *YouGov*. https://yougov.co.uk/news/2017/06/13/how-britain-voted-2017-general-election/. Accessed October 23, 2017.

Curtice, J., & Simpson, I. (2018). *Why turnout was higher in the 2017 general election and the increase did not help Labour*. NatCen Social Research. http://natcen.ac.uk/our-research/research/why-turnout-was-higher-in-the-2017-general-election/. Accessed June 4, 2018.

Curtice, J., Fisher, S., Kuha, J., & Mellon, J. (2017). Surprise, surprise! (again) The 2017 British general election exit poll. *Significance, 14*, 26–29.

Electoral Commission. (2016). *The December 2015 electoral registers in Great Britain: Accuracy and completeness of the registers in Great Britain and the transition to individual electoral registration*. Electoral Commission, London. http://www.electoralcommission.org.uk/__data/assets/pdf_file/0005/213377/The-December-2015-electoral-registers-in-Great-Britain-REPORT.pdf. Accessed February 6, 2017.

Electoral Commission. (2017). *2017-UKPGE-Electoral-Data.XLS*. https://www.electoralcommission.org.uk/__data/assets/excel_doc/0007/234979/2017-UKPGE-Electoral-Data.xls. Accessed June 13, 2018.

Fieldhouse, E., Green, J., Evans, G., Schmitt, H., van der Eijk, C., Mellon, J., et al. (2016). *British election study, 2015: Face-to-face post-election survey (SPSS dataset), version 4.0*. The University of Manchester. http://www.britishelectionstudy.com/data-object/version-3-0-2015-face-to-face-post-election-survey/. Accessed June 15, 2018.

Fieldhouse, E., Green, J., Evans, G., Schmitt, H., van der Eijk, C., Mellon, J., et al. (2017). *British Election Study Internet Panel Waves 1–13 (SPSS dataset)*. The University of Manchester. http://www.britishelectionstudy.com/data-object/british-election-study-combined-wave-1-13-internet-panel/. Accessed June 7, 2018.

Fieldhouse, E., Green, J., Evans, G., Schmitt, H., van der Eijk, C., Mellon, J., et al. (2018). *2017 Face-to-face post-election survey (SPSS dataset), version 1.0.* The University of Manchester. http://www.britishelectionstudy.com/data-object/2017-face-to-face/. Accessed June 15, 2018.

Hanmer, M. J., Banks, A. J., & White, I. K. (2014). Experiments to reduce the over-reporting of voting: A pipeline to the truth. *Political Analysis, 22,* 130–141.

Heath, O., & Goodwin, M. (2017). The 2017 general election, Brexit and the return to two-party politics: An aggregate-level analysis of the result. *The Political Quarterly, 88,* 345–358.

Hillygus, D. S. (2011). The evolution of election polling in the United States. *Public Opinion Quarterly, 75,* 962–981.

Kellner, P. (2015, June 8). General election 2015: How Britain really voted. *YouGov.* https://yougov.co.uk/news/2015/06/08/general-election-2015-how-britain-really-voted/. Accessed May 31, 2018.

Kellner, P. (2018, January 30). The British Election Study claims there was no 'youthquake' last June. It's wrong. *Prospect.* https://www.prospectmagazine.co.uk//blogs/peter-kellner/the-british-election-study-claims-there-was-no-youthquake-last-june-its-wrong. Accessed May 15, 2018.

Mortimore, R., Baines, P., Worcester, R., & Gill, M. (2017). BPC/MRS enquiry into election polling 2015: Ipsos MORI response and perspective. *International Journal of Market Research, 59,* 285–300.

Price, R. (2017, June 8). This alternative election exit poll shows how young British voters may have caused a political earthquake. *Business Insider.* http://uk.businessinsider.com/young-people-labour-jeremy-corbyn-shock-exit-poll-victory-nme-2017-6. Accessed June 4, 2018.

Prosser, C., Fieldhouse, E. A., Green, J., Mellon, J., & Evans, G. (2018). *Tremors but no youthquake: Measuring changes in the age and turnout gradients at the 2015 and 2017 British general elections.* SSRN Scholarly Paper No. ID 3111839, Social Science Research Network, Rochester, NY. https://papers.ssrn.com/abstract=3111839. Accessed January 29, 2018.

Robinson, W. S. (1950). Ecological correlations and the behavior of individuals. *American Sociological Review, 15,* 351–357.

Skinner, G., & Mortimore, R. (2017). How Britain voted in the 2017 election. *Ipsos MORI.* https://www.ipsos.com/ipsos-mori/en-uk/how-britain-voted-2017-election. Accessed May 30, 2018.

Stewart, M., Clarke, H., Goodwin, M., & Whiteley, P. (2018, February 5). Yes, there was a 'youthquake' in the 2017 snap election—And it mattered. *New Statesman*. https://www.newstatesman.com/politics/staggers/2018/02/yes-there-was-youthquake-2017-snap-election-and-it-mattered. Accessed February 8, 2018.

Sturgis, P., Baker, N., Callegaro, M., Fisher, S., Green, J., Jennings, W., et al. (2016). *Report of the inquiry into the 2015 British general election opinion polls*. Market Research Society and British Polling Council, London. http://eprints.ncrm.ac.uk/3789/. Accessed September 5, 2016.

van Elsas, E. J., Lubbe, R., van der Meer, T. W. G., & van der Brug, W. (2014). Vote recall: A panel study on the mechanisms that explain vote recall inconsistency. *International Journal of Public Opinion Research, 26*, 18–40.

Whiteley, P., & Clarke, H. D. (2017, July 3). Understanding Labour's 'youthquake'. *The Conversation*. http://theconversation.com/understanding-labours-youthquake-80333. Accessed June 1, 2018.

Why Polling Matters: The Role of Data in Our Democracy

Keiran Pedley

An important lesson to learn when studying politics is that democracy is about more than the process of having elections and counting votes. It should be seen, not as a series of events every four or five years— where an election takes place and a winner is crowned—but instead as an ongoing process that describes the relationship between government and the governed. That process is a complex one involving many actors; from political parties and their leaders to the media, law and the electors themselves. It is messy, imperfect and ever-changing. For these reasons, it is often very difficult to understand.

Opinion polls are rarely mentioned as important actors in our democracy. Yet that is exactly what they are. Political parties use them to win and the media obsesses over them when covering campaigns. In fact, how parties and their leaders are performing in "the polls" is a constant thread woven through how our politics is presented and understood. In some ways this is their most superficial use. Used well, polling data can shed light on the big trends shaping our society and political life beyond

K. Pedley (✉)
GfK, London, UK
e-mail: Keiran.Pedley@gfk.com

© The Author(s) 2019   265
D. Wring et al. (eds.), *Political Communication in Britain*,
https://doi.org/10.1007/978-3-030-00822-2_18

who is up or down in a given week, such as how age and education have replaced social class as the great British political divides in 2018.

Yet opinion polling faces something of an existential crisis. The perception, fair or otherwise, that polls have called successive election campaigns "wrong" has led to a crisis of confidence in the industry. This chapter examines the role that polling plays in our democratic process and some of the challenges the industry faces. It makes suggestions for how we might use polling data better in the future, though it does not claim to have all of the answers. As we will see, polling does not occupy a vacuum in our political life. Pollsters can be held responsible for "getting things right," but they alone cannot be held responsible for how their data is used. That requires the support of others, many of whom have their own agendas to pursue beyond those of academic rigour.

The scale of the challenge that pollsters face should not be underestimated. Their purpose is to reach a representative sample of voters. However, this apparently simple mission statement masks a myriad of problems. Reaching voters is difficult in a world where how we communicate (and therefore how they can be reached) is changing. Others in this book will comment on the merits of different methodological approaches, but the important point is that there are no "magic wands" that pollsters can wave. Younger voters may be easier to reach online, older voters by telephone. New approaches will doubtless emerge in the future, yet they too will contain their own benefits and flaws.

The biggest challenge faced by pollsters is that they are constantly trying to hit a moving target—the voter. There are two main problems here. The first is that not all voters are the same. One of the explanations for the polling miss at the 2015 General Election was that opinion polls picked up too many "politically engaged" respondents and that this group thought and behaved a certain way. Therefore, by capturing too many of them in their samples, as the "less engaged" were naturally harder to reach, pollsters were skewing the headline voting intention figures that they published in Labour's favour, ultimately reaching the wrong conclusions about the General Election result.

The second problem with reaching voters reflects a more fundamental truth that keeps pollsters up at night. Put simply, who "the voters" are can change from one election to another. Even if you have the perfect sample of voters this time around you might not next time. This is not just a hypothetical problem. Turnout in the 2016 EU referendum was significantly up on the 2015 General Election and though a contested point, at least *some* younger voters showed up in greater numbers at the 2017 General Election than many expected. Therefore, despite three campaigns taking place in three short years, the composition of the voting population was different each time.

These problems might not be so bad for pollsters if they could assume that their surveys would naturally pick up any changes in the voting population from one election to another. In reality, no pollster assumes this entirely. All make assumptions on how they should convert the raw survey data they collect into a representative view of voting intentions. These assumptions might take into account past voting behaviour or the likelihood of different groups to show up on Election Day. They are judgement calls and difficult to make. The wrong assumptions lead to the wrong conclusions. All in an unforgiving media environment where pollsters are judged against the eventual result. There are no hiding places when the polls close.

POLLING IN THE DOCK: HOW POLLSTERS HAVE FARED SINCE 2015

So if polling is so difficult, with such a patchy record of calling election results correctly in recent times that begs a question; should we still take it seriously? Does it even matter anymore? The answer is "yes" and "yes". To explain why, we must first challenge the notion that the polls have "always been wrong" since 2015. The story is more complex than it may first appear. Pollsters did get the 2015 General Election wrong as a group, leading to an inquiry by the British Polling Council, but their record at the 2016 EU referendum and General Election of 2017 deserves a more nuanced assessment.

Six pollsters regularly produced voting intention figures during the 2016 EU referendum campaign: if we take a strict average of their final published polls ahead of the referendum, it is true that they (wrongly) point to a Remain victory. Yet there is a more complex methodological issue at play here. If only online polls had been produced during the campaign, an entirely different story is told. Online polls typically pointed to a close and unpredictable race whereas telephone polls were more likely to have Remain solidly ahead. Indeed, two online pollsters—TNS and Opinium—actually had Leave ahead going into polling day.[1] There were notable exceptions, such as Populus, who produced an online poll the week of the referendum with Remain 10 points ahead. Nevertheless, the absence of telephone pollsters producing solid leads for Remain during the campaign would have left us with a different impression of what was happening to the one we had in June 2016. In this context, it is too simplistic to say that the polls "got Brexit wrong". It may be, as we will explore later, that punditry failed to properly examine what the polls were saying—but this is an entirely different question.

A similar pattern is observed when looking back at the 2017 General Election this time for different reasons. We mentioned earlier that pollsters make assumptions on how to convert their raw survey data into voting intention figures. In 2017, it was variances in these assumptions, rather than survey methodology itself, that led pollsters to produce quite different figures from one another using raw survey data that was actually quite similar. We could spend a whole chapter on what was behind these differences and again others will explain in more detail. The heart of the matter was that some pollsters—namely BMG, ICM and ComRes—assumed that different demographic groups would turnout roughly in line with how they had done so in past elections whereas others, correctly, took changes in the composition of the voting public in their data at face value.

Once again, if we were to take a raw average of the final polls produced we would have incorrectly assumed that the Conservatives were on course for a convincing victory when, in fact, they lost their parliamentary majority. However, again, it is inaccurate to simply say "the polls got it wrong". Although it is true that Survation stand alone, in voting intention figures at least,[2] as the pollster that called the election correctly, if we were to take ICM, ComRes and BMG out of any final polling average we might have produced, then the eventual result of a hung parliament would have been far less surprising.

None of this seeks to exonerate pollsters from the mistakes that have been made in recent years. Nevertheless, it is right to challenge the

---

[1] Of the online pollsters, TNS put Leave ahead by 43–41% (with 16% don't know), and Opinium by 45–44% (with 9% don't know), while YouGov's final two polls put Remain ahead by 51–49% and 52–48%. All the final telephone polls put Remain ahead, Survation by 45–44% with 1% don't knows, Ipsos MORI by 52–48% and ComRes by 54–46%. Populus, who had not published regular polls during the campaign, published a final online poll showing Remain ahead by 55–45%. ORB's final telephone poll showed Remain ahead by 54–46%, but they had ended fieldwork five days before the referendum.

[2] YouGov's seat prediction model was of course also highly accurate as we will explore later.

notion that polls have "just been wrong" since 2015. The reality is far more complex, without even highlighting polls produced in Scotland, Wales and London that have fared much better than nationwide polls in that time. This complexity is important when examining the question of "does polling still matter?" If the data is just wrong—as it was in 2015—then the answer might be "no". However, if some pollsters are getting things right and some are getting things wrong (and we can explain why) then polling data is still valuable in understanding the state of our politics. Even if that data is imperfect and unable to provide the certainty that is sometimes expected of it.

WHY THIS MATTERS: HOW POLLING INFLUENCES OUR POLITICAL DISCOURSE

Another, perhaps less satisfactory, answer to the question of "why are opinion polls still important?" is "because they just are". Meaning that the influence they have on our public life is clear and lasting. Opinion polls remain extremely important in how our politics is understood and (crucially) the decisions that our politicians make. To show why, we must first return to the scene of polling's "darkest hour"—the 2015 General Election.

The polling miss at the 2015 General Election is well documented—see, for example, the previous volume in this series—and we do not propose to revisit it in detail here. In short, the opinion polls pointed to a close election and a hung parliament of some kind, whereas David Cameron's Conservatives actually won a surprise parliamentary majority. This polling failure led to an inquiry set up by the British Polling Council, which suggested a number of ways that pollsters might improve in the future (Sturgis et al. 2016).

The 2015 polling miss held significance far beyond its implications for the British polling industry. The Conservatives based their entire campaign on the idea that Britain faced a hung parliament, with the prospect of a Labour government led by Ed Miliband being held hostage by the SNP in Scotland. Posters were produced depicting Ed Miliband literally in the pocket of former SNP Leader Alec Salmond, and the then Prime Minister David Cameron tweeted a warning to his followers that, "Britain faces a simple and inescapable choice – stability and strong Government with me, or chaos with Ed Miliband".

It is difficult to underestimate the significance of the role that polling played in the 2015 General Election. The Conservatives were able to leverage public doubts about Ed Miliband as Prime Minister because the prevailing political narrative was that the election was close and that the SNP—who had only recently fought a bitter independence campaign in 2014—might very well play kingmaker in Westminster. This narrative was driven by the polls. Had they shown the Conservatives six points ahead, it is reasonable to suggest the entire tone of the campaign might have been very different.

Understandably, this is a sore point for some who blame the failure of pollsters in 2015 for the nature of that campaign and subsequent political events that followed—notably Brexit. This anger leads many to suggest that we should somehow simply ignore the polls and pay no attention to what they say. In practice this is wishful thinking. The reality is that the media continues to use polling in its coverage of politics and political leaders—whatever they might say—use polling in the decision making process. Who, for example, really believes that David Cameron did not factor in the rise of UKIP in the polls when deciding to call an in/out referendum on Britain's membership of the EU or that Theresa May ignored polls showing her 20 points ahead when deciding to call a General Election in 2017? Even leaving aside the defence of polling's recent record that we have made above, the truth is it is important and here to stay. Therefore—as with any data—what we must do is learn to use it better.

Uneasy Bedfellows: Polling, the Media and Political Punditry

In examining how to use polling data better, we must turn to the relationship between pollsters and the media. It is here where things get difficult. Pollsters are not always entirely in control of how their data is used by media clients. Furthermore, these clients have their own agendas when commissioning polls. To understand who is "winning" an election campaign, yes, but also to create compelling content for their newspaper or website or to further the editorial line that a particular outlet might have. For many in the media, nuanced analysis of polling data is not on the menu, the aim is clicks, shares and front-page scoops. In some cases, this creates a real problem.

A good example of how the media can use polling very badly can be found on the front page of *The Sun* from 23 November 2016. The front page in question, published shortly after the Paris terror attacks of that month, screamed, "1 in 5 Brit Muslims' sympathy for Jihadis" alongside a picture of notorious terrorist Mohammed Emwazi dressed all in black holding a knife. The article claimed that "nearly one in five British Muslims has some sympathy with those who had fled the UK to fight for IS [so-called Islamic State] in Syria". It prompted more than 3000 complaints and was censured by the Independent Press Standards Organization (IPSO) for being "significantly misleading" (BBC News 2016).

So why was this article misleading? The problem was that there was a complete disconnect between the claims being made in the article and the data produced by Survation on which it was based. Respondents had been asked which statement was closest to their own view, "I have a lot of sympathy...", "I have some sympathy..." or "I have no sympathy..." with "young Muslims who leave the UK to join fighters in Syria". The "one in five" figure is taken from those that said they had either "a lot of sympathy" (just 5.3%) or "some" (14.5%); 71.4% said they had "no sympathy" and 8.8% that they didn't know. It is not really clear what "some sympathy" means here and we could easily use the same data to show that "seven in ten British Muslims have no sympathy with young Muslims travelling to Syria". Whatever your views on the broader subject, the use of data here is highly questionable—as IPSO ruled. There is ambiguity in the data not reflected in how it was presented to the reader.

Fortunately, extreme examples like this are reasonably rare and can be dealt with when they occur. A wider problem, more difficult to address, is the relationship between polling and punditry. Here, journalists and political commentators often use polling data selectively to advance their particular causes or to confirm their prior assumptions about public opinion on a certain issue or who might win an election. This is much harder to deal with because it relates not to using polling data improperly but drawing the wrong conclusions from it. Which is hardly a crime in itself.

For example, consider the front page of *The Guardian* on 10 April 2015. Under the headline "The day the polls turned", Ed Miliband was shown beside the voting intention figures from three polls, all with Labour ahead. The sub-heading added that "Figures suggest support of non-dom move and dislike of negativism" (Wintour and Nardelli 2015). But, contrary to the *Guardian*'s interpretation, this did not prove to be an indication that the polls were turning in Ed Miliband's favour. Also, consider the tweet from political commentator Dan Hodges the day before the 2017 General Election, claiming that the Conservatives would get a three figure majority. They didn't. These examples are not meant to pick on *The Guardian* or Dan Hodges, there are too many examples of pundits and journalists drawing the wrong conclusions from polling data to count. They are just examples. The point is that polling does not operate in a vacuum. Once put in the public domain, it is subject to the interpretation of others and sometimes these interpretations are wrong.

This is an important point. If we return to our example of the 2016 EU referendum earlier, we know that online and telephone polls were painting a different picture of the campaign. Yet, at the time, political commentators and journalists were much more willing to believe the telephone polls because they confirmed the expected Remain victory. Likewise, at the 2017 General Election, Survation's final prediction poll and YouGov's successful election model—both pointing to a hung parliament—were dismissed because they did not fit the media narrative that Theresa May was on course for a convincing victory.

It is difficult to come up with a workable solution to some of these problems. The reality is that different people can interpret the same data in different ways. Sometimes this might be because a media outlet has an editorial agenda to pursue, but often the issue is not one of malicious intent. Sometimes, an unexpected event—such as Brexit or the election of President Trump in the United States—is so unexpected that intelligent people almost subconsciously ignore the signs it could happen and exaggerate the probability that it will not, regardless of what the data says. Perhaps this reflects a lack of diversity of opinion in our media or perhaps it is just human nature when faced with the unexpected. Whatever the case, there are no easy answers in how we address the problem and the problem is not polling's alone.

FINDING SOLUTIONS: THE PROBLEM WITH STATE REGULATION OF POLLING

So far in this chapter, we have simultaneously defended polling from the charge that it has "always been wrong since 2015" whilst acknowledging that it is a difficult exercise, vulnerable to the misuse or misinterpretation of others. We have shown that it has a profound effect on our democratic process and suggested that despite obvious challenges, it is here to stay because it is firmly embedded in how British politics works. If we accept the premise of these conclusions, then a logical next question is "where do we go from here"? How can we ensure that polling plays an appropriate role in our democracy that provides insight rather than does harm?

Some have suggested that state regulation is the answer. The argument goes that if opinion polling is more firmly regulated then this can stamp out the misuse of survey data and ensure that best practice is used in all circumstances. The House of Lords Select Committee on Political Polling and Digital Media has recently reported on some of the issues raised in this chapter, stopping short of proposing state regulation for now but firmly demanding that the polling industry "get its house in order".[3]

Although it is welcome that the Lords has stopped short of proposing state regulation for now, the polling industry will have to be open-minded and constructive in how it addresses such questions. In reality, until the industry can show that it consistently calls elections unambiguously right, it should expect the question of state regulation to persist. Yet there are reasons to worry about state regulation. Though done for the right reasons, there is the potential for unintended negative consequences. For example if, as some have suggested, opinion polls were banned at an agreed interval before polling day, this might not stop the media reporting on private polling from individual campaigns, selectively leaked to influence public opinion. Likewise, what would stop newspapers conducting unscientific polls of their own readers designed with the same aim?

Such issues can probably be worked out but the biggest potential risk of state regulation is that it stifles innovation. One of the great success stories of the 2017 General Election was YouGov's regression model that correctly used polling data and other information to project a hung parliament (Shakespeare 2017). Not only successfully predicting the result at a macro level but also calling some improbable results at a constituency level too. Yet when this model was first published during the campaign, it was met with howls of derision. We should ask the question therefore: would YouGov have been allowed to publish this model under state regulation? If the polling industry is to avoid damaging "group-think" in the approaches permitted, then innovation must be allowed to

[3] House of Lords Select Committee on Political Polling and Digital Media HL Paper 106 Report of Session 2017–2019 'The politics of polling', https://publications.parliament. uk/pa/ld201719/ldselect/ldppdm/106/106.pdf.

succeed (and sometimes fail). The framework under which that operates is secondary but it makes state regulation at least appear quite difficult, almost unworkable.

LOOKING TO THE FUTURE (AND MOVING BEYOND THE HORSE RACE)

Debates about the state regulation of polling and how polling data is presented in the media will continue. In the meantime, pollsters can only focus on what they can control. Namely continuing to refine their methods in the hope of improving accuracy and more broadly demonstrating value in their work. These are difficult challenges, but in succeeding opinion polling can secure its role as a trusted actor in the British democratic process.

The question of "demonstrating value" is an important one. It goes to the heart of the question "what is polling for?" In this writer's view, pollsters should do all they can to move the focus of their work away from the so-called "horse race" (e.g. who is going to win) towards explaining the broader trends shaping our society and politics and what this "might" mean for people's voting behaviour. For example, pollsters would have been better served in 2017 saying that "The Conservatives look like they are ahead but the scale of their victory depends on turnout among younger voters or the extent to which Remain voters back Labour". Having made such a statement (perhaps through the British Polling Council) individual pollsters could have drawn their own conclusions, but by at least collectively acknowledging this uncertainty from the outset, the industry could have partially protected itself against the accusation that the polls "got it wrong – again".

At the heart of such a nuanced yet ambitious shift in focus is a more transparent acknowledgment from pollsters as to the, already pretty obvious, limitations of voting intention polls. By being more open about the uncertainties in headline figures, more focus could then be placed on the genuine insight that polling can provide on the important trends shaping society. Such as how young people are moving towards Labour (some) working class voters to the Conservatives or voting patterns in market towns and the societal shifts behind them. These trends matter and outside of election time they will only be uncovered by robust, independent, opinion polling. Here good polling and good journalism can provide a genuinely positive public service.

Making such a shift would probably require a rethink from pollsters as to who their clients are and how their data will be presented. If media outlets continue to be the main clients for pollsters then it will be hard to move away from a short term focus on "who is winning" and "what the public think of news story X?" However, if clients were universities or other academic bodies and the media merely reported on the published reports, then the content and presentation of polling could change in the future, closer to the vision outlined above.

This chapter outlined several challenges that the polling industry faces and made some suggestions on how these can be met. In the end, the industry will decide both individually and collectively how to proceed. Earlier we said that polling matters "because it does", in reality the most important reason it matters is that it provides us with the best independent way to understand what voters want and how our society is changing. The priority now is to make sure that this remains the case in the future.

References

BBC News. (2016, March 26). The Sun's UK Muslim 'jihadi sympathy' article 'misleading', Ipso rules. *BBC News*. http://www.bbc.co.uk/news/uk-35903066. Accessed April 3, 2018.

Shakespeare, S. (2017, May 31). Introducing YouGov's 2017 election model. *YouGov.* https://yougov.co.uk/news/2017/05/31/yougovs-election-model/. Accessed April 4, 2018.

Sturgis, P., Baker, N., Callegaro, M., Fisher, S., Green, J., Jennings, W., et al. (2016). *Report of the inquiry into the 2015 British general election opinion polls.* London: Market Research Society and British Polling Council. http://eprints.ncrm.ac.uk/3789/. Accessed March 29, 2018.

Wintour, P., & Nardelli, A. (2015, April 10). The day the polls turned. *The Guardian*, p. 1.

Index

© The Editor(s) (if applicable) and The Author(s), under exclusive license to Springer Nature Switzerland AG 2019
D. Wring et al. (eds.), *Political Communication in Britain*,
https://doi.org/10.1007/978-3-030-00822-2

C13, Antony Rowe,
Eastbourne, UK
November 2019

CPI Antony Rowe
Eastbourne, UK
August 06, 2019